POPULATION SCHEDULE OF THE UNITED STATES CENSUS OF 1860 FOR COCKE COUNTY, TENNESSEE

Transcribed by

David H. Templin and
Cherel Bolin Henderson

Heritage Books
2024

HERITAGE BOOKS

AN IMPRINT OF HERITAGE BOOKS, INC.

Books, CDs, and more—Worldwide

For our listing of thousands of titles see our website
at
www.HeritageBooks.com

A Facsimile Reprint
Published 2024 by
HERITAGE BOOKS, INC.
Publishing Division
5810 Ruatan Street
Berwyn Heights, MD 20740

Originally published:
Maryville, Tennessee
1983

International Standard Book Number
Paperbound: 978-0-7884-8762-0

FOREWORD

Of all the censuses we have transcribed from microfilm, the Cocke County 1860 was the most difficult to read. Although W. F. Morris signed each page as the enumerator, the census appears to have actually been taken by several different individuals. There were many different styles of handwriting and spelling - not only of surnames, but of first names also. These variances made it almost impossible to establish a pattern which would enable us to transcribe difficult names with confidence as to their correctness.

In addition to the usual problem letters, such as uncrossed t's and undotted i's, M, W, and H were often identical, as were r, n, s, c, and e. For this reason we suggest that you consult the microfilm copy if you have any question as to our interpretation of a particular name.

Each page of the census was headed as District 8, but the general location of a family's residence can be identified through the post office headings.

The Cocke County Courthouse burned in 1876 with almost complete destruction of the county records.

We wish to extend our appreciation to the East Tennessee Historical Center in Knoxville and the Blount County Library in Maryville for the use of their microfilm readers.

David H. Templin

Cherel Bolin Henderson

1860 U. S. CENSUS OF COCKE COUNTY, TENNESSEE

P. O.: Newport   June 4, 1860

	Name		Age	Occupation	Real	Pers.	Birthplace
1	Jehu	STOKELY	46	Farmer	8,000	30,000	Tenn.
	Jane A.		40				N. C.
	Jane A.		18				Tenn.
	Susan E.		16				"
	John B.		14				"
	Louisa E.		12				"
2	Joseph	OTTINGER	20	Farmer		700	"
	Sarah						"
3	Michael	OTTINGER	59	Farmer	8,600	5,100	"
	Elizabeth		58				"
	Elizabeth		16				"
	Narcissus (f)		15				"

NEWPORT COUNTY SEAT

	Name		Age	Occupation	Real	Pers.	Birthplace
4	Jacob P.	RAGAN	45	Collecting Officer	300	300	Tenn.
	Charity		44				"
	Robert		22				"
	Alexander		20				"
	Laura		17				"
	Creed F.		15				"
	Jas. C.		13				"
	Mary E.		10				"
5	Peter H.	CLINE	30	Grocer	1,050	300	"
	Elizabeth		25				"
	James H.		8				"
	Andrew M.		7				"
	George W.		4				"
	William R.		2				"
6	James W.	BROOKS	28	Grocer	1,500	1,000	"
	Sidney L.		24				"
	Emma C.		1				"
	Sarah		77				S. C.
	Judith		47				"
7	Alex	STUART (mwy)	28	Trader		5,000	Tenn.
	Adalizar		21				"
8	J. H.	RANDOLPH	34	Lawyer	1,800	1,650	"
	Malinda J.		30				"
	Rolph M.		9				"
	Townsella		4				"
	Nancy		63				"

Page 2   June 4, 1860

	Name		Age	Occupation	Real	Pers.	Birthplace
9	Lucinda	DAWSON	48		5,000	5,435	Tenn.
	James C.		21	Farmer			"
	Sarah		17				"
	Rebecca		15				"
	Laura		10				"
	Ellen		8				"
	John		6				"

	Name		Age	Occupation	Real	Pers.	Birthplace
10	Wm.	CURETON	48	Minister M. E.	1,000	975	"
	Mary		40				"
	Samuel		15				"
	Robert		12				"
	Wm.		8				"
	Martha A.		5				"
	N. L.	WRIGHT	26	Physician		1,900	Va.
11	Sarah A.	CRAWFORD	28		2,500	1,350	Tenn.
	William		6				"
	Ellinora		4				"
	Charles		2				"
	Sarah D.		3/12				"
	William H.	FINE	32	Trader		2,000	"
	Daniel	SMITH	12				"
12	H. H.	BAIR	40	Circuit Clerk	1,200	3,500	"
	Mary A.		35				"
	Laura C.		14				"
	Mary E.		12				"
	William H.		10				"
	John M.		9				"
13	William	McSWEEN	50	Lawyer	8,250	10,630	N. C.
	Catharine		48				Tenn.
	Nancy E.		19				"
	Mary S.		16				"
	Cynthia M.		14				"
	Wm. J. M.		12				"
	James		37	Stock Driver		5,400	"
14	W. P.	BADGET	27	Physician		100	"
	Timinary(f)		27				"
	Thomas H.		6				"
	George F.		4				"
	John C.		1				"
	Mary A.	BALLENGER	29			100	"

Page 3   June 4, 1860

	Name		Age	Occupation	Real	Pers.	Birthplace
15	C. D.	FAIRFIELD	35	Physician	1,200	800	Mass.
	Mary		36				"
	Mary		8				Maine
	Minnie		5				Ky.
	Dexter		5/12				Tenn.
	Alphous	OSBORN	69	Carpenter			Mass.
	W. W.		22	Tobacinist			"
	G. W.	SATERFIELD	23	Laborer			Tenn.
16	Thomas E.	FLINN	31	Tanner	700	2,500	Tenn.
	Elizabeth R.		26				"
	Martha F.		1				"
17	Henry	GONCHENOUS	30	Merchant	1,250	8,197	Va.
	Elizabeth		30				Tenn.
	Robert		8				"
	Charlie		6				"
	Blanche		4				"
	Julia		2				"

	Name		Age	Occupation	Real	Pers.	Birthplace
	W. L.	DEWITT		Merchant		8,250	"
	Baptist	McNABB		Mcht. Clerk		160	"
18	R. A.	DEWITT	30	Farmer	1,500	10,330	"
	Julia E.		26				"
	Harriet		6				"
	Margaret A.		4				"
	Mary W.		3				"
	Fanny		10/12				"
19	W. H.	SMITH	40	Minister N.S.P.	2,300	2,000	"
	Adaline M.		36				"
	William M.		6				"
20	James	RANKIN	51	Merchant	1,200	15,000	"
	Nancy		54				"
	Menerva J.		27				"
	William D.		23	Merchant			"
	Chatarine E.		19				"
21	William G.	ROADMAN	44		8,000	24,000	"
	Elizabeth		27				"
	Mary L.		9				"
	Chesley		2				"
22	Addison A.	RYAN	47	Tailer	900	1,500	Tenn.
	Michael C.		44				"
	Sarah		21				"

Page 4   June 4, 1860

	Name		Age	Occupation	Real	Pers.	Birthplace
	Martha		19				"
	Jacob P.		14				"
	Marion (m)		12				"
	Phillip		9				"
	William		2				"
	Julius	RAGEN (mul)	25	Saddler			"
23	Stephen	BASINGER	34	"	350	1,225	"
	Jane		29				"
	Alice		9				"
	James R.		7				"
	Sarah M.		5				"
	William L.		2				"
	Malissa	SHELTON	18				N. C.
24	Mahala	PORTER	48		1,000	2,800	Tenn.
	Martha K.		29				"
	David L.		15				"
	William H.		13				"
	Florence J.		11				"
	Charlie R.		6				"
	Eliza		50				"
	A. W.	RHEA	21	Physician		850	"
25	P. W.	MURPHY	30	Blacksmith		200	"
	Nancy A.		22				"
	Allice		6				""
	Henry B.		4				"
	William L.		2				"

1860 U. S. CENSUS OF COCKE COUNTY, TENNESSEE

	Name		Age	Occupation	Real	Pers.	Birthplace
	George		1				"
	John P.		26		300		"
26	Lewis A.	CURETON	32			60	"
	Elizabeth		15				"
27	James	NORRIS	23	Tanner	250	100	"
	Elizabeth J.		22				Va.
	Charles A.		1				Tenn.
28	John	CAMERON	40	Saddler	2,500	3,000	"
	Mary H.		36				"
	James H.		10				"
	Penelope D.		8				"
	Benjamin D.		7				"
	Julia A.		7				"
	Mary G.		4				"

Page 5   June 6, 1860

	Name		Age	Occupation	Real	Pers.	Birthplace
	Louiza C.		17				Tenn.
	Hannah	HUNT (bl)	18	House girl			"

CONCLUDED

	Name		Age	Occupation	Real	Pers.	Birthplace
30	J. H	ROBINSON	28	Farmer		9,000	Tenn.
	Nancy M.		24				"
	Mary E.		5				"
	Sarah Roena		3				"
	Brance		11/12				"
31	JAMES C.	MURRAY	36	Farmer	5,000	4,000	Tenn.
	Elizabeth		31				"
	Thomas J.		4				"
	Harriett S.		2				"
	Lucinda J.		10/12				"
	Sarah	ODELL	20				"
32	G. J.	THOMAS	38	Farmer	5,000	2,425	Tenn.
	Matilda		35				"
	Mary C.		14				"
	Sarah E.		13				"
	George M.		12				"
	Rity J.		10				"
	John A.		7				"
	James H.		3				"
	William B.		1				"
33	A. E.	SMITH	59	Farmer	76,180	67,600	Tenn.
	Julia R.		52				"
	Thomas L.		23				"
	Mary		21				"
	Julia		18				
	Theodore M.		17				"
	Elisabeth Irene		12				"
	Mary		78				S. C.
	Wm. R.		31	Merchant		9,000	Tenn.
	Elisabeth		28				"
	Mary		3				"
	Dewitt		1				"

1860 U. S. CENSUS OF COCKE COUNTY, TENNESSEE

	Name		Age	Occupation	Real	Pers.	Birthplace
34	A. R.	GARRISON	50	Farmer	1,500	500	N. C.
	Susan		58				S. C.
	Cristan (f)		20				S. C.

Page 6   6 June 1860

	Name		Age	Occupation	Real	Pers.	Birthplace
	Solomon		18				N. C.
	Susan		16				"
	Laura		15				"
	David		13				"
	Robert		11				Tenn.
35	Isaac W.	HASKIN	22	Fisher		20	Tenn.
	Sarah		20				"
	Wm. S.	ALLEN	21	Mail Rider		2	Va.
36	Jobe	ODELL	45	Farmer	1,500	900	Tenn.
	Martha		35				"
	Mary A.		9				"
	Nancy		6				"
	Andrew J.		1				"
	Mary J.		7				"
	Jane	PARKS	22	None			"
37	H. H.	WARE	65	Farm Laborer		20	N. C.
	Mary		48				"
	Sidney	VICK	20	Farm Laborer			"
	Mary E.		18				"
	Calvin W.		17	Farm Laborer			"
	Edward J.		15	" "			"
	Alexander		4				"
	Julia F.		2/12				Tenn.
38	James A.	ANDERSON	26	Farm Laborer		15	Tenn.
	Mary A.	ANDERSON	25				"
	Nancy E.		3				"
	James A.		1				"
	Rachel A.		5/12				"
39	James M.	THOMAS	32	Farming	2,400	2,000	Tenn.
	Phebe		31				"
	Andrew Johnson		2				"
	Lydia		10/12				"
	G. B. L.	MOODY	12				N. C.
40	David	ODELL	47	Farmer	6,800	16,000	Tenn.
	A.	ODELL	42	"			"
	Febe		57				"
	Nancy		55				"
	William	HENRY	18	Farm Laborer			"
	Sarah		13				"
	Thomas	MALOY	8				"

Page 7   6 June 1860

	Name		Age	Occupation	Real	Pers.	Birthplace
41	Jacb	THOMAS	28	Farming	4,000	2,400	Tenn.
	Nancy		28				"
	Nancy Jane		5				"
	Elisabeth		3				"
	Murray		1				"
	Catharine	THOMAS	75	None		5,700	Tenn.

	Name		Age	Occupation	Real	Pers.	Birthplace
42	Wm. H.	TAYLOR	26	Farm Laborer		50	N. C.
	Jane		19				Tenn.
	Sarah		1				"
43	Richard	EVANS	23	Farm Laborer		24	N. C.
	Martha		22				Tenn.
	Nancy J.		1				"
44	Eli	HILL Jr.	22	Farm Laborer		100	"
	Mary		30				"
	J. M.		8				"
	Daniel A.		3				"
	George W.		1				"
45	Thomas	HILL	30	Farm Laborer		10	N. C.
	Phebe E.		37				"
	Emeline		13				"
	Eli		10				Tenn.
	H. C.		4				N. C.
46	Eli	HILL	42	Farm Laborer		40	N. C.
	Sarah C.		39				"
	Royal		18				Tenn.
	Elisabeth		14				"
	Thomas		11				"
	Green B.		10				"
	Alexander J.		7				"
	Margarett E.		2				"
	Mary A.		1/12				"
47	Ambrose	WILLET	45	Miller		20	Tenn.
	Mary		47				"
	Margarett		17				"
	Jacob R.		16				"
	Phillip J.		14				"
	Hailda C. (f)		12				"
	Martha J.		10				"
	Catharine E.		8				"
	Sarah E.		6				"

Page 8   6 June 1860

	Name		Age	Occupation	Real	Pers.	Birthplace
	William		4				Tenn.
	William M.	BAKER	26	Laborer			S. C.
49	Doctor Wm. McCLERKING (bl)		43	Farm Laborer		1,000	S. C.
	Elisabeth (bl)		39				N. C.
	Monroe (bl)		20	Farm Laborer			S. C.
50	David	McKOY	34	Blacksmith		300	Tenn.
	Juda		28				"
	Mary		11				"
	Martha		8				"
	Nancy		6				"
	Juda		4				"
	James P.		2				"
	John T.		3/12				"
	Robert		36	Farmer		450	"

	Name		Age	Occupation	Real	Pers.	Birthplace
51	Wm. M.	MALOY	31	"	3,000	500	Tenn.
	Rachel		22				"
	Elisabeth A.		5				
	Elisa Jane		3				
	John		11/12				
52	John	MALOY	29	Farmer	4,000	500	Tenn.
	Nancy J.		25				"
	Martha F.		1				"
	Elisa E.		1/12				"
53	John	GORRELL	57	Miller	10,000	2,530	Maryland
	Sarah		53				Tenn.
	Joseph R.		24	Carpenter			"
	Benjamin W. D.		20	Farm Laborer			"
	Mary A.		17	None			"
	Sabra S.		16				"
	George W.		13				"
	Charley A.		10				"
54	David	DUMTON	45	Laborer		400	S. C.
	Risah		44				"
	Andrew		16				Tenn.
	James		15				"
	Henry		12				"
	Rufus		9				"
	Porter		3				"
	Not Named (f)		4/12				"
55	Preston	SUTHERLAND	36	Farm Laborer		40	S. C.
Page 9							6 June 1860
	Susan		4/12				Tenn.
56	Preston	SUTHERLAND	36	Laborer		40	S. C.
	Jane		36				Tenn.
	Sarah A.		17				"
	William		14				"
	Mary J.		12				"
	John M.		9				"
	Marcus L.		7				"
	Luther		6				"
	Alexander		5				"
	Tilghman		2				"
	Emaline		1				"
57	John	BROWN	50	Farmer	3,600	2,265	"
	Selina		50				"
	Sarah F.		18				"
	Selina H.		15				"
	Bethany	LAREW	55			35	"
58	James	HOLT	52	Laborer	3,600	2,265	N. C.
	Margaret		46				"
	Julia A.		30				"
	Rebecca		13				"
	Mary		9				"
	Jesse		6				"

	Name		Age	Occupation	Real	Pers.	Birthplace
	Margaret		9				"
	Elvira		24				"
	Nancy D.		1				S. C.
59	Mary	MOORE	52			20	N. C.
	Catharine	"	20				"
60	Abraham	McKOY	75	Farmer	1,200	1,130	Va.
	Sarah J.		68				"
61	Christina	ELWOOD	65			50	N. C.
	James		29				"
	Mary A.		26				"
	Charles N.		25				"
	Thomas C.		24			50	S. C.
	George H.		20				
62	Henry	BOLCH	54	Farmer	1,000	600	N. C.
	Sarah		50				"
	Gerdine (m)		18	Laborer			"
	Hartwell (m)		15				"

Page 10   7 June 1860

	Name		Age	Occupation	Real	Pers.	Birthplace
	Candus (f)		13				N. C.
	Ellinora		22				"
	Carnellus (f)		4				"
63	David	BOYER	23	Farmer	1,800	400	Tenn.
	Nancy		24				"
	Alexander		2				"
	Sarah A.		7/12				"
64	J. L.	SUGGS	23	Laborer		250	N. C.
	Etha E.		20				"
65	Sarah	CURETON	50		110	150	Va.
	Mary		22				Tenn.
	Robert		21				"
	Richard		17				"
	Margaret		12				"
	Thomas		10				"
	Sarah		6				"
66	Edom	KINDRICK	83	Miller		5,170	Va.
	Elisabeth		83				N. C.
67	Harriet	KINDRICK	38		8,000	6,632	Tenn.
	William D.		16				"
	Caroline		14				"
	Joseph E.		12				"
	Emma		10				"
	Harriet O.		8				"
	Mary V.		6				"
	Florence A.		4				"
68	William	ROBINSON	61	Farmer	15,000	35,000	"
	Mary		55				"
	William A.		32	Musician		1,000	"
	Edom K.		27	Merchant		1,000	"
							"

	Name		Age	Occupation	Real	Pers.	Birthplace
	Mary L.		23				"
	Martha		21				"
	Josephine		16				"
	Laura		14				"
	David		12				"
	J. P. (m)		5				"
69	Daniel	FARNER	25	Laborer		51	"
	Judy E.		25				"
	Mary J.		6				"
	Elizabeth		3				"

Page 11   7 June 1860

	Name		Age	Occupation	Real	Pers.	Birthplace
	Caleb		11/12				Tenn.
70	James M.	HURLEY	43	Farmer	12,000	10,680	"
	Sarah E.		41				"
	John G.		21	Student			"
	James H.		15				"
	Rachel		11				"
	Sarah J.		9				"
	Daniel W.		4				"
	Florence P.		2				"
71	Abraham	BARNET	25	Laborer (Idiotic)		52	"
	Nancy		28				"
	Sarah E.		1				"
72	James	BARNET	29			50	S. C.
	Anna C.		23				"
	George W.		4				Tenn.
	Florence M.		9/12				"
	Abel	MATHIS	35				S. C.
73	Jane	BASSET	48			970	N. C.
	Wm. W.		24				"
	Daniel F.		21				"
	Robert W.		19				"
	John F.		16				"
74	Mary	WILSON	45			300	"
	William		21				"
	Elijah		19				Tenn.
75	Samuel	SWATSEL	31			230	"
	Caroline		20				"
	Mary J.		11/12				"
76	Meradith	BARNET	65	Farmer	300	200	S. C.
	Sarah		55				Tenn.
	Susannah		19				"
	Elizabeth J.		15				"
	Thomas D.		13				"
	James H.		12				"
77	James A.	PARKS	25			400	"
	Catharine W.		23				N. C.
	Layfatte		2/12				Tenn.

	Name		Age	Occupation	Real	Pers.	Birthplace
78	Martha	WARD	24			25	S. C.
	Sarah J.		9				Tenn.
	James H.		7				"

Page 12   7 June 1860

	Name		Age	Occupation	Real	Pers.	Birthplace
	Francis (f)		6				Tenn.
79	James	PARKS	24	Farmer		150	"
	Margaret		20				"
80	Wright	BROOKS	36	"	1,000	640	N. C.
	Jane		24				Tenn.
	William E.		4				"
	Saphronia		3				"
	Alonzo		2				"
	Edom		2/12				"
	Merdith	BARNET	24				"
	Jane		23				"
81	William R.	BROOKS	30	Farmer	700	300	"
	Sarah		30				"
	Eugene A.		4				"
	Lafayette F.		3				"
	Angeline B.		2				"
	Allice V.		1/12				"
82	Samuel	HOLT	56	Laborer		150	N. C.
	Mary		43	"			Tenn.
	Jesse		16	"			S. C.
	Augustus		18				Tenn.
	Jane		14				S. C.
	Emma		12				"
	Louise		7				"
	Lucretia		4				"
83	Royal	BROOKS (mwy)	23	"		40	Tenn.
	Jane		16				"
	Margaret		50				Ga.
	Nancy		25				Tenn.
	John		17				"
	William		13	"			"
84	P. M.	BROOKS	32	Farmer	700	300	"
	Sarah E.		27				N. C.
	Alexander C.		5				Tenn.
	Luallen E.		3				"
	Helen O.		1				"
85	Alexander	PARKS	49			150	"
	Margaret		48				"
	Elizabeth		19				"
	Nancy		18				"

Page 13   7 June 1860

	Name		Age	Occupation	Real	Pers.	Birthplace
	Martha		15				"
	Eliza		12				"
	Daniel		10				"
	William		7				"
	Margaret		6				"

	Name		Age	Occupation	Real	Pers.	Birthplace
	Emeline		6				"
	Andrew J.		3				"
	John	BROOKS	1				"
86	H. A.	McKAMY	36	Farmer	500	200	"
	Catharine		38				N. C.
	Nancy J.		16				Tenn.
	Elizabeth		15				"
	Lydia		12				"
	Samuel J.		9				"
	Lucinda		4				"
	David S.		1				"
87	Tidings	HOLT	35	"	450	200	N. C.
	Nancy		31				"
	Elizabeth		14				"
	Jessee (m)		12				"
	Susannah		9				"
	Sarah		5				"
88	George	BOLEYPAN	52	Laborer		15	Va.
	Candus		50				N. C.
	Benjamin		31				"
	Mathew		25				Tenn.
	Sarah		28				"
	Henry		18				"
	James		14				"
	Catharine		8				"
	Nancy E.		3				"
89	John	GRAGG	46			125	"
	Sarah		34				N. C.
	Martha J.		15				Tenn.
	Elizabeth		16				"
	Henry		14				"
	William A.		11				"
	Thomas W.		9				"
	James A.		5				"
	Jonathan		3				"

Page 14   7 June 1860

	Name		Age	Occupation	Real	Pers.	Birthplace
	Mary	HOLT	10				Tenn.
	Sarah	GRAGG	7/12				"
90	Matilda	RUSSEL	36			500	N. C.
	Elizabeth		16				"
	Leander M.		14				"
	Margaret		13				"
	William N.		9				"
	Harrit J.		5				Tenn.
91	Joseph	BURGESS	60	Laborer		70	Ga.
	Purcy		60				S. C.
	Asbury		22				"
	Nancy		14				"
92	Samuel S.	WARREN	47	Shoe Maker		250	Va.
	Amelia		36				Va.

- 11 -

	Name		Age	Occupation	Real	Pers.	Birthplace
	James F.		18	Laborer			"
	Judy		16				"
	John K.		15	Laborer			Tenn.
	Rebecca A.		12				"
	Louisa C.		10				"
	William		5				"
	Sarah E.		2				"
93	Allen	HIGHTOWER	48	"		200	S. C.
	Driscilla		28				N. C.
	Jane		19				Tenn.
	John		14				"
	Nancy		8				"
	Joseph M.		7				"
	Harrit		4				"
	James R.		2				"
	Annanias		10/12				"
94	John	STUART	67	Farmer	24,300	21,845	"
	D. Ward	STUART	35	County Clerk		1,000	"
	George	STUART	22	Fox Hunter			"
95	William	McNABB	42	Trader		2,000	"
	Minerva		41				"
	John		15				"
	Nancy J.		8				"
	Elias		6				"
96	Henry	JACK	80	Hunter		9,800	"
	Delilah		25				"

Page 15   8 June 1860
	Joel N.	COWAN	7				Tenn.
97	Alvy	JACK	43	Farmer	15,000	7,335	"
	Laura E.		14				"
	Emma		12				"
	Henry		10				"
	Florence		6				"
	John	CLARK	86				S. C.
98	F. R.	WHITE	64	Laborer		25	"
	Mary		50				Unknown
	Martha	SHELTON	25				N. C.
	Elizabeth		6				Tenn.
	John H.	WHITE	6				N. C.
99	Aaron	HATLEY	41			50	Tenn.
	Eliza J.		10				"
	John H.		8				"
	G. W.		6				"
	Mary A.		4				"
	William		2				"
	Telitha	LUMILLA	23				"
	Sarah S.		1				"
100	William F.	WHITE	30	Laborer		40	N. C.
	Sarah J.		28				Va.
	William C.		8				N. C.
	Jane A.		5				"

	Name		Age	Occupation	Real	Pers.	Birthplace
	John		6				"
	Sarah N.		1				Tenn.
101	Charles	MORELL	58	Farmer	1,200	800	Va.
	Eliza		52				Tenn.
	Joseph		20				"
	John		17				"
	Jane		14				"
	Nancy		12				"
	James R.		10				"
102	Grigsby	WOOD	39	Farmer	6,500	3,588	"
	Rachel		36				"
	John		15				"
	Jaly (f)		13				"
	Columbus		11				"
	Lewis		9				"
	Sarah E.		7				"

Page 16   8 June 1860

	Name		Age	Occupation	Real	Pers.	Birthplace
	Fanny		5				Tenn.
	Andrew J.		2				"
103	Lafayette	STOREY	25	Farmer	2,000	600	"
	Mary A.		35				"
	Eliza		18				"
	John		15				"
	Sarah		13				"
	Thomas	MOORE	20	Laborer			"
	Chance	COOPER	21	"			Ky.
	Sarah J. McCLERKING (bl)		18				S. C.
	Doctor W.	(mul)	16				"
	Martha S.	"	14				"
	Mary E.	(bl)	12				"
	John N.	"	9				Tenn.
	Harrit L.	"	8				"
	Francis C.(f)	"	5				"
	Amanda J.	"	3				"
104	William	BROTHERTON	77	Laborer	350		N. C.
	Margaret		67				Tenn.
	George		30				"
105	Lawson H.	BRIDGES	25	"		30	"
	Plassee (f)		26				"
	James D.		4				"
	Mary E.		2				"
	Nathaniel		11/12				"
106	Austin	TAYLOR	34	"		20	"
	Mary		22				"
	Major		8				"
	Mary J.		6				"
	Benjamin		4				"
	Sarah E.		1				"
107	James	DAWSON	29	Farmer		500	"
	Margaret		33				"
	James R.		1				"
	Sarah C.		7/12				"

	Name		Age	Occupation	Real	Pers.	Birthplace
108	B. F.	HARRIS	30	"	1,000	100	N. C.
	Oliva A.		34				Tenn.
	Theodore H.		3				"
	Julia A.		6/12				"
109	Thomas L.	SMITH	26	Laborer			"

Page 17   8 June 1860

	Name		Age	Occupation	Real	Pers.	Birthplace
	Margaret		20				Tenn.
	Franklin		1				"
	Julia A.		1/12				"
110	George P.	HUFF	24	Sawyer	2,000	1,500	"
	Catharine J.		21				"
	Sarah E.		2				"
111	Sarah	HUFF	58		15,000	5,000	"
	Julia		33				"
	William H.		30	Farmer			"
112	Bryson	KELLY	50	"			Va.
	Sinia		48				S. C.
	Sarah J.		8				Tenn.
	Harris		6				"
	Lucy		79				N. C.
113	George W.	PRATER	22	Laborer		20	Tenn.
	Jane	"	25				N. C.
114	Daniel M.	GRAHAM	49	Miller		100	Tenn.
	Elizabeth		40				"
	James M.		19				"
	Margaret		17				"
	Amanda F.		14				"
	John W.		6				"
	Elizabeth		3				"
	William A.	HIEFNER	1				"
115	James	CLARK	65	Farmer	9,000	5,000	"
	James A.		18	Laborer			"
	Issabella C.		13				"
116	Adam	HOLT	38	Carpenter	1,100	800	"
	Elizabeth		38				"
	Martha		16				"
	Mary		13				"
	Elizabeth		12				"
	Joseph A.		10				"
	Laura		7				"
	Joseph	SHAVER	14				"
117	David	MANNING	65	Farmer	2,000	700	"
	Tabitha		41				"
	Elsa		36				"
	Lucy		33				"
	Deberah		31				"

Page 18   8 June 1860

	Name		Age	Occupation	Real	Pers.	Birthplace
	Nancy		29				Tenn.
	Ellinora		21				"
	Charity A.		6				"

- 14 -

	Name		Age	Occupation	Real	Pers.	Birthplace
118	Oliver	FRESHOUR	45	Farmer		150	N. C.
	Peggy		26				"
	George		11				Tenn.
	Alexander		4				"
	Samuel		1				"
119	Calvin M.	HUTSON	37	"	800	400	"
	Martha		32				"
	John J.		8				"
	Laomy (f)		5				"
	Rachel		4				"
	Sarah J.		1				"
	Obediah		69	Laborer			Va.
120	Sarah	HULL	30			75	Tenn.
	Joseph		16				"
	Martin		84				N. C.
	Drusilla		75				"
121	William	MURPHY	55	Farmer		300	Va.
	Robert		24	Blacksmith		200	Tenn.
	William B.		21				"
	Martha J.		20				"
	Mary E.		18				"
	David C.		14				"
	James		7				"
	Caroline		10				"
122	James H.	CLARK	31	Farmer	7,000	2,500	"
	Sinia		29				"
	James N.		10				"
	John L.		8				"
	Joseph S.		4				"
	Thomas M.		2				"
	Elizabeth E.		8/12				"
123	Nancy A.	CLARK	58			350	"
124	John	WISE	30	Laborer		55	"
	Elizabeth		30				"
	Sarah		12				"
	Andrew		9				"
	Rachel		5				"

Page 19   8 June 1860

	Name		Age	Occupation	Real	Pers.	Birthplace
	Howard		3				Tenn.
	Calaway		9/12				"
125	Calaway	ATKINS	23	Laborer		100	"
	Martha		30				"
126	Mary G.	CLARK	55		3,500	2,000	"
	Seth R.		27	Farmer			"
127	George B.	ROGERS	46	"	7,000	2,000	"
	Priscilla D.		33				"
	Mark M.		15				"
	James C.		14				"
	William F.		12				"
	Penelope H.		10				"

	Name		Age	Occupation	Real	Pers.	Birthplace
	Amanda J.		8				"
	George D.		4				"
128	Creed	RANKIN	38	"		500	"
	Martha J.		34				"
	George S.		10				"
	Thomas W.		6				"
	Elizabeth J.		3				"
129	John	MOORE	29	Laborer		100	"
	Lydia		30				"
	William		6				"
	James		5				"
	Amanda		3				"
130	James	BUCKNER	63	"		75	Va.
131	Calvin	ATKINS	21	"			Tenn.
	Elizabeth		22				"
	Alexander		1				"
	Andrew J.		3/12				"
132	George W.	JONES	22	"		30	"
	Mary		22				"
	Amanda M.		3				"
	Telitha P.		1				"
133	William	JONES	58	"		12	"
	Hannah		45				"
	Rebecca		18				"
	Elizabeth		13				"
	Emily		10				"
	Martha		9				"
	Nancy		7				"

Page 20   NEWPORT   8 June 1860

	Name		Age	Occupation	Real	Pers.	Birthplace
	Simon		7				Tenn.
	Margaret		1				"
134	Elijah	WOOD	45	Laborer		5	N. C.
	Jane	(Blind)	35				Tenn.
	Rachel		22	"			Va.
	James		18				"
	Sarah		15				Tenn.
	Elizabeth		10				"
	Martha		7				"
	David		5				"
	Benjamin F.		2				"
	Francis M.	(m)	2				"
	Benjamin F.		5/12				"
	Francis M.	(m)	5/12				"
135	James A.	BUCKNER	39	Farmer		500	"
	Lavisca		37				"
	Robert W.		12				"
	Marvel M.		9				"
	Joseph		8				"
	Amanda		7				"
	James H.		6				"

1860 U. S. CENSUS OF COCKE COUNTY, TENNESSEE

Name		Age	Occupation	Real	Pers.	Birthplace
Martha		2				"
Lawsen D.		3				"
Calvin		5/12				"
Sarah	SHAVER	13				"
136 Levi	GUINN	45	"		50	"
Mary		33				"
Gabriel		15				"
Isaac J.		14				"
Rebecca		12				"
Cristina		9				"
Margaret E.		7				"
137 Andrew	WISE	44	"		300	"
Rachel		47				"
Susannah		16				"
Martha J.		14				"
Mary		9				"
Rachel F.		8				"
138 Levi	ATKINS	21	Laborer		75	"
Nancy		18				"

Page 21   9 June 1860

Name		Age	Occupation	Real	Pers.	Birthplace
Sarah C.		1				Tenn.
Nancy		63				Va.
139 William	MOORE	67	Farmer	1,800	1,000	"
Settelia		33				Tenn.
William		27				"
Clarissa		22				"
George		21				"
140 Elijah	BUCKNER	27	"		175	"
Catharine		30				"
Lemuel		3				"
Laura		2				"
Millard F.		8/12				"
141 Franklin DICKSON (mwy)		22	"		25	N. C.
Martha		18				Tenn.
142 G. P. H.	TALLEY	29	"		200	"
Emeline		28				"
Nancy E.		6				"
Noah		3				"
Cordelius (m)		2				"
Rachel		6/12				"
143 Moses P.	FREEMAN	36	"		55	N. C.
Margaret		37				"
William G.		13				Tenn.
John A.		9				N.C.
Mary		4				Tenn.
Joseph M.		2				"
Enos	SHIELDS	1/12				"
Martha	WRIGHT	26				"
Elizabeth		4				"

	Name		Age	Occupation	Real	Pers.	Birthplace
144	Andrew	RAMSEY	37	Farmer	20,000	15,000	"
	Dorcus		38				"
	Harriet		39				"
145	Coleman	BURGES	29	Laborer		50	S. C.
	Ferbily	(f)	29				Tenn.
	Martha C.		5				"
	Mary J.		1				"
	Joseph M.		2/12				"
146	White	MOORE	69	Farmer	5,000	14,065	Va.
	Hannah		58				Tenn.
	Mary E.		23				"

Page 22   13 June 1860

	Name		Age	Occupation	Real	Pers.	Birthplace
	Margaret M.		19				Tenn.
	Esabella W.	PERDLAND	37				"
	James T. W.		14				"
	Harvy	INMAN (bl)	35				"
147	Alvin	BRADY	42	Laborer			N. C.
	Sarah		18				Tenn.
	Simon		17				"
	Dolly		16				"
	George		14				"
	Nancy		13				"
	James F.		11				"
	Mary		7				"
	Priscilla		6				"
148	John H.	GLAZE	38	Farmer	1,500	3,838	"
	Martha J.		30				"
149	John W.	SLADE	25	Laborer		220	"
	Martha		24				"
	Rebecca M.		53				Va.
150	John	BRADY	38	Farmer	1,500	400	Tenn.
	Harriet		37				"
	William		6				"
	Thomas		5				"
	Hugh J.		4				"
	Nancy E.		3				"
	John W.		4/12				"
	Nancy		44				"
151	David	WAYMIRE	40	Farmer	350	400	N. C.
	Mary		18				Tenn.
	Irene		17				"
	James W.		14				"
	Susannah		12				"
	Elizabeth		11				"
	Jonas		9				"
	Nancy		24				"
152	Ransom	FOX	56	"		400	N. C.
	Penelope		62				Tenn.
	Carter		20	Laborer			"
	Robert		16				"

	Name		Age	Occupation	Real	Pers.	Birthplace
153	Preston	CAMPBELL	34	Farmer	500	350	"
	Emaline		33				"
Page 23 Leadvale							13 June 1860
	Isabella		12				Tenn.
	Jonas		6				"
	Mary M.		6/12				"
154	William B.	REAMS	30	Farmer	600	500	"
	Martha L.		34				"
	John W.		8				"
	Howard O.		6				"
	Frances	(m)	5				"
	Catharine J.		2				"
155	Isaac	FOWLER	33	"	400	300	"
	Nancy A.		25				"
	Joseph L.		6				"
	Francis A.	(f)	3				"
	Cassa H.	(f)	1				"
	Joseph		23	Laborer			"
	Elizabeth	RISSATOR	90				Va.
	Lucinda	FOWLER	15				Tenn.
	John	DEAN	30	(Idiotic)			"
156	David	WAYMIRE	25	"		100	"
	Amanda		24				"
	Clarinda		2				"
	William A.		11/12				"
	Margaret	MAYNOR	16				"
157	Jonas	WAYMIRE	48	Farmer	1,000	400	N. C.
	Charles		20	Laborer			Tenn.
	Thomas		18	"			"
158	William W.	DICKSON	36	"		100	"
	Susannah E.		27				"
	Eliza A.		8				"
	David		7				"
	Mary J.		5				"
	Jonas		3				"
	Joseph		4/12				
159	Baldwin H.	SOLOMAN	28	"		200	"
	Catharine		26				"
	Pauline		3				"
	William		1				"
160	Benoni C.	TALLY	51	Farmer	650	2,400	"
	Nancy		54				"
161	John	LESTER (mwy)	27	"	900	500	"
Page 24							13 June 1860
	Julia	(mwy)	22				Tenn.
	John	OWENS	23	Laborer		100	Va.
162	Calvin	SOLOMAN	34	Farmer	2,000	400	Tenn.
	John H.		12				"
	James M.		9				"

	Name		Age	Occupation	Real	Pers.	Birthplace
	Tilghman H.		5				"
	Josiah		3	(Idiotic)			"
163	Thomas W.	INMAN	57	"		700	"
	Mary J.		18				"
	Lincoln A.		15				"
	Thomas J.		8				"
	Rachel	FOX	34				"
164	Tilghman H.	SOLOMAN	30	"		300	"
	Sarah		38				"
165	Samuel	REED	33	Laborer		20	"
	Martha		25				"
	Hamilton		9				"
	Mary		7				"
	Elijah		6				"
	Charles		3				"
166	Calloway H.	BRAGG	44	Farmer		375	"
	Mary A.		32				"
	Ellender		17				"
	Julia A.		15				"
	Caroline		12				"
	William		10				"
	Mary		8				"
	James L.		1				"
	Thomas		11				"
167	Joseph H.	THRASHER	42	"	1,450	600	"
	Elizabeth		45				"
	Sarah J.		11				"
	William L.		10				"
	Joseph G.		7				"
	Isaac F.		4				"
	Louisa A.		2				"
168	Jane	SOLOMAN	70		500	200	Md.
	Ellender		29				Tenn.
	John W.		4				"
	Andrew J.		2				"
Page 25						13 June 1860	
169	Mary	SOLOMAN	64		1,300	500	Tenn.
	John		24				"
170	C. C.	TURNER	44	Farmer	6,500	2,200	"
	Martha		46				Ky.
	Andrew J.		20				Tenn.
	Isaac A.		18				"
	Susannah		15				"
	Charles C.		12				"
	Joseph D.	(mwy)	24	Laborer			"
	Sarah E.		16				"
171	James	TURNER	22	Farmer		100	"
172	George W.	INMAN	29			1,000	"
	Dorthula		23				"
	Rufus		10/12				"

	Name		Age	Occupation	Real	Pers.	Birthplace
173	George W.	WARD	50	Laborer		275	N. C.
	Martha		30				"
	William		18	"			Tenn.
	Mary		17				"
	Sarah		13				"
	Richard		12				"
	George W.		1/12				"
174	Joseph	TALLY	60	Farmer	2,600	1,800	"
	Sarah		59				"
	Dudley		27	Laborer			"
	Benjamin		25	"			"
	Jeremiah		24	"			"
	Alexander		22	"			"
	Daniel F.		20	"			"
	Mary A.		17				"
	Sarah		14				"
175	David	DRISKILL	42	"	60	100	"
	Sarah		42				"
	Eliza		17				"
	Orlena		16				"
	James P. H.		14				"
	John		11				"
	William		9				"
	David		6				"
	Hardin B.		3				"
	Sarah E.		1				"

Page 26   13 June 1860

	Name		Age	Occupation	Real	Pers.	Birthplace
176	John	INMAN	64	Farmer	15,000	4,840	Tenn.
	Margaret		32				"
177	William	SMITH	40	Laborer		25	"
	John		14				"
178	James H.	TURNER	29	Farmer		200	"
	Martha		23				"
	Elizabeth		4				"
	John		3				"
	Charles C.		8/12				"
179	James	FOX (mwy)	30	Laborer	-	125	"
	Jane		24				N. C.
	G. W.	DICKSON	23		1,000	130	Tenn.
180	Mary J.		25				"
	Nancy A.		4				"
	John		2				"
	Thomas		1				"
181	S. H.	INMAN	47	Farmer	4,000	2,350	"
	Julia		44				"
	James C.		22				"
	Ruth		19				"
	John		16				"
	Thomas		61		1,000	200	"
	Osbern (bl)		50			75	"

	Name		Age	Occupation	Real	Pers.	Birthplace
182	Jonas B.	CASTILLES	44	Minister Bapt.	2,500	4,000	N. C.
	William		22	Carpenter			Tenn.
	Isabella		15				"
	Mary F.		10				"
183	James	TALLEY	64	Farmer	3,500	4,248	"
	Prudence		60				"
	Mary		37				"
	Bradley W.		30				"
	Elizabeth		15				"
184	Thomas J.	BRIZANDIM	27	Laborer		150	"
	Nancy		28				"
	Anna		8				"
	Joel		7				"
	Mary J.		5				"
	Thomas		4				"
	Isabella		1				"
185	Thomas		73	"		50	Va.

Page 27   14 June 1860

	Name		Age	Occupation	Real	Pers.	Birthplace
	Martha		68				Va.
186	William Y.	MARTIN	48	Farmer	1,000	400	Tenn.
	Mary A.		38				"
	Jubra (?)		14				"
187	Bradley W.	TALLEY	56	"	3,000	400	"
	Carter B.		21				"
	James M.		17				"
	William B.		11				"
	Edward		9				"
188	Charles M.	FOX	25	"	350	350	"
	Mary		23				"
	Rithy M.		3				"
	Sarah	TALLY	47				"
189	George	REED	37	Laborer		75	"
	Mary		36				"
	William		16				"
	John		16				"
	Thomas		12				"
	Louisa J.		9				"
	Robert		6				"
190	Elizabeth	FOX	48		650	250	"
	Maranda		20				"
	Priscilla		18				"
	John		13				"
	Jonas		11				"
191	John	DICKSON	22	"		300	"
	Susannah		21				"
	Elizabeth		3				"

	Name		Age	Occupation	Real	Pers.	Birthplace
192	Martha	REED	58		1,000	300	"
	Caroline		26				"
	Elizabeth		18				"
	Isabel		15				"
193	London	REED	28	"		200	"
	Margaret		23				"
	Martha		4				"
	Sarah		2				"
	London		3/12				"
194	Arthur	REED	24		400	100	"
	Martha		20				"
	Caroline		2				"
Page 28							14 June 1860
	Robert		10				Tenn.
195	Elijah	REED	36	Farmer		250	"
	Harriet		19				"
	Mary		3				"
	Edney		2				"
	Jane		4/12				"
196	John	TURNER	55	Farmer	2,000	1,217	"
	Mary A.		61				"
	John		22				"
	Isaac		23				"
	Russel		3				"
	Absalem	FOX	9				"
197	P. M.	TURNER	27	"		300	"
	Mary J.		18				"
	John		1				"
	Lavina J.		4/12				"
198	John	TALLEY	65	Farmer	900	400	Va.
	Joseph		20				Tenn.
	John		18				"
	Julia		17				"
	James		15				"
	William		14				"
	Alexander B.		8				"
199	Wiley	NOLEN	62	Farmer	350	175	N. C.
	Elizabeth		56				Va.
	Mary		37				N. C.
	Benjamin		25				Tenn.
	Charles J.		21				"
	David		18				"
	William		13				"
	Caroline		15				"
	Penelope		12				"
200	Sarah	WALDEN	43		150	20	N. C.
	Narcissus		17				Tenn.
	Sarah J.		14				"
	Lucinda		11				"
	Clara E.		2				"

	Name		Age	Occupation	Real	Pers.	Birthplace
201	Beverly B.	TALLY	23	"		250	"
	Mary S.		20				"
	Bradly W.		2				"

Page 29   15 June 1860

	Name		Age	Occupation	Real	Pers.	Birthplace
	Lucinda		8/12				Tenn.
202	Jesse	CRUMLEY	59	Farmer	300	720	N. C.
	Emily		40				S. C.
	Lucinda		14				Tenn.
	John		13				"
	Rufus M.		12				"
	Louisa		10				"
	Sina		8				"
	Jesse A.		6				"
	Parthula (f)		4				"
	Winnie		3				"
	Emily		1				"
203	William	CRUMLEY (mwy)	23	Laborer		50	"
	Margaret		22				"
204	James	CAFFY	27	Farmer	750	300	"
	Martha		21				"
	Benjamin		5				"
	Darthula		3				"
	William		9/12				"
	Isaac		26	Laborer			"
205	Charles P.	TALLY	26	"		200	"
	Susannah		23				"
	Ransome		1				"
	Sarah E.		10/12				"
206	Rufus M.	KELLY	33	Farmer	400	240	"
	Kissiah		28				"
	Josephus		13				"
	Mary A.		9				"
	Rufus M.		2				"
	Kissiah B.		3/12				"
207	Moses	DRISKILL	50	"	2,000	1,122	Va.
	Brittana N.		48				Tenn.
	Mahal (m)		25				"
	Benjamin F.		20				"
	Moses E.		15				"
	Mary H.		12				"
	Martha P.		12				"
	Elizabeth	SMITH	60	Spinster (Idiotic)			"
208	Lemuel	WILDER	56	Wheel Wright		50	N. C.
	Elizabeth		58				Va.

Page 30   15 June 1860

	Name	Age	Occupation	Birthplace
	Ellen	18		Tenn.
	Lemuel	16	Laborer	"
	Mary J.	14		"
	William	32	Chairmaker	Va.
	Phebe E.	6		Tenn.

	Name		Age	Occupation	Real	Pers.	Birthplace
209	R. A. STEPHENSON (mwy)		26	Wagon Maker		125	Va.
	Martha		17				Tenn.
	Seth	CAFFY	21	Laborer			
210	William H.	ELLIS	37	Farmer	650	250	"
	Mary A.		35				"
	Adaline		13				"
	Martha L.		11				"
	Temperance E.		9				"
	Isaac H.		7				"
	Lawson F.		5				"
	Sarah M.		1				"
211	Elbert	ELLIS	67	"	1,000	1,456	N. C.
	Temperance		54				Tenn.
	Richard		21	"			"
	Darcus M.		18				"
	Elbert		15				"
	Jefferson		13				"
	Moses		12				"
212	Daniel	WHITE	35	"	700	850	N. C.
	Sarah		36				Tenn.
	Martha J.		16				"
	Sarah E.		15				"
	Mary		13				"
	Margaret		11				"
	Catharine D.		8				"
213	Sampson	WARD	69	Laborer		100	N. C.
	Liles (f)		48				Tenn.
	Sarah		14				"
214	William	HOLT	42	Farmer		325	"
	Martha		39				"
	Josiah		18	Laborer			"
	William		15	"			"
	Basdell G.		12				"
	James A.		11				"
	George P.		8				"
Page 31 Warnsburg							16 June 1860
	Preston J.		6				Tenn.
	Calafornia (f)		4				"
	Martha J.		11/12				"
215	Elizabeth	DRISKEL	76		3,500	200	Va.
	Catharine	INMAN	8				Tenn.
	Elizabeth	WILLIAMS	44				"
	Minerva		13				"
	Ora		10				"
	Petolonia		5				S. A.(?) ————
216	Robert Y.	SCULLY (mwy)	28	B. Smith		200	Tenn.
	Elizabeth		16				"
217	Dempsey	MOORE	58	Farmer	3,000	300	"
	Mary J.		18				"
	Dempsy		16	Laborer			"
	Joseph		15				"

	Name		Age	Occupation	Real	Pers.	Birthplace
	John		14				"
	Thomas S.		12				"
	Sarah C.		9				"
	Martha		5				"
	Pleasant W.		5/12				"
218	William	MOORE	28	Farmer		325	"
	Mildred A.		27				"
	Lafayett		1				"
219	Thos. M.	JONES	40	Farmer	1,000	4,114	"
	Eliza		25				"
	Daniel D.		16	Laborer			"
	Robert M.		10				"
	Richard J.		4				"
	Lavica L.	(f)	2				"
220	Tilghman	LEDFORD	46	Laborer		75	N. C.
	Mildred		42				"
	Carlene		27				"
	Jessee (m)		15				S. C.
	Adam		12				Tenn.
	Sarah		8				"
	Sims		8				"
	Mildred		4				"
	Nancy		2				"
221	John	KELLY	63	Farmer	633	710	N. C.
	Mary		64				Tenn.
Page 32							16 June 1860
	Nancy		39				Tenn.
	Mary		34				"
222	John	KELLY, Jr.	21	Farmer		300	"
	Agnus		22				"
	Mary		6/12				"
223	John W.	NOLEN	34	Farmer		470	N. C.
	Sarah		40				Tenn.
	John W.	WORTH	16	Laborer			"
	Mary		14				"
	Nancy	NOLEN	9				"
	Mary C.		7				"
	Sarah M.		5				"
	John W. W.		2				"
224	Simon	KELLY	26	Farmer	200	400	Tenn.
	Christina		22				"
	Sarah		3				"
	Mary E.		2				"
	William D.		9/12				"
225	William	KELLY	24	"			"
	Elizabeth		21				"
	Sarah J.		3				"
	John H.		2				"
	Simon M.		1				"

	Name		Age	Occupation	Real	Pers.	Birthplace
226	Lovina	FOX	32			75	Tenn.
	Nancy P.		9				"
	Josiah J.		8				"
	Mary A.		6				"
	Susannah E.		4				"
	Rufus M.		10/12				"
227	James S.	HOLT	51	Laborer		150	Va.
	Mahaly		45				"
	Edward		21	Laborer			Tenn.
	Mary		18				"
	Sarah		16				"
	James W.		10				"
	Isaac		6				
	Lydia		4				"
	James	BOSWELL	2				"
228	Henry	HALL	32	Farmer		300	"
	Manerva		23				"

Page 33   NEWPORT   16 June 1860

	Name		Age	Occupation	Real	Pers.	Birthplace
	Martha		9				Tenn.
	Willoby		7				"
	Drucillah		5				"
	William		3				"
	Amanda (f)		1				"
229	Anthony	CHRISTIAN	37	Farmer	3,000	1,100	Tenn.
	Sarah		37				"
	Julia A.		16				"
	John W.		14				"
	Elizabeth M.		11				"
	Mary E. A.		8				"
	W. B.		10				"
230	Judith	BAILY	50			40	N. C.
	William		19	Laborer			"
	Rubin		17				Tenn.
	John		13				"
	Sarah	ELLIS	60				N. C.
231	F. D.	TAYLOR	40	Laborer		10	Va.
	Martha		40				N. C.
	James		15	"			Tenn.
	Jane		12				"
232	Samuel	MALONE	59	Laborer		50	"
	Mary		48				Va.
	William		22	(Idiotic)			Tenn.
	John		10				"
	James		7				"
233	OMITTED						
234	Fanny	FARMER	80			5	Va.
235	John	WISE	48	Farmer		235	Tenn.
	Luanda		36				"

	Name		Age	Occupation	Real	Pers.	Birthplace
	Anderson		15				"
	Nelson		12				"
	John		8				"
	Coleman		4				"
	Rachel		67				Va.
	Sarah		32				Tenn.
	Anderson		33	Laborer			"
	Sarah		5				"
	John		4				"
236	Jane	WARD	67				N. C.
	Julia (mul)		22				"

Page 34   18 June 1860

	Name		Age	Occupation	Real	Pers.	Birthplace
237	Young E.	BROOKS	39	Farmer	1,000	900	S. C.
	Sarah		36				Tenn.
	Elizabeth		15				"
	Lucy C.		14				"
	William C.		12				"
	Obediah		11				"
	Jane		7				"
	John		5				"
	James		4				"
	Andrew		4/12				"
238	Sarah	WOOD	56		9,000	15,316	S. C.
	David		31	Farmer			Tenn.
	William		27				"
	Thomas		25				"
	Jeptha		20				"
	Agnus (f)		17				"
239	James	JONES	47	Laborer		20	"
	Elizabeth		38				"
	Thomas		12				"
	Alex		2				"
240	Maxwell	BIBEE	28	Farmer	600	350	"
	Elizabeth		34				"
	John W.		8				"
	Sarah M.		7				"
	Joseph H.		4				"
241	Tipton	BIBEE	34	Farmer	2,000	800	Tenn.
	Pateince		33				In.
	William		7				Tenn.
	Joseph M.		3				"
	July (f)		4/12				"
	Elizabeth	GILLETT	47				"
242	John	MIDCALF	50	Farmer		350	N. C.
	Mahaly		34				Tenn.
	Elizabeth		16				"
	William D.		13				"
	Selina		11				"
	Joseph		9				"
	Sarah F.		7				N. C.
	James R.		4				"

	Name		Age	Occupation	Real	Pers.	Birthplace
243	William	BUCKNER	60	Farmer	2,000	1,160	"

Page 35   18 June 1860

	Name		Age	Occupation	Real	Pers.	Birthplace
	Leher (f)		58				N. C.
	Nancy		23				Tenn.
	Leher (f)		19				"
	John		18				"
	Jasper		16				"
	Newton		16				"
	Samuel		14				"
	Sarah		11				"
244	Charles	KELLY	48	Farmer	2,000	1,320	"
	Lucinda E.		42				N. C.
	William		20	Laborer			Tenn.
	Sarah E.		14				"
	Lucy C.		11				"
	Jaly (f)		3				"
	Charles		3				"
245	John	GILLETT	65	Farmer	6,000	22,478	N. C.
	July		63				Tenn.
246	John	FOX	29	Farmer			"
	Martha		25				"
	Sarah E.		6				"
	Mary J.		4				"
	John		2				"
	Benonie C.		1				"
247	John	HARPER	56	Laborer		90	S. C.
	Malinda		45				"
	Nancy		17				"
	Sarah		15				"
	Mary		13				"
	Robert		6				"
	Martha J.		5				"
	John		3				"
	William B.		2/12				Tenn.
	John F.		2				"
248	Wiot	MAYFIELD	45	Laborer		35	"
249	John	MAYFIELD	40			30	"
	Disa		40				"
	Samuel		14				"
	Henry		12				"
	George		8				"
	John		2				"

Page 36   18 June 1860

	Name		Age	Occupation	Real	Pers.	Birthplace
250	Elijah	FOX	30			260	Tenn.
	Carline		32				S. C.
	Gilford		9				Tenn.
	Ransom		7				"
	Benonie C.		2				"

	Name		Age	Occupation	Real	Pers.	Birthplace
251	George D.	HOLT	26	Laborer		300	"
	Mary		27				"
	Matilda	COPLEN	15				S. C.
252	A. J.	GILLET	43	Farmer	4,760	6,655	Tenn.
	Mariah		42				"
	Sarah E.		16				"
	John		15				"
	Mary J.		11				"
253	Thomas	DOCKINS	46	Laborer		40	S. C.
	Esther J.		21				Tenn.
	James R.		2				"
	William		9/12				"
254	Thomas	STEPHENSON	24	Waggon Maker		100	Va.
	Sarah E.		21				Tenn.
	Andrew J.		4				"
	Sarah J.		2				"
255	William	THOMAS	27	Farmer	1,750	1,612	"
	Eliza A.		27				"
	James P.		1				"
	Eliza		1/12				"
256	John	THOMAS	51	Farmer	2,500	3,610	"
	Louiza		45				"
	Mary		14				"
	Jeremiah		11				"
	Mildred		7				"
	Amanda		3				"
	William	DUGLES	41	Gunsmith		10	N. C.
257	Lowry	THOMAS (mwy)	19	Laborer		40	Tenn.
	Nancy		17				"
258	Samuel	ROGERS	49	Laborer		25	N. C.
	Nancy		52				Tenn.
	Lucinda		15	(Idiotic)			"
259	George	THOMAS	25	Farmer	800	570	"
	Binda		26				"
	George J.		2				"
Page 37							18 June 1860
	Jacob		1				Tenn.
	James		6/12				"
260	Drury	DAWSON	32	Farmer	2,000	1,050	"
	Elizabeth		31				"
	Britana		12				"
	Mary		10				"
	Isaac		8				"
	James		6				"
	Temperance		5				"
	Shadrack		2				"
261	Alfred	DAWSON (mwy)	22			275	"
	Elizabeth		22				Va.

1860 U. S. CENSUS OF COCKE COUNTY, TENNESSEE

	Name		Age	Occupation	Real	Pers.	Birthplace
262	Joseph E.	CONWAY	28			300	Tenn.
	Elizabeth		23				"
	Elizabeth		9				"
	James		7				
	Mary J.		6				"
	Penelope		4				
	Ruth A.		1				"
263	Elisha	BUCKNER	28	Laborer		390	"
	Susannah		27				
	John W.		7				
	Samuel		5				
	Daniel		3				
	Leah E.		2/12				
264	John	BUCKNER	65	Farmer	960	745	N. C.
	Rachel		58				"
	John L.		23				Tenn.
	Rebecca		20				"
	Levi		19				
	Lucinda		14				
265	Nancy	MOSS	54			5	Va.
	James H.		16	(Idiotic)			N. C.
266	Alexander	FOWLER	29	Farmer		300	Tenn.
	Lucinda		29				"
	Phebe		6				"
	Andrew		4				"
	Heward (m)		1				"
	Jane		18				"
267	David	DRISKILL	36	"		350	"

Page 38   WARRENSBURG   19 June 1860

	Name		Age	Occupation	Real	Pers.	Birthplace
	Elizabeth		36				Va.
	Francis M.	(m)	14				Tenn.
	Elizabeth E.		12				"
	Robert A.		10				"
	Eliza E.		7				"
	David T.		5				"
	Charles P.		4				
	Daniel		2				
268	Robert	INMAN	37	Farmer	3,000	1,495	"
	Mary		30				
	John		4				
	Sarah		3				
	Margaret P.		1				
	Mary	MURRY	66				Va.
269	Alexander	TALLEY	41	"		6,350	Tenn.
	Elvira		37				
	Catharine		15				
	Nancy E.		13				
	Richard D.		9				
	Lucy C.		7				
	Maranda P.		5				
	Hannah		3				"

	Name		Age	Occupation	Real	Pers.	Birthplace
270	James H.	JONES	30	"	6,000	2,696	"
	Sarah M.		25				"
	Reps		2				
271	James	MARTIN	46	Laborer		640	"
	Nancy		46				"
	Martha		27				"
	Mary A.		26				"
	James F.		21	"			
	Thomas		19	"			
	Josiah		19				
	Alexander		13				
	Margaret		11				
	Laura		10				
	Rebecca		8				
	Susannah		4				
	Eliza J.		8				
272	Daniel	JONES	50	Farmer	12,000	6,147	"
	Utalla C.		44				

Page 39   20 June 1860

	Name		Age	Occupation	Real	Pers.	Birthplace
	William R.		17				
	Mary D.		15				
	Nancy A.		12				
	Thomas M.		8				
	James D.		6				
	Daniel A.		3				
	Branch J.		1				
273	Thomas	BUCKNER	41	Laborer		175	Tenn.
	Elizabeth		37				N. C.
	William H.		18				Tenn.
	Nancy E.		4				"
	Sarah	ALEXANDER	34				N. C.
	Sarah		9				Tenn.
274	Ambrose	CARTWRIGHT	32	"		50	"
	Elizabeth		29				
	William		10				
	Nancy		5				
	James H.		7/12				
275	Thomas	CHRISTIAN	36	Farmer	7,500	6,400	"
	Elmira C.		27				"
	Sarah E.		6				
	Mary A.		3				
	Margaret		6/12				
276	Isham	EDDINGTON	27	"		800	
	Jane		30				"
	Elizabeth		7				"
	John	SHAVER	9				"
	Henry	EDDINGTON	25	Laborer			"
277	Pierce	CAMPBELL	55	"		25	N. C.
	Lutitia		55				"
	Anna		14				Tenn.

	Name		Age	Occupation	Real	Pers.	Birthplace
278	Mary	EDDINGTON	55			20	"
	William H.		20				"
	Nancy		16				
	John		12				
	Joseph		7				
279	William	MARTIN	27	"		50	"
	Catharine		30				"
	William		5/12				
280	John	STANSBERRY	21	"		110	N. C.

Page 40   20 June 1860

	Name		Age	Occupation	Real	Pers.	Birthplace
	Elizabeth		35				Tenn.
	Joseph H.		2/12				
281	Rebecca	HEATH	59				N. C.
	Eliza		29				"
	Mary		21				"
	William G.		24				"
	Hulda C.		19				"
282	Mary	ERVIN	40			40	Tenn.
283	James	MURRY	37	Farmer		235	"
	Elizabeth A.		40				"
	Menirva E.	EVANS	13				
284	Abraham	DAWSON	84	"	400	200	Va.
	Martha		65				"
	Thomas		23	(Idiotic)			Tenn.
285	Abraham	DAWSON, Jr.	28	Laborer		30	"
	Catharine		29				"
	Isaac B.		2				"
286	Lemuel	BIBLE	27	Farmer	3,000	3,475	"
	Perlina		32				
	Albert J.		2				
287	John W.	GILBERT	39	Cooper		50	S. C.
	Nancy		37				N. C.
	Eliza M.		13				Tenn.
	Mary J.		12				N. C.
	Emma A.		10				Tenn.
	Rosaline E.		8				
	Laura C.		7				
	Andrew J.		5				
	Henry A.		4				
	Caswell T.		3				
	Martha		1				
288	C. L. P.	CONWAY	30	Farmer	60	500	"
	Ellender		30				
	Charles		8				
	Mary J.		7				
	James C.		6				
	John		4				

	Name		Age	Occupation	Real	Pers.	Birthplace
289	Hezekiah	MOORE	25	"	1,000	220	
	Martha		23				
	Sarah J.		2				

Page 41   20 June 1860

	Porter C.		4/12				Tenn.
290	Simon	WISE	38	Laborer		17	"
	Mildred		37				
	James H.		11				
	George W.		9				
	Isaac W.		7				
	Martha J.		5				
	Phillip		11/12				
291	Henry	WILLIAMS	37	"		210	N. C.
	Elizabeth		32				Tenn.
292	Ann C.	SMITH	53		800	1,520	"
	Coleman		30	Farmer			"
	John C.		3				"
293	James	MOORE	26	Farmer		250	"
	Lavina		26				"
	Robert		22	Laborer			"
294	William	SMITH	26	Farmer	1,000	378	"
	Sarah		19				"
	Mary J.		3				"
	Stephen D.		1				"
295	Martin	EDINGTON	45	Farmer		200	N. C.
	Martha S.		44				Tenn.
	William		17	Laborer			"
	Fowler F.		15				"
	Alexander		13				"
	Martha J.		9				"
	Jacob S.		2				"
	Mary S.		4				"
296	Rachel A.	ELKINS	48			10	N. C.
	Sarah E.		19				Tenn.
	Christina S.		15				"
	Thos. S.		8				"
297	Juda	BROWN	35			40	"
	Elender		14				"
	Martha		9				"
	Manerva		12				"
	Drueillah		7				"
	Charly		6				"
298	Hal	HOLDAWAY	44	Farmer	1,000	500	"
	William		23	Mcht. Clk.		150	"

Page 42   20 June 1860

	Sarah	"	19				Tenn.
	James		17				
	Sarah		75				Va.

	Name		Age	Occupation	Real	Pers.	Birthplace
299	Martha M.	CAMPBELL	33			25	N. C.
	James R.		9				Tenn.
	Ida J.		5				"
	Joseph L.		4				"
	Sarah E.		2				"
	Mary A.		8/12				"
300	Marshall	HALL	24	Miller		200	"
	Carline		24				"
	Sidna (f)		9				"
	Sarah		8				"
	Elizabeth		5				"
	Eliza		3				"
	Lydia		1/12				"
301	William	HALL	46	Farmer	1,300	1,310	N. C.
	Nancy		40				"
	John A.		21				Tenn.
	Carline		15				"
	Catharine		14				"
	Conway		11				"
	Mary		9				"
	Barshaba		7				"
	Nancy		3				"
	Loueza		3				"
302	Philip	HALL	24	Farmer		450	"
	Mary J.		21				"
	Charles W.		9/12				"
303	Jonathan	BIBLE	52	Farmer	5,000	378	Tenn.
	Sarah J.		26				"
	Patrik		25				"
	Preston		23				"
	Elbert		20				"
	Henry	(mul)	7				"
304	Josiah J.	HOLT	45	Farmer	1,800	3,576	Va.
	Mildred		40				Tenn.
	Sarah E.		16				"
	Mary		15				"
	Sarah M.		12				"

Page 43   20 June 1860

	Name		Age	Occupation	Real	Pers.	Birthplace
	Martha P.	"	11				Tenn.
	Basdell A.		7				"
	David A.		3				"
	Hariett		1				"
305	Lewis	SMITH	43	Farmer	2,000	1,025	"
	Mary		53				"
	Porter		16	Laborer			"
306	Joel M.	SMITH (mwy)	25	Laborer		25	"
	Mary E.		23				"
307	Arch	THOMAS	22	Laborer			Va.
	Rutha A.		18				Tenn.
	Ann	HOG	28				"

	Name		Age	Occupation	Real	Pers.	Birthplace
	James		8				"
	John		5				"
	Joseph	MOSS	11				"
308	Sarah	MAYSON	69		3,000	13,500	Va.
309	John	HOLT	44	Farmer	1,000	2,220	Tenn.
	Lydia		40				"
	Asad (m)		18	Laborer			"
	Susanah		14				"
	Thomas		12				"
	Prudence		10				"
	Pleasant		9				"
	Joseph		7				"
	Margaret		5				"
310	Nancy	REECE	45		200	350	"
	Thomas		18				"
	Eliza J.		17				"
	France (m)		15				"
	Julia		14				"
	Mary		4				"
	James		12				"
311	Mary	HOG	22			30	"
	James G.	(mul)	2				"
	William	(mul)	6/12				"
312	David	SMITH	38	Farmer		500	"
	Eliza		36				"
	Durthula		12				"
	Pelina		10				"
	Pleasant		9				"

Page 44   20 June 1860

	Name		Age	Occupation	Real	Pers.	Birthplace
	Sarah	"	7				Tenn.
	John		6				"
	Mildred		3				"
	Susanah		1				"
313	Jesse	MATHIS	39	Laborer		250	S. C.
	Mary E.		19				Tenn.
	Elvira		3				"
	James S.		2				"
	Hariett		4/12				"
314	Sarah	MATHIS	45			30	S. C.
	Abell	MATHIS	32				"
	Clara		25				"
	James		20	"			"
	Allen		17	"			"
	Elizabeth		14				"
	Jane		12				Tenn.
315	George	MATHIS	25	Laborer		80	S. C.
	Rachel		25				Tenn.
316	Thomas J.	TALLEY	27	Farmer	1,360	415	"
	Sarah C.		22				"
	James K.		3				"

	Name		Age	Occupation	Real	Pers.	Birthplace
317	Sarah	DUN	36			20	N. C.
	James H.		13				Tenn.
	Sarah A.		8				"
	Margaret		2				"
	William		2/12				"
	Sarah	MAYFIELD	25				"
	William		2				"
318	Thomas	KESTERSON	31	Farmer	2,500	728	"
	Carline		30				"
	Sarah A.		5				"
	Emaline		4				"
	Catharine		2				"
319	William	HOLDAWAY	43	Farmer	4,000	4,250	"
	Frances		44				"
	Joseph		21	Laborer			"
	Stephen D.		20				"
	Mary J.		17				"
320	Charles	TALLEY	34	Farmer	1,360	450	"
	Sarah		29				Va.

Page 45   21 June 1860

	Elizabeth		3				Tenn.
	Mary		1				"
	Pernicilia	HARPER	30				S. C.
321	Valentine	CLINE	35	Farmer	24	500	N. C.
	Margaret		32				"
	Andrew J.		10				Tenn.
	Mary		7				"
	Joseph M.		6				"
	Mariah		4				"
	Harriett		3				"
322	Berry	HOLT	33	Farmer	500	680	"
	Martha E.		26				"
	Catharine D.		3				"
	Julia		1				"
323	George	HOLT	25	Laborer		180	"
	Darcus E.		23				"
	Penelope		5				"
	Edward		3				"
	Noah		1				"
324	Richard	CURENTON	67	Farmer	40,000	13,846	Ga.
	Winnaford		63				S. C.
	S. F.	CURENTON	28	Laborer		1,500	Tenn.
325	R. M.	CURENTON	24			2,500	"
	Mary		21				"
326	Elijah J.	DIKE	37		1,000	650	"
	Mary		16				"
	Samuel W.		6				"
	Nancy F.		4				"

	Name		Age	Occupation	Real	Pers.	Birthplace
327	John	BANKS	45	Laborer		40	N. C.
	Margaret A.	McMAHAN	54				"
	Kisiah	BAKS	40				"
	Thomas		21	Laborer			"
	Matilda	McMAHAN	16				"
	George M.		10				"
328	James	WALKER	41	"		25	Tenn.
	Margaret		41				N. C.
	Barbary A.		17				Tenn.
	William		15				"
	John W.		8				"
	Phebe		5				"

Page 46   PARROTTSVILLE   21 June 1860

	Name		Age	Occupation	Real	Pers.	Birthplace
329	Andrew J.	HOLT	26	Farmer		500	N. C.
	Elizabeth		24				"
	Nancy A.		8				"
	Andrew J.		4				"
	Martha M.		2				"
	John		2/12				Tenn.
330	William S.	ORY	37	Farmer		3,856	Va.
	Judeth A.		34				"
	William		9				"
	Catharine E.		6				Tenn.
	John A.		4				"
	Edwin		1				"
331	Louiza	BIBLE	42		1,500	386	"
	Morgan		21				"
	Elender		20				"
	John		18	Laborer			"
	Levina		14				"
	Lafayett		12				"
	Laura		9				"
	Lewis		5				"
332	Isaac	DAWSON	50	Farmer	800	460	"
	Elizabeth		52				"
	Sarah		23				"
	Deless (?)	WHITE	10				"
	R. E.	SWINEA	32	Physician			Tenn.
333	William	CARMIKLE	54	Laborer		100	N. C.
	Sarah		54				Tenn.
	George		20	Carpenter			"
	William		18	Laborer			"
	Martha		14				"
	Sarah		10				
334	Jeptha	YARBER	60	Farmer			N. C.
	Elizabeth		46				"
	Tolbert C.		22				"
	Lucinda		20				"
	McDaniel		16				"
	Barnet R.		13				"
	Elizabeth		8				Tenn.

	Name		Age	Occupation	Real	Pers.	Birthplace
335	Joseph	DAWSON	39		800	600	"
	Jane		37				"

Page 47   21 June 1860

	Name		Age	Occupation	Real	Pers.	Birthplace
	John		11				"
	Franklin		9				
	Caroline		7				
	Thomas		4				
	Mollie		6/12				
	Marion	WHITE	24	Laborer			S. C.
336	Henry J.	SMITH	42	Farmer	300	100	"
	Mary		35				N. C.
	Susannah J.		17				S. C.
	Mary C.		14				"
	Martha G.		8				"
	Joseph A.		12				Tenn.
	John J.		6				"
	Elizabeth		2				
	Nancy		4/12				
337	Abraham	OTTINGER	61	"		220	Va.
	Cynthia		58				N. C.
	Rachel L.		20				Tenn.
	Eliza		14				
	Sarah S.		8				
338	Elisha	NOTT	41	"	1,000	370	S. C.
	Malissa		44				Tenn.
	Martha		15				
	Joseph		13				
	William A.		11				
	Charles H.		7				
	Sarah S.		2				
339	Israel	CLINE	34	"		250	"
	Penelope		30				"
	William		13				
	Caleb A.		11				
	George W.		9				
	Sarah M.		7				
	Rachael E.		6				
	John M.		3				
	Joseph H.		4/12				
340	William	GUIN	34	"		130	S. C.
	Hester		34				Tenn.
	Porter		9				
	Martha		7				

Page 48   21 June 1860

	Name		Age	Occupation	Real	Pers.	Birthplace
	Isaac		3				Tenn.
	Florence		7/12				
341	William	GAMMON	31	Farmer		80	"
	Sarah		25				
	Mary L.		5				
	Joseph M.		3				

	Name		Age	Occupation	Real	Pers.	Birthplace
342	Harvey	GAMMON	65	Laborer		350	N. C.
	Lutitia		55				Tenn.
	Ellen		23				
	Sarah		21				
	Martha E.		19				
	William	KELLY	4				
343	W. H.	BUNTING	51	Farmer		240	N. C.
	Mary		45				"
	Uriah		19	Laborer			"
	William		16				"
	Noah		14				"
	Fanny		13				Tenn.
	Jimmy I.		11				"
	Josiah		9				
	Syrona (f)		7				
	Margaret		6				
	Arronten G.		4				
	Jane E.		24				
	Vilenah H.	(m)	5				
344	Alonzo	YARBER	24	"		475	N. C.
	Nancy		33				Va.
	David		10				Tenn.
	Margaret		6				
	Andrew J.		3				
345	Oscar	MOORE (m̄wy)	21				"
	Martha		19				
346	Timothy	SHAVER	37	Farmer	600	350	"
	Marrinda		29				"
	Mary E.		9				
	Sarah J.		8				
	Julia A.		6				
	Joel A.		4				
	Francis M.		2/12				
	Mary	SHAVER	66				N. C.
Page 49						21 June 1860	
347	Samuel	HICKY	43	Farmer		170	Tenn.
	Agnes		44				"
	John		19	Laborer			"
	Edom		16				"
	Isaac		13				
	Margaret		12				
	True (m)		9				"
	Catharine		8				"
	Martha		5				"
348	Joel	WAIN	51	Minister M.E.P	1,000	1,782	N. C.
	Elizabeth		45				"
	John W.		21				Tenn.
	Rebecca		19				
	Jacob S.		17				
	Joel L.		14				

	Name		Age	Occupation	Real	Pers.	Birhplace
	William		10				
	Mary A.		7				
	Robert W.		2				
349	William	GREEN	25	Farmer	1,500	1,325	Tenn.
	Harriett		20				"
	Westly		2				"
	James A.		2/12				"
350	John	REDIX	23	Laborer		260	"
	Jaly		23				"
	Andrew		3				"
	Martha A.		4/12				"
351	Levi	DUN	32	Farmer		70	"
	Cinthia		26				"
	Catharin		8				"
	Harriett		6				"
	Mary		5				"
	John		3				"
	Harriett		8/12				"
352	John	HARRISON	54	Laborer		30	Va.
	Lucinda		45				Tenn.
	Robert		32	(Idiot)			"
353	John	GREEN	20	Farmer	1,200	504	"
	Catharine		27				
	Martha S.		9				
	George A.		2				

Page 50   22 June 1860

	Name		Age	Occupation	Real	Pers.	Birhplace
354	William N.	PALMER	27	Farmer		500	Tenn.
	Mary J.		29				"
	Jaly		8				"
	William H.		5				"
	Frances M.	(m)	3				"
355	William	PALMER	68	Farmer	7,000	1,445	"
	Jaly		58				
356	Jacob E.	PALMER	25		300	2,037	"
	Mary		35				
357	John	DIKE	21	Farmer		250	"
	Eliza J.		20				"
	William H.		1				"
358	Thomas	BLACK	48	Laborer		90	"
	Elizabeth		30				S. C.
	John		14				Tenn.
	Mary		13				"
	James		11				"
	David		7				"
	Jane		4				"
359	Jasper	PALMER	30	Farmer	1,450	2,500	"
	Martha E.		28				"
	Sarah J.		6				"
	Mary A.		3				"
	Thomas N.	DYKE	11				"

	Name		Age	Occupation	Real	Pers.	Birthplace
360	Rubin	WATSON	56	Laborer		25	"
	Elizabeth		37				N. C.
	Nancy M.		21				Tenn.
	Susanah		16				"
	Mary A.		7				"
	Jacob		6				"
	Jasper		5				"
	Julia A.		5				"
	Sarah J.		1				"
361	William	BURGES	39	Laborer		100	S. C.
	Winny		22				Tenn.
	James		15				S. C.
	Nancy		13				"
	Sarah A.		11				"
	Perry		9				"
	Rufus		8				Tenn.

Page 51   22 June 1860

	Name		Age	Occupation	Real	Pers.	Birthplace
	William		5/12				Tenn.
362	M. J.	MIMS	24	Farmer	3,500	5,400	"
	Mary A.		20				"
	Jaly E.		1				"
363	W. H.	EVANS	45	"	4,000	4,186	S. C.
	Emillie		35				Tenn.
	Alfred W.		17				S. C.
	Malissee		15				"
	Mary E.		13				Tenn.
	Margaritt		11				"
	John A.		10				"
	Eliza J.		8				"
	Laura A.		6				"
	Margaret	MIMS	52				"
	A. L.	MIMS	26	Laborer			"
364	George	BANKS (mwy)	23			100	"
	Margaret R.		18				"
365	Sarah	WHITE	45			10	S. C.
366	Joseph	BANKS	25	Farmer		310	N. C.
	Nancy		23				"
	Saphrona E.		1				Tenn.
	William	WATSON	18	Laborer			N. C.
367	John H.	LOVEL	44	Farmer		748	Va.
	Martha		38				Tenn.
	Mary		16				"
	John		16				"
	Obedeince		14				"
	Mildred		11				"
	Louisa		10				"
	Rachel		5				"
	Charles		5				"
	Susanah		3				"
	Moses		1				"

	Name		Age	Occupation	Real	Pers.	Birthplace
368	John	LOVEL	92	Cooper	2,000	25	Va.
	Fanny		75				Tenn.
369	Mary	ONEIL	37			250	"
	John		15				"
	Marshal		10				"
	Elizabeth		4				"
	Mary J.		1				"

Page 52   23 June 1860

	Name		Age	Occupation	Real	Pers.	Birthplace
370	Martha	GREEN	59		8,850	1,281	Tenn.
	Wade		25	Farmer			"
	Joseph		21	"			"
	Harrison		19	Laborer			"
371	Alfred	GREEN (mwy)	23	Farmer		350	"
	Lowenda		20				"
372	Porter A.	GWINN	60	Teach		175	"
	Lueind		35				"
	Robert		8				"
	James S.		5				"
	Daniel F.		2				"
	Mary J.		1				"
372	William	SMITH	44	Farmer		225	"
	Elizabeth		33				"
	Mary A.		8				"
	Rubin		7				"
374	Abner	JONES	50	Wheel Right		100	Va.
	Chloe		44				N. C.
	John J.		18				Id.
	Deborah E.		14				"
	Henry		11				"
	Mary		8				Tenn.
375	John	SWATSEL	48	Blacksmith	20	420	"
	Sarah		49				"
	Thomas W.		12				"
	Maron (m)		9				"
	Catharine		3				"
376	Joseph	BAYSINGER	47	Farmer	1,500	570	"
	Catharine		36				"
	Amanuel		17	Laborer			"
	Jacob		10				"
	Catharine		14				"
377	Catharine	KINAMON	71			25	Va.
	Mary		29				Tenn.
	Sarah A.		7				"
378	W. A. A.	FOWLER	19	Farmer		125	"
	Lovinda		19				"
	Joseph		1				"
379	John M.	SHELTON	31	Farmer		90	"
	Emaline		24				Ind.

	Name		Age	Occupation	Real	Pers.	Birthplace
Page 53							25 June 1860
	Nancy J.		7				Tenn.
	William F.		6				"
	Catharine		3				"
	Martha		2				"
	Amanuel		2/12				"
	Mary A.		21				"
	Nancy		23				"
380	George	KEEKER	45	Laborer		65	"
	Delilah		38				"
	Jacob		15				"
	Mary J.		8/12				"
381	Westly	SWATSEL	49	Waggon Maker	1,200	550	"
	Barbary		49				"
	Louisa N.		18				"
	Angaline R.		15				"
	Elbert	DIKE	23	Laborer			"
382	William	WORTH	52	Farmer	2,500	750	"
	Malinda		45				"
	Sarah J.		22				"
	Rebecca		20				"
	Mary P.		17				"
	Malinda		15				"
	William J.		13				"
	Lucinda		11				"
	Thomas N.		8				"
383	Thomas	SMITH Jr.	26	Farmer		60	"
	Catharine		22				"
	Lawson		8				"
	Sarah		2				"
384	Henry M.	WORTH	28	"		70	"
	Sarah		25				"
	Martha		3				"
	Catharine		3				"
	Mary		1				"
	Martin	CLINE	67	(Blind)			N. C.
	Elizabeth		68				"
385	Willis	AVENTON	27	Laborer			"
	Mary A.		21				Tenn.
	Saphrona E.		6				"
	William		4				"
Page 54				NEWPORT			25 June 1860
	Sarah		2				Tenn.
	James D.		7/12				"
386	Wyly	SATERFIELD	46	Laborer		20	S. C.
	Elanora		31				Tenn.
	Manerva	MAYSON	13				"
	Jacob		10				"
	Adolphus		5				"
	Martha	MOORE	20				
	N. S. (f)	MALOY	24	Farmer	3,500	800	"

- 44 -

	Name		Age	Occupation	Real	Pers.	Birthplace
387	D. V.	STOKELY	31	Farmer	6,000	2,650	"
	Sarah H.		29				"
	N. E. W. (m)		4				"
	James C. M.		2				"
	Thomas D. B.		7/12				"
	Cassa (f)	CLARK	20				"
	Marion (f)	HOLAWAY	23				"
388	Alfred	HALL	26	Carpenter		200	"
	Darcas		18				"
	Rachal		1				"
	Malinda		4/12				"
	William		20				"
389	James	SWAGERTY, Jr.	59	Farmer	20,000	56,355	Tenn.
	Nancy		49				"
	Alexander S.		27	Merchant	300	1,300	"
	George		22	Laborer			"
	William		18	"			"
	Margarett		13	"			"
	David		12				"
	Florence		8				"
390	John	ROREX	50	Farmer	30,000	30,000	"
	Carline		38				"
	Samuel		17				"
	Martin		12				"
391	William	CARTER	48	Farmer	18,000	8,590	"
	Elizabeth		45				"
	Esther		8				"
	Esther		79				Va.
	Jane D.	EVANS	14				Tenn.
392	John	KENYON	53	Tinner	1,120	600	England
	Mary F. C.		32				N. C.

25 June 1860

	Name		Age	Occupation	Real	Pers.	Birthplace
	Edward C.		20				England
	Louisa		15				"
	Ellen		13				"
	Margarett		5				Tenn.
	Theadoeia		2/12				"
393	F. M.	WARD	30	Farmer		800	"
	Elizabeth		27				"
	Sarah		4				"
	John C.		2				"
	Alexander		2/12				"
394	Jonas	ALMAN	44	Farmer	1,800	1,000	N. C.
	Pernetta		16				S. C.
	Joseph		16	Laborer			Tenn.
	Lewis		15	"			"
	Mary		12				"
	Thomas A.		9				"
	Stephen		8				"
	Laura A.		6				"
	Cambell J.		2/12				"

	Name		Age	Occupation	Real	Pers.	Birthplace
395	Thomas	ELLISON	45	Farmer		1,459	N. C.
	Susannah		38				Tenn.
	Mary		19				"
	Jonathan		17	Laborer			"
	Rashal (f)		15				"
	Thomas C.		13				"
	Charles		9				"
	Sarah		7				"
	William M.		4				"
	Matilda		3				"
	George		2				"
	Carline		9/12				"
396	Philip M.	NEAS	27	Farmer	3,000	4,539	"
	Margarett E.		23				"
	Mary J. F.		6				"
	Martha J.		4				"
	Alies O.	(f)	9/12				"
397	A. F.	SHEPPARD	26	Carpenter		200	N. C.
	Nelly E.		25				Tenn.
	James M.		5				"
	Mary J. D.		4				"

Page 56   25 June 1860

	Name		Age	Occupation	Real	Pers.	Birthplace
	William D.		3				Tenn.
	Martha		4/12				"
	Martha		85				N. C.
398	Jesse	BREWER	48	Laborer		50	"
	Louisa		30				"
	John R.		19				"
	William		17				"
	Martha		13				Tenn.
	Rebecca J.		11				"
	Priscella		9				"
	Samuel		7				"
	Sarah		2				"
	Frances (f)		7/12				"
399	David	EISENHOWER	33	Farmer	3,500	1,300	"
	Catharine		30				"
	Arva		7				"
	Jane		4				"
	Mary C.		2				"
	Josephine		1				"
	Mary	BARNETT	25				"
400	Farris (f)	JONES	38			25	N. C.
401	Henry J.	RARD (?)	65	Farmer		275	"
	Elizabeth		52				"
	David M.		15				"
402	Hiram	BALCH (?)	43	Farmer	2,000	1,200	"
	Elizabeth		32				"
	Jane D.		12				"
	Francus (f)		10				"

Name		Age	Occupation	Real	Pers.	Birthplace
Butalaw (m)		8				Tenn.
Lovenia (f)		6				"
Elizabeth		4				"
Genelly (f)		1				"
403 Andrew	OTTINGER	34	Farmer	4,000	1,205	"
Sarah		25				"
Laura E.		6				"
Allen D.		5				"
Francis (m)		3				"
Lafayett		9/12				"
404 Elizabeth	BOYIER	58		2,000	2,755	S. C.
Creed		14				Tenn.
Page 57			PARROTTSVILLE		27 June 1860	
Josiah		12				Tenn.
Robert	ELLISON	19	Laborer	1,800		"
Martha		16				"
405 Conrad	EISENHOUR	42	Farmer	10,000	3,329	N. C.
Eve		39				Tenn.
Martin S.		20				"
Jacob		19	Laborer			"
Quenius (m)		18	"			"
Powel		16	"			"
Candrew F.	(f)	14				"
Sarah C.		13				"
Harriett M.		10				"
Mary D.		6				"
Martha A.		5				"
Tilghman F.		3				"
406 Aden	SMITH	32	Farmer	3,000	1,400	"
Loucinda		31				"
Elizabeth		9				"
Penelope		6				"
Sarah S.		2				"
407 Thomas	BUGG	55	Farmer		300	N. C.
Mary		50				Tenn.
John		28	Laborer			"
Jane		26				"
Charles		24	"			"
Franky (f)		22				"
Elias J. (m)		4				"
408 Benjamin	BUGG	27	Laborer		50	"
Susanah		24				"
Jane		1				"
Elizabeth		6/12				"
409 Alfred	ELISON	39	Farmer	2,500	865	"
Loucinda		42				"
Powel W.		12				"
James M.		9				"
John D.		5				"
Lucinda	REEVES	50				"

	Name		Age	Occupation	Real	Pers.	Birthplace
410	Thomas	GRAGG	67	Laborer		25	"
	Elizabeth		67				"
411	Benjamin	GRAGG(mwy)	22	Laborer		20	"

Page 58   27 June 1860

	Name		Age	Occupation	Real	Pers.	Birthplace
	Margaret	(mwy)	22				Tenn.
412	Noah	PACK	23	Laborer		20	"
	Sarah		24				"
	Mary		5				"
	Lucinda J.		10/12				"
413	Edward	PATERSON	45	Carpenter	120	500	"
	Susannah		47				"
	Joel		12				"
	Sarah		10				"
414	Martha S.	SNEED	51			50	"
	George		20	Laborer			"
	Elizabeth		18				"
	Isabella		16				"
	Henderson		13				"
	Allen		2				"
415	Thomas	SMITH	87	Minister (Pr. Bapt.)	3,000	6,476	Va.
	Mary B.		82				"
	Sarah		52				Tenn.
416	Thomas	SMITH, Jr.	45	Miller	600	250	"
	Obedience		28				"
	Alexander		7				"
	Susanah		6				"
	Thomas		3				"
	Mary		3				"
	Edmond		1				"
417	W. C.	COOPER	26	Farmer		200	Tenn.
	Margarett		27				"
	John B.		5				"
	William	HALE	65	Laborer			Unknown
418	Sarah	COOPER	52	"		250	Tenn.
	John		22				"
	Dolly E.		16				"
419	James	COOPER	23	"		75	"
	Elizabeth		23				S. C.
	George W.		2				Tenn.
420	George	STUART	35	Farmer	1,800	1,162	"
	Lydia C.		35				"
	John G.		8				"
	Catharine J.		6				"
	Samuel		4				"

Page 59   27 June 1860

	Name		Age	Occupation	Real	Pers.	Birthplace
	Isaac		1				Tenn.

	Name		Age	Occupation	Real	Pers.	Birthplace
421	Sarah	BLACK	55		600	75	"
422	Lettice	COOK	56			25	S. C.
	Mary		30				"
	Lucinda		28				"
	John		26	Laborer			"
	Edwin		25	"			"
	Julia		21				"
	Boice (m)		19	"			"
	Lettice		17				"
423	Cuthia (f)	SMITH	35			25	S. C.
	Amanda		12				Tenn.
	Elender		10				"
424	Thomas	STAFFORD	27	Laborer		40	Va.
	Delilah		46				Ga.
	James A. W.		18				Tenn.
	Joseph M.		16				"
	Sarah C.		13				"
	George		11				"
	Senia (f)		8				"
	Havar C. (?)		7				"
425	John	WORTH	49	Farmer		2,375	"
	Elizabeth		40				"
	James T.		7				"
	William S.		5				"
	George S.		4				"
	Joseph M.		2				"
	John B.		1				"
426	Jobe	ODELL	30	Laborer	200	265	"
	Elender		32				"
	William		12				"
	Margarett		10				"
	Mary A.		8				"
	Sarah C.		6				"
	Hannah		6				"
	Saphronia		4				"
	Louiza		1				"
427	L.D.	FOX	31	Farmer		1,244	"
	Nancy		31				"
	John		9				"
Page 60						27	June 1860
	Elizabeth		7				Tenn.
	George		5				"
	Sarah		4				"
	Margarett		2				"
428	Washington	DAVIS	50	Farmer	300	200	N. C.
	Elizabeth		40				"
	Thomas		21				"
	John H.		16				"
	Sarah J.		13				"
	William		11				"
	Wily		6				Tenn.

	Name		Age	Occupation	Real	Pers.	Birthplace
429	David	WINNYFORD	65	Farmer	1,200	400	Va.
	Elizabeth		66				"
430	David R.B.	WINNYFORD (mwy)	22	Laborer			"
	Mary		18				Tenn.
	John	ARROWOOD	26	"			N. C.
431	William	MIMS	26	Farmer	4,500	2,453	Tenn.
	Jaly		19				"
	John		3				"
	Albert W.		9/12				"
432	Emma J.	WRITAGE ?	38			25	N. C.
	Vinetta		10				Va.
	James T.		8				N. C.
	John		16	Laborer			N. C.
	Emily		14				"
	Mary E.		3				Tenn.
433	Anderson	WALKER	50	Farmer		515	"
	Lydia		47				"
	David		20				"
	Sarah J.		18				"
	Mary L.		14				"
	Carline		12				"
	Catharine		9				"
	Charles		6				"
	Harriett		3				"
	Barbary		70				Va.
434	George	CLINE	30	Farmer	600	433	Tenn.
	Lear		34				"
	Rebecca A.		12				"
	Maron (m)		10				"

Page 61   28 June 1860

	Name		Age	Occupation	Real	Pers.	Birthplace
	Creed		7				
	Mary J.		5				Tenn.
	James B.		3				"
	Malinda C.		1				"
435	W. C.	HOLT	24	Laborer		100	"
	Margarett S.		24				N. C.
	George W.		1				Tenn.
436	William R.	WALKER	47	Farmer	200	150	Ireland
	Catharine		27				Tenn.
	Sarah M.		7				"
437	Peggy	WORRIX	40			2	N. C.
	Elizabeth		16				Tenn.
	James		20				"
	John		10				"
438	John W.	HOLT	36	Farmer		380	Va.
	Catharine		39				Tenn.
	Mary J.		18				"
	George L.		14				"
	Louisa		12				"

	Name		Age	Occupation	Real	Pers.	Birthplace
	Mildred E.		9				"
	Andrew J.		5				"
439	Hosa	HARDEN	22	Laborer		25	N. C.
	Nancy		21				"
	Jesse		1				Tenn.
	Parilee		1/12				"
440	William	FOWLER	59	Farmer	1,200	480	S. C.
	Susanah		64				"
	Elizabeth		34				Tenn.
441	Isaac	FOWLER	24	Laborer		135	"
	Catharine J.		20				"
	Mary N.		11/12				"
442	William	FOWLER	21	Laborer		235	"
	Editha		23				"
443	Amos	DAWSON	56	Farmer	5,000	2,200	"
	Rachal		19				"
	David		17				"
	Alexander		15				"
	Eliza		14				"
444	Isaac	DAWSON	27	Farmer		675	"
	Phebe		28				"

Page 62   28 June 1860

	Name		Age	Occupation	Real	Pers.	Birthplace
	William		4				Tenn.
	Mary B.		2				"
	Amos A.		10/12				"
445	Elizabeth	FOWLER	70	(Idiotic)	800	220	N. C.
	Colman		29	Laborer			"
	Nancy		19				S. C.
446	James	FOWLER	25	"		120	"
	Roseanna		22				N. C.
	Mary E.		1				Tenn.
447	Daniel	HEIFNER	46	Farmer	1,500	500	N. C.
	Barbary		45				"
	Louiza		18				"
	Sylvina		16				"
	Susanah		14				Tenn.
	Flora		12				"
	Elizabeth		9				"
	Loranza		9				"
	Loucinda		6				"
	Daniel		4				"
	Daniel		3				"
448	Merit	DUNCAN	30	Laborer		100	N. C.
	Mary		19				"
	Samuel		1				Tenn.
449	Mark	FOWLER	22	"		20	N. C.
	Mary		20				Tenn.

	Name		Age	Occupation	Real	Pers.	Birthplace
450	John B.	OTTINGER	47	Farmer		650	"
	Elizabeth		38				"
	David L.		18	Laborer			"
	Duglass		16				"
	James A.		14				"
	Reps G.		12				"
	Laura		9				"
	Martha		9				"
451	Peter	REECE	33		450	100	"
	Emaline		43				N. C.
	Julia		12				Tenn.
	Luceinda		11				"
	Martha E.		10				"
	Sidney E.	(f)	8				"
452	A.	DAWSON	25	Farmer		600	"
Page 63							28 June 1860
	Jane P.		23				Tenn.
	Alfred M.		1				"
453	Christly	FAUBION	30	Farmer	800	350	"
	Sarah A.		18				"
	Nancy		2				Ky.
	Mary		28				Tenn.
454	N. W.	EASTERLY	47	Farmer	8,000	3,500	"
	Jalea		40				"
	S. E. (f)		13				"
	Mary C.		12				"
	Eliza M.		9				"
	Carisa A.		7				"
455	Alfred	DAVIS	39	Laborer			N. C.
	Margarett		34				S. C.
	Sarah J.		12				N. C.
	Nancy M.		10				"
	William F.		8				S. C.
	James P.		7				"
	Zubron (m)		4				"
	Alfred		1				"
456	James	CARTER	26	Laborer			N. C.
	Martha		24				Tenn.
	Susanah		1				"
457	Joshua	CLANTHAM	25	Miller		25	N. C.
	Emily		41				S. C.
	Mary		21				"
	Thomas		20	Laborer			N. C.
	Christian		18				"
	Charlott		16				S. C.
	Malinda E.		14				"
	George M.		12				N. C.
	Francis (m)		11				Tenn.
	Robert		6				"
	William R.		4				"
	John E.		2				"

	Name		Age	Occupation	Real	Pers.	Birthplace
458	William	OTTINGER	41	Farmer	3,000	2,875	"
	Carisa		47				"
	Hester A.		21				"
	Stephen		10				"
	Mary G.		8				"

Page 64   29 June 1860

	Name		Age	Occupation	Real	Pers.	Birthplace
459	George	EASTERLY	48	Farmer	5,000	12,730	Tenn.
	Elizabeth		45				"
	Robert P.	FAUBION	26	Laborer		600	"
460	Elizabeth	MIMS	50			150	S. C.
461	Eliza	BUSTLER	30		3,000	1,000	"
	Calvin		9				Tenn.
462	David	OWENS	33	"		140	"
	Sarah		33				S. C.
	George		10				Tenn.
	Marion (m)		8				"
	Martha S.		6				"
	Mary E.		3				"
	Julia A.		1				"
463	Elias	OWENS	69	Laborer		120	Va.
	Phobe		60				N. C.
	Sarah		38				Tenn.
	Mary		23				"
	Mahaly		21				"
	Abraham		19	Laborer			"
	Jacob		17	"			"
464	John R.	OTTINGER	44	Farmer	2,000	1,160	"
	Sarah		48				"
	George A.		16	Laborer			"
	Martha J.		13				"
	David P.		11				"
	Isaac L.		10				"
	Beard		4				"
465	William	FANCHER	41	Laborer		150	"
	Sarah		40				S. C.
466	Anderson	SWATSEL	34	"		1,050	Tenn.
	Sarah		32				"
	William A.		4				"
	Samuel H.		2				"
	David		9/12				"
467	David	VARNELL	65	Farmer	12,000	2,020	"
	Mary		62				"
	Samuel		26				"
	William		24				"
	Delilah		18				"
	Editha		12				"

Page 65   29 June 1860

	Name		Age	Occupation	Real	Pers.	Birthplace
	Jacob	PARROTT	62	Laborer	500	450	Tenn.

	Name		Age	Occupation	Real	Pers.	Birthplace
468	George	WHITLOCK	55	"		40	S. C.
	Darcus	WRIGHT	55				N. C.
	Mary		27				"
	Catharine		17				"
	Saphronia		13				"
	William		3				Tenn.
469	J. K.	LOWE	29	Blksmith		615	"
	Zererah		31				"
	Jacob M.		10				"
	Nancy E.		7				
	Samuel		5				
	Amanda		2				
470	Adam	FLEENER	33	Minister Lutheran	200	910	Va.
	Lavina		27				Tenn.
	Joseph A.		7				
	Mary E.		5				
	Abraham M.		3				
	Narcissus		2/12				
471	Jonas	TOBY	30	Laborer		225	"
	Elizabeth M.		26				N. C.
	George H.		12				Tenn.
	Mary E.		11				
	Catharine		10				
	Martha A.		6				
	James E.		6				
	William D.		4				
	Jorden M.		1				
472	Allen	PETERS	40	Farmer		450	
	Rebecca		26				
	Assarona		19				
	William F.		17	Laborer			
	James T.		14				
	Martha J.		9				
	Joseph D.		7				
	Eliza A.		4				
	Thomas A.		1				
473	Meredith	GOSLIN	38	Laborer		200	N. C.
	Sarah A.		36				Tenn.
	Isaac A.		15				
Page 66							29 June 1860
	Mary M.		11				Tenn.
	Rebecca A.		5				"
	Margart		2				
	Columbus N.		5/12				
	John	COFFMAN	65	Whilting	1,050	50	"
474	David	HILL	45	Carpenter		25	N. C.
	Minton (f)		39				"
	Mary		20				"
	Hannah J.		19				"
	Joseph		11				"
	James W.		5				"

	Name		Age	Occupation	Real	Pers.	Birthplace
	David W.		4				"
	George W.		3				Tenn.
	Margaret M.		1				"
475	Henry	HEADRICK	31	Mechanic	1,200	474	N. C.
	Minerva		27				"
	Catharine		3				Tenn.
	Garrett		7/12				
476	Wiley	PRUTT	30	Laborer		50	Va.
	Mary		27				"
	Lutitia		10				Tenn.
	Marcus		10				
	Joseph		7				
	Jane		5				
477	Dudly	HARRIS	31	Laborer		50	N. C.
	Rebecca		29				"
	John Q. A.		8				Tenn.
	Robert J.		6				
	Mary S.		4				
	William M.		7/12				
478	John	MOORE (MOON?)	56	"			N. C.
	Mary		55				"
	Martha J.		21				Tenn.
	Joseph		20				
	Caleb		17				
	William R.		16				
	Eliza J.		15				
	Thomas D.		7				
479	Jorden	MIMS	29	Farmer	5,000	900	S. C.
	Jane		30				Tenn.
Page 67							29 June 1860
	Soperna		9				Tenn.
	Albert		1				"
480	William	OWENS	34	Laborer		125	Va.
	Francis		33				Ga.
	Elizabeth		12				Tenn.
	Sarah		10				
	Jane		8				
	Jacob		6				"
481	Margaret	ETHERTON	35			4	"
	Mary A.		14				
	John W.		12				
	Laurilla (?)	(f)	8				
	Paralee		6				
	James A.		4				
	Sarah J.		1				
482	W. A.	MALONE	32	"		150	"
	Sarah		30				"
	Susannah		9				
	Binda E.		7				
	Aaron		5				

	Name		Age	Occupation	Real	Pers.	Birthplace
	Isaac A.		4/12				
	Mary		56				
	Mary		29				
483	Peter	BURREL	52	"		160	S. C.
	Nancy		51				"
	Giles		21	"			Tenn.
	Eliza J.		16				
	Samuel		14				
	David		9				
	John W.		5				
484	William	BURREL	22	"		30	"
	Mary A.		17				
485	John	COOK	25	"			S. C.
	Rebecca A.		27				"
486	Samuel J.	FOWLER	43	Farmer	640	500	"
	Hannah		48				Tenn.
	Joseph		13				"
487	C. P.	MILLER	32	"	2,200	725	"
	Catharine		28				"
	Martha J.		8				"

Page 68   29 June 1860

	Name		Age	Occupation	Real	Pers.	Birthplace
	Lourina M.		4				Mo.
	Marcus R.		6				Ind.
	Michael E.		2				Tenn.
	Saranah	DRYMAN	17				"
	Zhurah (f)	OTTINGER	7				"
	William C.		4				"
488	Nancy	FANCHIER	63		1,000	1,000	"
	Salina P.		22				"
	David A.		37	Farmer			
	John D.		14				
	Harrison		13				
	Paralee		10				
	Sophronia A.		8				
489	Joseph	BALCH	47	"	2,250	500	N. C.
	Mary		47				"
	Abel		24	Laborer			
	Emeline		21				
	Perlina		19				
	Amanda		16				
	Sylvanus (f)		14				
	John		10				
490	Jesse	LAMBERT	54	"		100	Unknown
	Elizabeth		42				Tenn.
	Mary A.		20				
	Emaline		17				
	Sarah J.		16				
	Nancy		15				
	Joseph		13				

	Name		Age	Occupation	Real	Pers.	Birthplace
	James		11				
	Margart		9				
	Julia A.		3				
491	Mark	SOUTHERLAND	34	"			N. C.
	Ruthy		37				Tenn.
492	Mary	ALLEN	73		5,000	17,625	"
	G. W.	ALLEN	45	Farmer	5,500	16,000	"
	Emma						"
	Martha E.	HOUSTON	17				"
	West	HARRIS	20				"
493	Green	ALLEN	41	"	2,000	5,500	"
494	William	WARE	25	Laborer		50	"
Page 69							29 June 1860
	Nancy A.		23				Tenn.
	George W.		6				
	Toby		4/12				
495	Jeremiah	CUMMINGS	30	Laborer		100	"
	Julia		25				N. C.
496	Augustus	SMITH (mwy)	26	Farmer		9,655	Tenn.
	Eliza J.		20				"
497	Bartlet	SISK	60	"	3,500	1,000	Va.
	Mary		57				"
	Nancy		24				Tenn.
	Elizabeth		22				
	Ira		19	Laborer			"
	Harriet		16				
	Sycha (f)		13				
498	William	HOLLAND	55	Farmer	10,000	6,835	
	Eliza		49				
	Reubin A.		26	Laborer			
	John		22				
	William A.		21	"			
	Laura		13				
	James T.		10				
	Elbert H.		7				
499	Charles	HOLLAND	24	Farmer		1,600	"
	Matilda		16				"
	William		7/12				
500	Balam	DOCKERY	65	Laborer		270	N. C.
	Mary		65				"
	Eliza	SMITH	13				Oh.
501	Stephen W.	JONES	41	Farmer	1,250	270	Tenn.
	John F.		6				
	Cameron J.		4				
502	Charles M.	MILLER	69	"	12,000	13,097	N. C.
	Sarah		69				"
	Washington		40				Tenn.

	Name		Age	Occupation	Real	Pers.	Birthplace
503	David	SPROUCE	30	"	100	310	S. C.
	Elizabeth		30				Tenn.
	Martha		9				S. C.
	Julia		7				Tenn.
	Regena		5				
	Margart		4				

Page 70   NEWPORT   2 July 1860

	Name		Age	Occupation	Real	Pers.	Birthplace
	William F.		5/12				Tenn.
	Palestine (f)		62				S.C.
504	Elison	SPROUCE	30	Laborer		150	"
	Nancy		25				"
	Alfred		8				"
	Alice		6				"
	Regena		3				"
505	Alexander	SPROUCE	27	"		150	"
	Sarah		25				"
	William		3				"
	Regina		2				"
	Jefferson	McKINY	19	Laborer			S. C.
506	J. R.	ALLEN	53	Farmer	6,820	16,566	Tenn.
	Rebecca		38				"
	Elbert		19	Laborer			"
	Lizzee		11				"
	David		8				"
	Amma		6				"
	Love (f)		4				"
507	George	McNABB	50	Farmer	6,000	3,348	"
	William		21	Laborer			"
	Jackson		19				"
	Margarett		18				"
	Maranda		15				"
	Rachel		10				"
	Lear		10				"
508	Jacob	McNABB	23	Farmer		325	"
	Hannah		23				"
	Elizabeth	ODELL	13				"
509	Joel	BROOKS	27	Farmer	2,500	2,900	"
	Parthena		26				"
	Sarah E.		5				"
	John		3				"
	David		1				"
	Royal S.		19	Laborer			"
	Maranda		13				"
510	Thomas M.	GRAGG	43	Farmer	2,000	900	"
	Mahaly		47				"
	Melvina		18				"
	James P.		17	Laborer			"

Page 71   2 July 1860

	Name		Age	Occupation	Real	Pers.	Birthplace
	Isabella W.		15				Tenn.
	Creed F.		14				"

- 58 -

	Name		Age	Occupation	Real	Pers.	Birthplace
	Mary A.		12				"
	Morgan T.		12				"
	Susanah		10				"
	John M.		8				"
511	Thomas	HOI WAY	30	Farmer		700	N. C.
	Fanny		20				Tenn.
	Willard C.		1				"
	Matilda	RAY	16				N. C.
512	Catrom	HOLAWAY	26	Farmer		235	"
	Eliza		19				Tenn.
	Rebecca	ONEAL	45				"
513	Elijah	WILY	46	Farmer	600	260	"
	Eliza		30				"
	Jane		13				"
	Absalum		11				"
	Priscilla		10				"
	Elijah		3				"
514	Green	INMAN	53	Farmer	1,800	795	S. C.
	Mary		29				Tenn.
	Sarah		21				"
	Isabella		18				"
	Green		14				"
515	Biddy	LINDER	60			25	S. C.
	William		20	Laborer			"
516	William	WILY	50	Farmer		131	Tenn.
	Martha		24				S. C.
	Carity		10				Tenn.
	Mary		7				"
	George		5				"
	Saphrona		2				"
517	George	WILY	45	Farmer		200	"
	Nancy		48				N. C.
	Mary		18	(Idiotic)			Tenn.
	Elijah		15				"
	Cenia (f)		13				"
	Daniel		12				"
	Jane		8				"
	Presten		3				"

Page 72   2 July 1860

	Name		Age	Occupation	Real	Pers.	Birthplace
518	Nathaniel	LINDER	65	Slay Maker		5	S. C.
519	W. A.	ROADMAN	32	Farmer	12,250	10,723	Tenn.
	Martha J.		31				"
	Jacob L.		8				"
	Laura E.		7				"
	Bonce		5				"
	Eugene		3				"
	Flora		1				"

	Name		Age	Occupation	Real	Pers.	Birthplace
				PARROTTSVILLE			
520	Alfred	KNISELY	25	Carpenter		2,000	Va.
	D. A.	MIMS	30	Merchant	2,000	9,500	Tenn.
	Margarett J.		21				"
	Charles		7/12				"
521	F. A.	FAWBION	36	Merchant	2,000	13,000	"
	Margarett		34				"
	James H.		15	Laborer			"
	William J.		12				"
	Saphrona		10				"
	Samuel		7				"
	Joseph		5				"
	Alexander		3				"
	Mary L.	DAVIS	18	Teacher			Va.
522	R. S.	ROADMAN	38	Merchant	21,200	51,200	Tenn.
	Susanah M.		34				Va.
	William C.		14				Tenn.
	Emma R.		16				"
	Florence		12				"
	Sanford		7				"
	Augustus E.		5				"
	Orlando (m)		1				"
	Aduson		16	Clk. in store			Va.
	Athan	McGINTY	36	Merchant		11,300	N. C.
523	D. G.	BOYD	39	Blacksmith		350	Tenn.
	Nancy		39				"
	John		18	"			"
	James		16	"			"
	Jane		13				"
	Mary		11				"
	William		10				"

Page 73   2 July 1860

	Name		Age	Occupation	Real	Pers.	Birthplace
	W. F.	COLY	23	Carpenter		400	N. C.
524	W. L.	WORTHINGTON	26	Bootmaker	550	200	Va.
	Mary E.		27				Tenn.
	Alexander		7				"
	Carline		5				"
	Nancy		3				"
	George W.		1				"
525	Jesse	HOLT	34	Shoe & Bootmaker		200	"
	Delilah		35				N. C.
	Mary E.		12				Tenn.
	Sarah L.		9				"
	Martha L.		7				"
	John F.		3				"
	Eliza C.		1				"
526	W. N.	HAYSE	39	Tanner	1,500	800	"
	Mary A.		37				"
	James A.		15	Laborer			"
	Thomas M.		12				"

	Name		Age	Occupation	Real	Pers.	Birthplace
	William A.		10				"
	John H.		7				"
	George M.		3				"
	Melvina		6/12				"
527	Mathias	FAWBION	42		1,000	7,290	"
	Matilda C.		33				N. C.
	Margarett J.		9				Tenn.
	Sarah E.		5				"
	James C.	LAREW	34	Teacher	2,500	7,000	"
528	Joseph	DUNCAN	45	Merchant	7,000	48,460	"
	Martha E. F.		26				N. C.
	Mary S.		6				"
	Joseph		3				Tenn.
	Jannie	DAVIS	22	Instructress			Va.
	William	GRAGG	22	Clk in store			Tenn.
529	James	McLAUGHIN	58	Cabinet Maker		800	"
	Abigail		50				"
	John A.		29	Merchant	250	3,500	"
	James R.		23	"	250	2,500	S. C.
	George W.		18	Laborer			S. C.
	Robert G.		12				Tenn.
530	G. W.	SUGGS	46	Farmer	450	432	N. C.

3 July 1860

	Name		Age	Occupation	Real	Pers.	Birthplace
	Margarett C.		44				N. C.
	Wily		15	Laborer			"
	Jane		13				"
	George C.		9				"
531	James	KILGORE	48	Saddler		3,300	Tenn.
	Louze J.		16				"
	Susanah		13				"
	Fielding K.		13				"
	Hugh M.		11				"
532	J. B.	GILLYLAND	37	Physician	1,000	1,500	"
	Catharine J.		25				"
	Mary J.		4				"
	Martha		7/12				"
533	Joseph J.	MICHAUX	44	Physician	2,900	3,250	Va.
	Jane		27				N. C.
	Helena		9				Tenn.
	Robt.		6				"
	John C.		4				"
	Elizabeth		7/12				"

CONCLUDED

	Name		Age	Occupation	Real	Pers.	Birthplace
534	W. W.	SUGGS	21	Laborer		100	N. C.
	Margarett		19				Tenn.
	George		3				"
	John		6/12				"
535	Thomas W.	WINNYFORD	30	Farmer	5,000	2,492	Va.
	Margarett		26				Tenn.

	Name		Age	Occupation	Real	Pers.	Birthplace
	Elizabeth		4				"
	George		3				"
	Sarah		2				"
	Martha		70				Va.
	Alexander F.	WINNYFORD	26	Farmer			"
536	Vina	BOULDEN	45				N. C.
	Louiza		20				"
	Eli		18	Laborer			"
	John		16	"			"
	Thomas C.		14				"
	Baxter		12				"
	Sarah		12				"
537	Elizabeth	CHANDLER	50			40	N. C.
	Martha		27				"

Page 75   3 July 1860

	Name		Age	Occupation	Real	Pers.	Birthplace
538	James	HEWING	50	Chairmaker		50	N. C.
	Elizabeth		45				"
	Samuel		19				"
	John		17				"
	Sol (m)		12				Tenn.
	Rebecca		10				"
	Thomas		9				"
	Charles		6				"
	Rachel	SIMMONS	90				N. C.
	Margaret		20	(Idiotic)			"
539	Jesse	BLACK	22			40	"
	Elizabeth		23				Tenn.
	Sarah E.		7				"
	William		3				"
	George W.		5/12				
540	W. B.	WALL	39	Farmer	7,700	2,182	N. C.
	Louise C.		38				Tenn.
	Mary		15				"
	Nancy E.		14				
	Susan J.		12				
	G. P. (m)		9				
	William J.		7				
	Willard F.		3				
	John W.		11/12				
541	Henry	PARROTT	52	"	3,000	1,130	"
	Elizabeth		51				
	Salina J.		26				
	Sarah E.		24				
	Martha W.		22				
	Susan L.		5				
542	Samuel	PARROTT	55	Tailer	2,000	350	"
	Elizabeth R.		51				
	Margart J.		26				
	Elizabeth		24				
	John		19	Laborer			

	Name		Age	Occupation	Real	Pers.	Birthplace
543	Catharine	WINNIFORD	32			100	"
	Virginia		12				
	Ellen		11				
	John G.		9				
	Nina	PARROTT (mul)	22	House Girl			"

Page 76   3 July 1860

544	Job	PARROTT	63	Farmer	2,500	1,500	Tenn.
	Alla		50				"
	Charles G.		23	Laborer			"
	Francis (f)		20				
	Martha		12				
545	John	HALL	47	Farmer	7,560	2,317	"
	Elizabeth		37				"
	James		18	Laborer			
	Samuel		16				
	William		14				
	Caroline		10				
	Malinda	MORROW	40				
546	Joseph D.	SMITH	28	Farmer	1,500	375	"
	Martha J.		20				
	Margart E.		1				
547	George	ETHERTON	30	Laborer		150	"
	Julia		29				
	Charles		17	"			
	James A.		13				
	Sarah M.		12				
	Mary M.		10				
	Job		7				
	Laura E.		5				
	William S.		3				
548	George	PARROTT	83	None	1,000	7,000	Va.
	Sarah		86				Pa.
549	L. B.	YOUNG	53	Saddler	1,400	350	Tenn.
	Elizabeth		58				
	Sarah		23				
	Mary		22				
	D. W. Clinton		18				
	Josephine C.		13				
550	Clara	YOUNG	26		50	100	"
	Clementine		7				"
	Margart		3				"
551	H.	YETT	43	Farmer	9,000	10.061	"
	Sarah		37				"
	Alexander C.		14				"
	Eliza E.		10				"
	Cora L.		8				"

Page 77   3 July 1860

| | Ida M. | | 4/12 | | | | Tenn. |

	Name		Age	Occupation	Real	Pers.	Birthplace
552	William	YETT, Jr.	19	Farmer		300	"
	Clementine		20				N. C.
	Tilghman		7/12				Tenn.
553	Jacob	STEPHENS	57	"	9,000	9,385	"
	Levina		50				"
	Margart L.		22				
	Isaac		14				
	Susannah J.		12				
	Catharine		9				
554	James	SWAGGERTY, Sr.	86	"	8,000	10,959	Pa.
	Nancy H.		64				Va.
555	Rufus	GOSLIN	27	"		200	Tenn.
	Malissa		24				
	James		5				
	John		1/12				
556	Alexander	FRESHOUR	29			360	N. C.
	Catharine		26				Tenn.
	Margart E.		5				
	Inatha (?) A.	(f)	4				
	James		2				
	Martha		1				
	Alfred	STUART	22	Laborer			
557	James H.	YETT	34	Farmer	16,000	22,235	"
	Maliscent E.		30				S. C.
	William C.		7				Tenn.
	Mary E.		5				
	Martha J. S.		3				
558	William	YETT, Sr.	78	"			Va.
	Mary E.		66				Tenn.
559	John	GARIS	61	Laborer		100	N. C.
	Rhoda		37				S. C.
	James		16				Tenn.
	William		12				
	William P.	TELSIN	25	Carpenter		500	"
560	W. B.	TEMPLIN	38	Farmer	2,000	2,255	"
	Emaline		38				
	Samuel		8				
	James		6				
	Jane	SUGGS	27				"

Page 78   4 July 1860

	Name		Age	Occupation	Real	Pers.	Birthplace
561	Henry	OTTINGER (Big)	66	Farmer	3,500	5,700	Va.
	George		23	Laborer			Tenn.
	Mary M.		22				
	Sarah	SMELSER	14				"
562	Henry	OTTINGER	31	Farmer	2,000	942	"
	Hannah		33				
	Emma E.		8				
	George D.		7				
	Joseph M.		5				
	Sarah		3/12				

	Name		Age	Occupation	Real	Pers.	Birthplace
563	Mahal	OTTINGER	29	"	100	958	"
	Catharine		29				
	John		5				
	Sarah L.		4				
	Wilie G.		1				
	Susanah	OTTINGER	83				
564	Jonathan	OTTINGER	34	"	1,500	1,056	"
	Rebecca		37				
	Phillip M.		16				
565	B. B.	HALL	59	"		737	"
	Minerva		42				
	John		20				
	Mary A.		15				
	Joseph W.		13				
	Albert	SCRUGGS	13				
566	Henry	RADER	49	Farmer	6,000	1,300	"
	Anna		45				
	Powell		15	Laborer			
	Granell (m)		12				
	Mary E.		10				
	Sarah J.		6				
567	John	RADER	32	Farmer	2,000	640	"
	Elizabeth		29				"
	Mary E.		10				
	Sarah A.		8				
	Amanda M.		6				
	Hiram H.		4				
	Hannah E.		3				
	Laura M.		1				
	Jacob	OTTINGER	22	Laborer			"
Page 79				CANEY BRANCH		4 July 1860	
568	John D.	OTTINGER	42	Farmer	2,500	4,000	Tenn.
	Mariah		42				
	Louisa B.		16				
	Samuel		16				
	Paul		12				
	Daniel M.		11				
	Martha A.		8				
	Susanah	RADER	65				
569	Adam	WINTER	54	"	3,000	1,943	"
	Sarah		52				
	Magdaline		22				
	Lavina		21				
	Joseph		19	Laborer			
	Hannah		17				
	Jacob		15	"			
	Mahal		15	"			
	Emily		11				
	Catharine		88				Md.
570	James	WARD	35	Farmer		200	Tenn.
	Jane		30				

	Name		Age	Occupation	Real	Pers.	Birthplace
571	Catharine	OTTINGER	70		1,800	700	Va.
	John	WINTER	31		1,000	900	Tenn.
	Mary		25				
	Paralee		2				
	Isaac M.		7/12				
572	Chrisly (m)	OTTINGER	28	"		586	
	Eve		26				"
	Peter		2				"
	Francis M.	(m)	1				"
	Laura E.		4/12				"
573	Mary H.	OTTINGER	65		1,200	410	Md.
574	Abraham	PETERS	50		1,500	945	Tenn.
	Magdalene		45				
	David F.		17	Laborer			
	Conradd		14				
	Jonathan		12				
	Jacob		10				
	Mary C.		6				
575	Henry	OTTINGER	66	Farmer	2,000	1,600	Va.
	Mary		55				"

Page 80   5 July 1860

	Name		Age	Occupation	Real	Pers.	Birthplace
	Elizabeth		26				Tenn.
	Hannah		24				
	George		23	Laborer		500	
	Andrew		22			350	
	Catharine		21				
	Henry		19				
	Mary M.		18				
	Ephraim		15				
	Samuel		14				
	Margart		10				
576	Ambrose	NEAS	23	Farmer		326	"
	Dolly Ann		23				
	Sarah		1				
577	David	OTTINGER	70	"	1,500	750	Pa.
	Catharine		65				Md.
	Sarah		36				Tenn.
	Catharine		28	(Idiotic)			"
	Noah		22	Laborer			"
578	Jacob	OTTINGER	28	Farmer	3,000	2,915	"
	Mary		26				
	Elizabeth		9				
	Sarah		5				
	Franklin		3				
	Eliza J.		1				
579	Patrick	COGBURN	31	Laborer		58	
	Anna		35				
	Davis		5				
	Malinda		4				
	Sarah		2				

	Name		Age	Occupation	Real	Pers.	Birthplace
580	Joseph	McMURTRY	60	Farmer	1,200	1,255	"
	Susannah		60				Pa.
	Abagil	MALEN	14				Tenn.
581	Elizabeth	BORDEN (mul)	40				S. C.
	Magdaline	(bl)	7				Tenn.
582	Joseph	RODES	37	"	800	663	"
	Barbary		36				"
	Sarah C.		14				
	Christian	(f)	12				
	Adam F.		10				
	David		8				

Page 81   5 July 1860

	Name		Age	Occupation	Real	Pers.	Birthplace
	Regenna		7				Tenn.
	Simpson		6				"
	Mary A.		4				
	Phillip M.		2				
583	John	WELTY	63	Farmer	4,000	401	Va.
	Mary A.		30				Tenn.
	Hannah J.		3				
	Peter		2				
	Martha L.		1				
	Sarah	NELSON	15				
584	Mathew	GOODSON	65	Laborer		75	N. C.
	Caly		60				"
	James M.	PARDON	24	"			"
	Elizabeth		20				"
	Samuel		15	"			"
	Thomas P.		17	"			"
585	George W.	GUINN	35	Farmer		370	Tenn.
	Anna		30				
	S phronia		10				
	Adolphus		7				
	Magdaline		2				
586	William	RUNNER	23	"		200	"
	Mary A.		20				
	Westly		6/12				
587	James	JOHNSON	50	Shoemaker		125	N. C.
	Harriet		55				Ga.
	Griza (?)	(f)	22				Tenn.
	Sarah J.		18				"
	Nancy		16				"
588	Amos	YOUNG	20	Laborer		10	Ga.
	Margaret		23				Tenn.
589	John	SHARP	46	Farmer		290	"
	Eliza		40				
590	Elizabeth	BLASER	50			183	Va.
	Andrew		22				Tenn.
	Daniel		15	Laborer			
	Sarah		12				
	Maly		10				

	Name		Age	Occupation	Real	Pers.	Birthplace
591	Phillip.	NEAS	35	Farmer			"
	Catharine		30				

Page 82   5 July 1860

	Name		Age	Occupation	Real	Pers.	Birthplace
	Amanda		6				Tenn.
	Samuel		4				
	George		3				
	Andrew		9/12				
592	Royal	MOORE	47	Farmer		150	N. C.
	Sarah		45				
	Aaron		20	Laborer			"
	Magdalen		18				"
	Moses		14				"
	Susannah		10				"
	Andrew		8				"
	Martha		5				"
593	Henry	RUNNER	48	Miller	1,200	1,245	"
	Orphy		51				
	Andrew		19	Laborer			
	Susannah		18				
	Elizabeth		17				
	Mary M.		15				
	Malissa		12				
	Henry B.		8				
594	Noah	RUNNER	23	Cabinetmaker		438	"
	Lucinda		21				
	Alfred D.		3				
	Orphy E.		2				
	Franklin	DRYMAN	8				
595	James	COOPER	58	Farmer	1,200	400	"
	Martha		29				
	Robert		9				
	James		8				
	William		5				
	Martha J.		4				
	John J.		2				
	Margaret		54				
596	John	GRAGG (mwy)	19	Laborer		200	"
	Nancy		27				
597	Peter	EISENHOUR	56	Carpenter	300	470	N. C.
	Sarah		51				Tenn.
	Sarah		22				"
	John		21	Laborer			"
	Emma		16				"

Page 83   5 July 1860

	Name		Age	Occupation	Real	Pers.	Birthplace
	David		12				Tenn.
	Susannah		9				
598	George M.	GRAGG	53	Farmer	1,000	700	"
	Mary		47				"
	Anna		23				"
	William		21	Laborer			"

	Name		Age	Occupation	Real	Pers.	Birthplace
	Samuel		18	"			"
	Sarah		16				"
	Andrew		15	"			"
	Isaac		12				"
	Alexander		6				"
	Lewis F.		4				
599	Robert	GRAGG	60	Farmer	600	431	"
	Jane		55				"
	Benjamin		21	Laborer			"
	Susannah		15				"
	Joseph		13				"
	George A.		6				"
600	James	GRAGG	29	Laborer	30	230	Tenn.
	Mary A.		30				"
	Catharine		6				"
601	John M.	SANE	73	Farmer	65	1,193	N. C.
	Margarett		54				Tenn.
	Sarah		37				"
	Joseph		24	Laborer			"
	Mary A.		23				"
	Andrew		21	Laborer			"
	Catharine		18				"
	William		4				"
602	Jacob	SANE	38	"		160	"
	Anna		35				"
	James		12				"
	Daniel		9				"
	Rachel		8				"
	Jefferson		6				"
	Margarett J.		4				"
603	William	GRAGG	35	Farmer	700	361	"
	Mary		37				"
	John		12				"
	Nancy J.		10				"

Page 84   5 July 1860

	Name		Age	Occupation	Real	Pers.	Birthplace
	George		7				Tenn.
	Samuel		5				"
	Lewis		6/12				"
604	Christopher	BLAZER	20	Farmer		160	Tenn.
	Elizabeth		18				"
	Joseph S.		3/12				"
	Joseph	SMITH	17	Laborer			"
605	George	NEAS	26				"
	Sarah		23				"
	Malinda		1				"
	Laura C.		1/12				"
606	Elijah	GRAGG	43	Farmer	1,500	1,013	"
	Sarah		37				"
	Nancy A.		12				"
	Emaline		7				"
	Josephine		4				"
	Francese		2				"

	Name		Age	Occupation	Real	Pers.	Birthplace
607	Joseph	WINTER	45	Farmer	2,000	2,000	"
	Rachel		33				"
	William		15	Laborer			"
	Sarah		14				"
	John		12				"
	George		11				"
	James M.		9				"
	Elizabeth		8				"
	Calvin		6				"
	Luther		4				"
	Florence		3				"
	Margarett		1				"
608	John W.	GRAGG	61	Farmer		102	"
	Anna		59				"
	Susanna		23				"
	John		21	Laborer			"
	Mary		11				"
	George L.	POTTER	25		2,500	800	"
609	Philip H.	EASTERLY	47	Farmer	3,000	1,550	"
	Elizabeth		45				"
	Thomas N.		21	Laborer			"
	Phebe		18				"
	Abraham H.		17	"			"

Page 85   5 July 1860

	Name		Age	Occupation	Real	Pers.	Birthplace
	Lydia C.		16				Tenn.
	Rachel		14				"
	Sarah		10				"
	Francese		9				"
	George		6				"
	James		4				"
	Martha		2				"
	Elbert		11/12				"
610	Elizabeth	WARD	53		113	50	S. C.
	Nancy		27				Tenn.
	Josiah		25	Laborer			"
	Florence C.	HOLT	2				"
611	John	REECE	55	Farmer	1,000	2,220	"
	Rachel		53				"
	Martha		20				"
	Sarah		17				"
	Charles	FANCHER	6				"
612	Rubin	REECE	26	Laborer		200	"
	Elizabeth		26				"
	Edith A.		4				"
	Lydia C.		3				"
	Rachel L.		1				"
613	Robert	COGBERN	32	"		40	"
	Winny		35				"
	Mary E.		12				"
	William		4				"
	Sarah		11/12				"

	Name		Age	Occupation	Real	Pers.	Birthplace
614	Henry	GRAGG	38	Farmer		375	"
	Ann	"	34				"
	Margarett	"	6				"
	William	"	4				"
	Charles A.	"	1				"
615	John	COOPER	64	"	2,000	1,800	Va.
	Emily C.	"	38				Tenn.
	Canzada (f)	"	30				"
	Rebecca M.	"	28				"
	Lucinda W.	"	27				"
	Nathan M.	"	24	Laborer			"
	Samuel H.	"	22				"
	Louiza A.	"	20				"

Page 86   6 July 1860

	Name		Age	Occupation	Real	Pers.	Birthplace
616	Green B.	EBBS	46	Farmer		120	Tenn.
	Nancy	"	38				"
	Loucretha	"	7				"
	Lydia	"	4				"
	John	"	1				"
617	Catharene	EBB	30		2,000	70	"
	Margaret	"	25				"
	Henry	"	27	(Idiotic)			"
618	Noah	NEAS	25	Farmer	3,000	1,204	"
	Catharine	"	29				"
	Francese	"	7				"
	Mary A.	"	4				"
	Wily G.	"	3				"
619	George	PRASEWATERS	70	Farmer	200	871	N. C.
	Tempy	"	50				"
	Timonty	"	24	Laborer			Tenn.
	Elanora	HODGE	18				"
620	Felh (m)	EBBS	38	Farmer		443	"
	Jane A.	"	30				S. C.
	Isaac N.	"	9				Tenn.
	William J.	"	7				"
	Frances C.	" (m)	6				"
	George W.	"	4				"
	John A.	"	3				"
	Nicholas	"	1				"
621	Henry	STUART	66	Laborer		75	Va.
	Mary A.	"	60				S. C.
622	Josiah	WILLIAMS	51	Farmer	4,000	1,827	Va.
	Tabitha C.	"	37				Tenn.
	Eliza J.	"	15				"
	Mary A.	"	11				"
	Sarah	"	8				"
	Pernetta	"	2				"
	James	COMPTON (bl)	6				"
	John	BENNER	20	Laborer			"

	Name		Age	Occupation	Real	Pers.	Birthplace
623	Michael	NEAS	56	Farmer	6,000	3,834	"
	Sarah	"	57				"
	John	"	21	Laborer			"
	Sarah	"	18				"
	Lavina	"	15				"
	Anna	EASTERLY	36				Tenn.

Page 87   6 July 1860

	Name		Age	Occupation	Real	Pers.	Birthplace
624	Martin	EISENHOUR	72	Farmer	4,170	3,052	N. C.
	Catharine	"	73				"
	Hellena	"	30				Tenn.
	Louiza J.	"	5				"
625	David	REDMAN	32	Laborer		353	N. C.
	Nancy	"	29				Tenn.
	Susanah	"	3				"
	Sarah J.	"	2				"
	James	"	6/12				"
626	Simeon	EISENHOUR	29	Farmer		2,065	"
	Mahaly	"	27				"
	James K.	"	2				"
	Nancy	COMPTEN	17				S. C.
627	Thomas	HENDERSON	41	Laborer		275	Tenn.
	Mahaly	"	27				"
	Emaly	"	10				"
	Mary E.	"	7				"
	Sarah	"	5				"
	Martha	"	5				"
628	John	SMITH	52	Laborer		588	"
	Anna	"	52				"
	Samuel	"	21				"
	Elijah	"	19				"
	John	"	18				"
	Robert	"	14				"
	Alexander	"	11				"
	Sarah A.	"	11				"
629	John S.	SMITH	53	Farmer	50	3,296	"
	Sarah	"	52				Va.
	Frances (m)	"	21	Laborer			Tenn.
	George	"	23				"
	Lydia	"	18				"
	Crocket	"	16				"
	John	"	15				"
	James	"	12				"
630	John	FAWBION	85	Farmer	6,000	11,775	Va.
	Henry	"	55				Tenn.
	Abraham	"	23	Laborer			"
	Margarett	"	21				"

Page 88   7 July 1860

	Name		Age	Occupation	Real	Pers.	Birthplace
	Moses	"	20	Laborer			Tenn.

	Name		Age	Occupation	Real	Pers.	Birthplace
631	William	SHIELDS	51	Farmer	3,500	2,700	"
	Mary A.	"	46				"
	John	"	16	Laborer			"
632	George	OTTINGER	60	Farmer	5,000	1,200	Va.
	Susanah	"	57				"
	Hannah	"	33				Tenn.
633	Jacob	OTTINGER	24	Farmer		600	"
	Neas W. (f)	"	20				"
634	Joseph	OTTINGER	32	Laborer		1,000	"
	Nancy	"	25				"
	Lydia E.	"	3				"
	Noah M.	"	2				"
	Mary M.	COBLER (?)	22				"
635	Aaron	BLAZER	44	Laborer		500	"
	Elizabeth	"	50				"
	Jacob	"	19	"			"
	Mary	"	16				"
	Susanah	"	15				"
	Mkael	"	10				"
	Hannah	"	9				"
	William	"	6				"
636	Peter	RADER	32	Farmer	500	750	"
	Rebecca	"	32				"
	Jacob D.	"	11				"
	Martha M.	"	8				"
	Melvina	"	3				"
637	William	OTTINGER	25	Farmer	850	1,370	"
	Dositha	"	28				"
	Mary Emily	"	33			60	"
	Charles	OTTINGER	1				"
638	Cornelius	SMELCER	47	"	2,500	1,425	"
	Mary	"	46				"
	Aaron	"	9				"
	Susanah	"	8				"
	George I.	"	7				"
	Sarah E.	"	2				"
639	Andrew	OTTINGER	34	"	1,000	750	"
	Elizabeth	"	34				"
	Martha	"	14				"

Page 89   7 July 1860

	Name		Age	Occupation	Real	Pers.	Birthplace
	Washington	"	12				Tenn.
	David F.	"	10				"
	Sarah	"	8				"
	Jacob D.	"	7				"
640	Michael	OTTINGER	25	Laborer		50	"
	Mary	"	20				"
641	Runius	BLAZER	23	"		100	"
	Rebecca	"	30				"

	Name		Age	Occupation	Real	Pers.	Birthplace
642	Michael	OTTINGER	30	F rmer	2,200	1,340	"
	Elizabeth	"	24				"
	James H.	"	3				"
643	Shaderic	DEBUSK	23	Laborer		610	"
	Martha	"	22				"
	Florence	"	2				"
644	Abraham	RADER	37	Farmer	4,100	1,475	"
	Matilda	"	37				"
	Isaac	"	13				"
	Samuel F.	"	10				"
	Catharine	"	8				"
	Susanah	"	6				"
	Noah	"	4				"
	Margarett P.	"	1				"
645	Lewis OTTINGER (mwy)		24	Laborer		100	Mo.
	Mary	"	21				Tenn.
646	George	NEAS	31	Farmer	1,500	1,160	"
	Mary M.	"	25				"
	Peter	"	2				"
	Douglas	"	2/12				"
647	John D.	SMITH	34	Sheriff		1,200	"
	Malinda M.	"	33				"
	Richard R. C.	"	4				"
	Joseph	"	2				"
	Nancy J.	LAREW	31				Ind.
648	Daniel	BLAZER	46	Laborer		275	Tenn.
	Margarett	"	45				"
	Mary A.	"	23				"
	Sarah C.	"	16				"
	Columbus	"	8				"
649	John E.	OTTINGER	47	Farmer	1,000	150	"
	Dolly	"	49				"

Page 90   7 July 1860

	Name		Age	Occupation	Real	Pers.	Birthplace
650	Philip OTTINGER (mwy)		24	Farmer	100	120	Tenn.
	Mariah A.	"	19				"
651	William COOK (mwy)		21	Laborer		75	"
	Emaline	"	24				"
652	Mahaly	MALOY	49		5,000	3,543	"
	Calvin	"	10				"
	Alice	"	8				"
653	Robt.	DAVIS	25	Farmer		250	"
	Margarett	"	22				"
	James	"	9/12				"
654	Henry	BLAZER	55	"	1,700	400	"
	Mary	"	46				"
	Calvin	"	13				"
	Rubin	"	12				"
	Martha	"	10				"

	Name		Age	Occupation	Real	Pers.	Birthplace
655	Solomon	BLAZER	34	Laborer		300	"
656	William	BLAZER	41		600	750	"
	Susanah	"	35				"
	Martha	"	14				"
	Thomas	"	12				"
	Loucinda	"	10				"
	Elizabeth	"	8				"
	Maranda	"	4				"
	Rachal	"	5/12				"
	Sarah	"	60				Va.
657	William	OTTINGER	43	Farmer	2,100	1,350	Tenn.
	Eda	"	44				"
	Anna	"	21				"
	Joseph	"	20				"
	Thomas	"	18				"
	Henry	"	16				"
	Malinda	"	14				"
	Timoth	"	11				"
	James	"	8				"
	Valentine	"	6				"
	Tempy	"	3				"
658	John	OTTINGER	37	Farmer	2,500	1,000	"
	Rebecca	"	34				"
	Alfred	"	12				"
	Moses	"	8				"

Page 91   7 July 1860

	Name		Age	Occupation	Real	Pers.	Birthplace
	Mary M.	"	7				"
	Susanah	"	4				"
659	David	OTTINGER	41	Farmer	1,332	960	"
	Eliza	"	34				"
	John C.	"	17	Laborer			"
	Lucinda	"	15				"
	Mary M.	"	7				"
	Susanah M.	"	7				"
	Catharine	"	5				"
660	Ranins	OTTINGER	25	Farmer	600	850	"
	Mary H.	"	26				"
	Lewis	"	7				"
	Elbert H.	"	6				"
	John W.	"	4				"
	Eliza	"	3				"
661	Lewis	OTTINGER	59	Farmer	2,000	925	"
	Eve	"	59				"
662	Thomas	OTTINGER	28	Laborer		700	"
	Sarah	"	28				"
	Eve	"	5				"
663	Philip	BLAZER	47	Farmer	1,600	990	"
	Sarah	"	46				"
	Mary A.	"	18				"
	Henry	"	16	Laborer			"

	Name		Age	Occupation	Real	Pers.	Birthplace
	Margarett	"	11				"
	Barbary	"	41				"
664	Thomas	OTTINGER	30	Farmer	2,000	1,300	"
	Lovina	"	30				"
	Eliza J.	"	14				"
	Henry	"	13				"
	Susanah M.	"	10				"
	Delilah	"	8				"
	Thomas	"	6				"
	Amanda E.	"	5				"
	Alfred D.	"	3				"
665	Moses	BLAZER	30	Laborer		100	"
	Laura	"	30				"
	Susanah	"	10				"
	Angaline	"	6				"
	McKinney	"	3				"

Page 92   7 July 1860

	Name		Age	Occupation	Real	Pers.	Birthplace
666	Samuel	BLAZER	37	Laborer		50	Tenn.
	Sarah A.	"	23				"
	Catharine	"	4				"
	Delilah W.	"	11/12				"
	Louiza	BOULDEN	22				S. C.
	Robert M.	SCRUGGS	16	"			Tenn.
667	James D.	BOULDEN	24	Miller			N. C.
	Elanora	"	25				"
	Mary J.	"	3	(Idiotic)			Tenn.
	John M.	"	1				"
	Lovina D.	"	4/12				"
668	Nicholas	SUESONG	32	Farmer	12,000	5,111	"
	Ellen	"	30				"
	Thomas A.	"	6				"
	William A.	"	2				"
	William	SMITH	24	Laborer			"
669	John	HAWK	38	Farmer	9,000	1,994	"
	Sarah	"	44				"
	Samuel L.	"	15	Laborer			"
	Mary C.	"	9				"
	Henry M.	"	7				"
	Martha J.	"	5				"
	Susanah	"	5				"
	Elizabeth	"	39				"
	Simpson	"	11				"
670	Davault	HEIDERICK	40	Laborer		100	N. C.
	Sarah	"	39				Tenn.
	John I.	"	17	"			"
	Eliza J.	"	15	"			"
	William	JOURDEN	15	"			"
	Elizabeth	HIDRICK	9				"
	Daniel P.	"	8				"
	Agnus	"	6				"
	Jacob	"	2				"
	Daniel	"	1/12				"

	Name		Age	Occupation	Real	Pers.	Birthplace
671	John	SMELCER	43	Farmer		654	"
	Catharine	"	25				"
	Sarah E. J.	"	1				"
672	John	BLAZER	47	Laborer		100	"
	Catharine	"	47				"

Page 93   7 July 1860

	Name		Age	Occupation	Real	Pers.	Birthplace
	Peter	"	20	Laborer			Tenn.
	Mary	"	19				"
	Julia	"	14				"
	Eliza	"	10				"
	Anderson	"	8				"
	Alice	"	4				"
673	Benjamin	BLAZER	56	Farmer	2,500	1,545	"
	Margarett	"	47				"
	Jacob	"	20	Laborer			"
	Sarah	"	19				"
	Lewis	"	17	"			"
	Andrew	"	15	"			"
	Martha	"	13				"
	Melvin	"	11				"
	Franklin	"	5				"
	Sarah M.	"	4				"
674	Joseph	OTTINGER	22	Farmer	1,120	300	"
	Rebecca	"	21				"
	Peter	"	19				"
	Andrew	"	18				"
	Benjamin	"	13				"
	Delilah	"	12				"
675	Andrew	COOK	52	Laborer		375	"
	Mary	"	48				"
	Carlene	"	16				"
	Peter	"	14				"
	Rachal	"	12				"
	Emaline	"	10				"
	Manerva	"	7				"
	Anderson	"	5				"
	Josephine	"	3				"
676	Joseph	COOK	23	"		50	"
	Catharine	"	24				"
677	Nanth	BLACK	53			200	N. C.
	Anna	"	19				Tenn.
	Anderson	"	14				"
	Nathan	"	12				"
	Sarah	"	10				"
	George	"	8				"
	Samuel	"	6				"

Page 94   7 July 1860

	Name		Age	Occupation	Real	Pers.	Birthplace
	Robert	"	4				Tenn.
678	Philip	OTTINGER	24	Laborer		75	"
	Anglin		19				"

	Name		Age	Occupation	Real	Pers.	Birthplace
679	Isaac	FANCHER	29	"		900	"
	Margaret S.	"	19				"
	Martha J.	"	4				"
	Sarah M.	"	3				"
	Robert M.	"	2				"
680	Robert	SMITH	58	Farmer	2,000	1,245	"
	Matilda	"	55				"
	William	"	30	Farmer			"
	Catharine M.	"	25				"
	Samuel R.	"	24	Laborer			"
	Jacob	"	20	"			"
681	John	FRESHOUR	42	Farmer		2,120	N. C.
	Hannah	"	33				"
	George	"	17				Tenn.
	Tillman	"	13				"
	Malvina	"	11				"
	Sarah	"	3				"
	Martha J.	"	10/12				"
682	Joseph	WHITACRE	34	Laborer		150	"
	Mary S.	"	33				"
	Catharine E.	"	11				"
	Margaret C.	"	9				"
	Martha J.	"	6				"
	William J.	"	5				"
	Mary R.	"	3				"
	Francis E.	"	1				"
683	John	HAYS	33	Laborer		125	"
	Martha	"	30				"
	William F.	"	10				"
	Mary E.	"	9				"
	Sarah S.	"	7				"
	Elizabeth	"	5				"
	Martha A.	"	2				"
	Francis E.	" (f)	1				"
684	David	SUSONG	39	Farmer	10,000	7,400	"
	Mary F.	"	22				"
	John M.	"	4				"

Page 95   7 July 1860

	Name		Age	Occupation	Real	Pers.	Birthplace
	John S.	"	2				"
	Jane	"	33				"
685	Joseph	TAYLOR	26	Laborer		40	N. C.
	Elizabeth	"	25				"
	Martha E.	"	2				Tenn.
	Lavina E.	"	7/12				"
686	Christian	BENNER	46	Shoemaker		100	"
	Elen	"	48				"
	Anderson	"	19	Laborer			"
	Mary A.	"	18				"
	Susan	"	17				"
	Jacob	"	16	Laborer			"

	Name		Age	Occupation	Real	Pers.	Birthplace
	Joseph	"	14				"
	George P.	"	13				"
	Elizabeth	"	10				"
	Christopher	"	7				"
	Eliza	"	10/12				"
687	Sarah	MOORE	26			65	N. C.
	Calvin	"	8				Tenn.
	Amanda	"	4				"
688	Elbert	GARREL (mwy)	23			720	"
	Maranda	"	20				"
689	Thursa (f)	YOUNG	39			158	"
690	James	GARREL	31	Carpenter		150	"
	Martha J.	"	25				Va.
	Susanah	"	7				Tenn.
	Alexander	"	5				"
	John	"	3				"
	Elbert	"	1				"
691	Daniel	BROOKS	36	Farmer	4,000	1,912	"
	Harriett	"	26				"
	Eliza	"	14				"
	Joel	"	12				"
	William	"	9				"
692	Jacob	HAYSE	23	Farmer		225	"
	Martha	"	20				"
	William H.	"	5/12				
693	Aste (f)	WHITEHEAD	40				N. C.
	James	"	14				"
	Jula	" (mul)	5				Tenn.

Page 96   9 July 1860

	Name		Age	Occupation	Real	Pers.	Birthplace
694	Nancy	BARNET	50			10	Tenn.
	Jane	"	23				"
	John	"	8				
695	Mary	MANOR	65		30	40	N. C.
	Elizabeth	"	40	-			"
	James	"	22	Laborer			S. C.
	Mathias	"	14				Tenn.
	Matilda	"	11				
696	William	BRAGDEN (mwy)	22	"			"
	Nancy C.	"	16				"
697	W. H.	MILLS	22	Blacksmith		234	N. C.
	Harriet E.	"	19				Tenn.
698	Alexander	TAYLOR	25	Laborer		40	Ky.
	Sarah E.	"	28				Tenn.
	Calvin	"	14				"
	Lucinda E.	"	7				
699	William	BRUNEFIELD	24	"		100	"
	Emiline	"	18				"
	Sarah	"	1				
	Mary	"	65				N. C.

	Name		Age	Occupation	Real	Pers.	Birthplace
700	W. H.	WILLIAMS	31	Cooper		100	Tenn.
	Elizabeth	"	23				"
	Martha J.	"	10				
	John A.	"	3				
	Sarah	"	6				
	James D.	"	2				
701	Isaac S.	BLANCHARD	33	Farmer	1,800	2,009	"
	Ruth C.	"	33				"
	John	"	13				
	William	"	12				
	David	"	8				
	Charles S.	"	6				
	Sarah	"	7				
	Stephen	"	4				
	Nancy	"	3				
E	Evaline	"	2				
	Ruth C.	"	5/12				
702	William	BLANCHARD	29	"		680	"
	Sarah	"	26				"
	John	"	4				"

Page 97 NEWPORT 9 July 1860

	Name		Age	Occupation	Real	Pers.	Birthplace
	Parthena	"					Tenn.
	Samuel	COGDELL	29				"
703	William	TALLENT	60	Farmer		100	N. C.
	Mary —	"	65				"
	Nancy	"	32				"
	Richard	"	33	Laborer (Idiotic)			"
704	Peter	TOWNSEND	50				"
	June L.	"	35				Tenn.
	Nebo	"	14				"
	Vina	"	12				"
	Laura	"	10				"
	Atla	" (f)	8				
	Louisa	"	3				
	Susannah	"	1				
705	John	LAMBERT	26	Farmer			N. C.
	Barbara	"	25				"
	Benjamin P.	"	9				Tenn.
	Mary A.	"	1				N. C.
706	Thomas	MOONEYHAM	27	Laborer		300	Tenn.
	Emaline	"	23				"
	William	"	6				
	Nancy J.	"	3				
	Sarah	"	8/12				
707	William	TALLENT	21	"		45	N. C.
	Nancy	"	20				Tenn.
	Mary A.	"	3/12				
	Sarah	BRAGDEN	16				
708	William	BROOKS	30	Farmer	2,000	715	"
	Mary	"	30				
	John	"	9				

	Name		Age	Occupation	Real	Pers.	Birthplace
	Rachel	"	8				
	Martha	"	6				
	Daniel	"	4				
	Harriet	"	1				
	Thomas	STEPHENS	17				
	John	"	13				
	Rachel	BROOKS	64				S. C.
	William	EVANS	27	Laborer			N. C.
709	Joseph	CASH	52	"			"
	Shadrack	"	21	"			S. C.

Page 98   9 July 1860

	Name		Age	Occupation	Real	Pers.	Birthplace
	Monroe	"	12				Tenn.
	Lorenzo	"	9				S. C.
	Alonzo	"	6				"
710	W. D.	GUINN (mwy)	25	Laborer		20	"
	Sarah	"	16				"
711	James	ROSS	64	Farmer	14,300	9,031	Tenn.
	Ellener	"	44				"
	George	"	13				
	Martha	"	10				
	Harriet	"	7				
	Nancy	"	2				
712	James	MOONEYHAM	33	"		70	"
	Sarah	"	33				
	Daniel	"	6				
	Sarah E.	"	1				
	Letta	MORGAN	37				
713	William	BOYER	37	"	7,500	1,175	"
	Sarah	"	32				
	Mary	"	11				
	Isaac	"	10				
	Michael A.	"	8				
	James A.	"	6				
	Catharine E.	"	4				
	David P.	"	2				
714	James	SMITH	26	Farmer		309	"
	Dorcas	"	24				
	Emma	"	6/12				
715	John	HOLT	26	Laborer		75	
	Elizabeth	"	27				
	Abagail	"	12				
716	Judith C.	HUFF	47		3,000	11,069	"
	Joseph	"	23	Farmer	1,000		"
	Leonard	"	20				
	James	"	18				
	Mary	"	16				
	Susannah	"	12				
	Emma	"	9				
	Laura	"	7				
	Florence	"	4				

	Name		Age	Occupation	Real	Pers.	Birthplace
	Stephen	" (mwy)	28	Farmer	500		

Page 99   9 July 1860

	Name		Age	Occupation	Real	Pers.	Birthplace
	Elizabeth	" (mwy)	22				Tenn.
	Sarah	Nichols	72				N. C.
717	Peter	HOWLET	29	Laborer		258	Tenn.
	Lydia L.	"	27				N. C.
	Sarah J. E.	"	9				Tenn.
	James W.	"	7				"
	John A.	"	6				"
	Robert T.	"	1				
718	David	FRESHOUR	32	Farmer	1,000	265	N. C.
	Nancy	"	28				Tenn.
	Mary	"	8				
	Sarah E.	"	6				
	Laura	"	5				
	William	"	2				
719	Robert	McCLANY	21	Laborer			"
	Catharine	"	21				"
	Marshal	"	3				
	Henry P.	"	10/12				
720	John	KEISLER	35	"		230	N. C.
	Cynthia	"	24				Tenn.
	Franklin	"	3				
	Mary E.	"	1				
721	Edward	McMAHAN	28	Farmer	900	4,050	"
	Sarah	"	34				
	Gentry	"	5				
	Stephen	"	2				
	Frank	GUIN	18	Laborer			N. C.
722	William	KILLIAN	37	"		337	"
	Mallissa	"	22				Tenn.
723	William	RUNNER	47	Farmer	2,600	2,354	"
	Mary M.	"	46				
	Rachel	"	19				
	Louisa J.	"	17				
	Rubin	"	15	Laborer			
	Franklin	"	11				
	Susannah	"	6				
724	J. R.	McKAY	36	Blacksmith		930	"
	Martha J.	"	31				
	Mary	"	8				
	Jeremiah	"	5				

Page 100   9 July 1860

	Name		Age	Occupation	Real	Pers.	Birthplace
	Isabella	"	5				Tenn.
	Laura	"	3				"
	William R.	"	2				
	John M.	"	5/12				

	Name		Age	Occupation	Real	Pers.	Birthplace
725	Luna (m)	CHAPMAN	61	Farmer	4,380	10,694	"
	Elizabeth		34				"
	John		21	Laborer			"
726	Elizabeth	CHAPMAN	85		3,975	7,543	"
	Mary		63				"
727	H. G.	KILGORE	39	Farmer		522	"
	Fanny		31				
	Zachariah W.		11				
	Simpson		9				
	Sarah A.		4				
	Thomas G.		2				
728	Jane	KILGORE	67		2,000	200	"
	Luciuda	MICHAL	15				
	Hannon (m)		13				
729	Martin	KILGORE	40	"		765	
	Ruth		27				
	Martha F.		9				
	Darth la M.		7				
	Jane		4				
	Mary		3				
	John		1				
730	Moses V.	NEAS	32	"	2,000	1,204	"
	Lydia		26				
	Martha		6				
	Amanda		4				
	Rufus		2				
	Mary G.	DRYMAN	13				
731	John	CRITSELOUS	49	Farmer	3,075	1,204	"
	June		41				"
	John P.		7				
	Noah R.		5				
	S phronia S.		2				
732	Martin	JUSTICE	54	"		100	N. C.
	Isabella		51				Tenn.
	John		21	Laborer			"
	Rubin		15	"			"
Page 101				PARROTTSVILLE			10 July 1860
	Eliza		12				Tenn.
	Ellen		9				
733	Powell	RUNNER	29	Laborer		491	"
	Elizabeth		25				
	Martha E.		5				
	Sarah L.		4				
	Louis B.		2				
734	Robert W.	HUFF	31	Farmer	2,000	708	"
	Delana		25				Ga.
	Henry A.		6				"
	Mary E.		4				"
	Margaret		1				"

	Name		Age	Occupation	Real	Pers.	Birthplace
735	Sarah	SWEEDEN	45			50	Tenn.
	Joseph		16	Laborer			"
	Stephen		16	"			"
	Susannah A.		14				
	William		11				
736	William	GRAGG	29	"		130	"
	Caroline		21				
	Sophronia		5				
	Marshal		3				
737	William	KELLY	32	Farmer		465	"
	Rebecca		31				
	Mary A. C.		10				
	Andrew J.		3				
	Susannah E.		5/12				
	Sarah E.		5/12				
738	B. F.	NEASE	46	"	3,600	1,726	"
	Magdalene		44				
	Martha E.		17				
	Narcissus		16				
	Leonard A.		12				"
	Laura S.		8				
	Jane		5				
	Julius F.		2				
739	Andrew	SANE	23	"		61	"
	Mary A.		24				"
	Mary J.		7/12				
740	William	KELLY, Sr.	70	"	1,000	1,000	Va.
	Elizabeth		68				"

Page 102   10 July 1860

	Name		Age	Occupation	Real	Pers.	Birthplace
741	Robert	KELLY	23	Laborer		450	Tenn.
	Lydia		19				
	Mary		1				
742	Joseph	KELLY	28	Farmer		500	"
	Sarah E.		22				
	Sarah		4				
	William E.		2				
743	Sarah A.	RICE	52			804	S. C.
	Margaret		24				N. C.
	Julius		26				"
	James		22				
	Sarah		21				
	Joseph		19				
	Carissa		15				
	Robert		13				
	Octavio	(m)	9				
744	Wiley	CHAPMAN	27	Farmer	800	530	Tenn.
	Mary E.		21				
	William E.		1				

	Name		Age	Occupation	Real	Pers.	Birthplace
745	William	CHAPMAN	33	Farmer	800	530	Tenn.
	Sarah H.		23				
	James H.		5				
746	William	STUART	58	"	880	962	Va.
	Mary		58				Tenn.
	George		27	Laborer			
	Alfred		21	"			
	James		18	"			
	Samuel		17	"			
	William		14				
747	Alfred	SPENCER	52	Farmer	2,500	750	Va.
	Harritta		50				Tenn.
	Mariam		28				
	Elizabeth		21				
	Joseph		17	Laborer			
	James		15				
	Alfred		9				
748	John	SHEPHARD	52	Farmer	2,500	100	N. C.
	Susannah M.	BALLEW	35				"
	Mary A.		16				"
	Caroline		14				"

Page 103   10 July 1860

	Name		Age	Occupation	Real	Pers.	Birthplace
749	Jacob	KILLIAN	31	Laborer		200	N. C.
	Martha		20				"
	William G.		3				Tenn.
	Susannah		1				
750	John	KILLIAN	31	Farmer		600	N. C.
	Barbara		72				"
	Rebecca	LINEBERGER	22				Tenn.
	Darthula	KILLIAN	17				N. C.
	William	LINEBERGER	8/12				Tenn.
751	Jacob	FRESHOUR	66	"		124	"
	Sarah C.		66				N. C.
	William		18	Laborer			S. C.
	John		17	"			"
	Jackson	ROBINSON	8				Tenn.
752	Susan	LILLARD	53		4,807	7,500	N. C.
753	William H.	DEWITT	65	Farmer	12,000	11,933	S. C.
	Hannah E.		60				Tenn.
	Richard		24				
	William		22				
	Alexander		18				
	Rebecca E.		15				
	James		12				
	William B.		12				Ark.
754	Daniel	HEADRICK	50	Farmer		949	N. C.
	Susannah		46				Tenn.
	Absalom		19				
	William H.		17				
	Mary		15				

	Name		Age	Occupation	Real	Pers.	Birthplace
	Parthena		12				
	Charlotte		10				
	Daniel		6				
	Andrew		1				
	Mary	MILLER	17				
755	Edmond	LAMBERT	34	Miller			N. C.
	Rosannah		25				"
	Sushanna		25				"
756	(Inmates of the Poor House)						
	David	WILLIAMS	84	(Blind)			Va.
	Sarah		90				S. C.
	Sarah	TAYLOR	59				Tenn.
	Prudence		39	(Blind)			

Page 104   NEWPORT   11 July 1860

	Name		Age	Occupation	Real	Pers.	Birthplace
	Benjamin	CARR	70				S. C.
	Catharine	INGRAM	60				"
	John	BARNET	88				Va.
	Job	HAMPTON	90	(Blind)			Tenn.
	John	DAVIS	84				Va.
	James	GALLAHER	40	(Idiot)			Tenn.
	Sarah	DAVIS	80				Va.
	Jane	LAKE	50	(Insane)			Tenn.
757	Rhoda	McMAHAN	41		1,500	900	"
	Royal A.		18	Farmer			"
	Mary		16				"
	John J. C.		13				"
	Ellen		8				"
	Evaline	MOORE	20				
758	Stephen	HUFF	63	"	20,000	11,127	"
	Eliza		43				Va.
	Jane		26				Tenn.
	Stephen		9				
	James		20	Laborer			
	Joseph	COGDELL	18	"			
	Robert		16	"			
	Jene	HOUSTON	22				
	Louisa		20				
759	John	HUFF	36	Farmer	3,500	1,765	"
	Jane E.		25				
	Elizabeth		2				
	Thomas N.		8/12				
	A. J.	FOREMAN	25	Teacher			"
760	Jacob	SHETLEY	45	Laborer			N. C.
	Jane		40				Tenn.
	William		18				"
	Elizabeth		16				
	John		13				
	Frank		9				
	Mary		7				
	Duncan		5				
	Harriet		1				

	Name		Age	Occupation	Real	Pers.	Birthplace
761	Sarah	BANKS	47		1,200	847	"
	Nathan		22	"			"
	Mary S.		20				

Page 105   11 July 1860

	Name		Age	Occupation	Real	Pers.	Birthplace
	Stephen		18	Laborer			Tenn.
	David		16				
	Rhoda A.		13				
	Sarah E.		11				
	Judy E. F.		7				
	William		4				
	Warren		1				
762	John	TOWNSEND	50	Farmer	2,000	746	N. C.
	Mary		50				"
	Phillip		20	Laborer			Tenn.
	Nancy		13				
	Mary		11				
	John W.		9				
	Royal S.		7				
	Margaret E.		5				
763	Franklin	STAMY	21	"		40	N. C.
	Martha		25				"
	Leander		3				Tenn.
	Jemima		2				
	Job		3				
764	James	TOWNSEND	24	Farmer		325	"
	Mary E.		18				
	William D.		1				
765	Elihu	MESSER	35	Miller		125	N. C.
	Martha		27				S. C.
	Thomas		15	Laborer			Tenn.
766	Thomas	MESSER	75	Farmer	150	200	N. C.
	Mary		50				"
	Royal		18	Laborer			"
	John		15				"
	Green B.		14				Tenn.
	George		16	"			N. C.
767	William	ELLISON	25	"		50	Tenn.
	Matilda		23				N. C.
	Mary J.		3				Tenn.
	John		1				
768	T. B.	HUFF	29	Farmer		900	"
769	Daniel H.	GOWAN	33	"	150	224	N. C.
	Elizabeth		28				"
	George	PRATER	5				Tenn.

Page 106   11 July 1860

	Name		Age	Occupation	Real	Pers.	Birthplace
770	Jesse M. L.	BURNETT	30	Minister (Baptist)	7,150	1,668	N. C.
	Charles T.		3				Tenn.
	Eliza E.		1				"

	Name		Age	Occupation	Real	Pers.	B rthplace
771	James N.	McKAY	43	Farmer		603	"
	Mary A.		40				"
	Abraham		19	Laborer			"
	Sarah		17				
	James		15				"
	Stephen		12				
	Judy		9				
	Eliza		4				
772	Americus	JONES	46	Dept. Sheriff	4,500	1,681	N. C.
	Eliza R.		43				Tenn.
	Charles C.		21	Laborer			"
	Mary E.		17				
	Nancy N.		15				
	Eliza J.		13				
	James N.		11				
	Sarah A.		7				
	William N.		4				
	John A.		1				
	Walter S.	BRANCH	25	Merchant	150	1,800	Va.
773	Peter	STAMEY	33	Cabinet Maker	500	110	N. C.
	Adaline		31				"
	Martha J.		12				
	Henry		10				Tenn.
	Nancy		7				
	Frances (f)		5				
	Stephen		3				
774	Arthur	SAWYERS	31	Farmer		285	Tenn.
	Mary J.		27				"
	Laura J.		8				
	William J.		6				
	Arthur M. L.		5				
	John L.		3				
	Sarah E.		10/12				
775	Merrit	BURGEN	23	Laborer		100	N. C.
	Mary J.		18				Tenn.
	Mary E.		10/12				"
776	John	WOOD	36	Farmer	6,000	3,817	"
Page 107							11 July 1860
	Nancy		37				"
	Tilman		13				"
	Elizabeth		12				"
	Mary J.		10				"
	James		8				"
	Martha		5				"
	Alexander		4				"
	Joseph		1				"
777	Elizabeth	WEAVER	55		5,000	8,403	"
	Laura		22			3,000	N. C.
	Ellinora		11				Tennessee
	William		9				Tenn.
	Lewis		17	Laborer		2,700	"

	Name		Age	Occupation	Real	Pers.	Birthplace
778	R. C.	WEAVER	30	Farmer	600	762	N. C.
	Mary J.		25				Ky.
	James		2				Tenn.
	Monroe		3/12				"
779	Peter	MILLER	79	Laborer	75	350	Montsome Scotland
	Nancy		71				Tenn.
	James	ELLENDER	4				
780	Rebecca	BROGDEN	48		30		"
	Margaret E.		8				"
781	J. B. S.	BURNETT	35	Farmer	300	580	N. C.
	Rebecca		33				Tenn.
	Mary A.		12				"
	Wm. J.		11				"
	Lydia J.		10				"
	John F.		7				"
	Jesse A. (m)		1				"
782	A. M.	WRIGHT	27	Farmer		100	N. C.
	Hannah		36				Tenn.
	Alice Ann		6				"
	Sarah		4				"
	Mary J.		2				"
	James R.		2/12				"
783	Wm.	MOONEYHAM	60	Farmer	800	730	Tenn.
	Winney M.		24				"
	Isaac		18				"
	Henry		14				"
	Samuel		6				"

Page 108   11 July 1860

	Name		Age	Occupation	Real	Pers.	Birthplace
	Robert F.		4				Tenn.
784	James	ASENTON	33	Farmer		300	"
	Sarah		37				"
	Daniel	NELSON	15	Laborer			N. C.
785	Thomas	MOONEYHAM	59	Farmer	200	202	Tenn.
	Sarah		57				"
	John N.		20	Laborer			"
	Elizabeth C.		16				"
	Elbert	TRENT	2				"
	Willis		22	Laborer			"
786	James	COGDELL	26	Farmer		150	"
	Elizabeth		24				"
	Thomas		6				"
	William		5				"
	Mary		2				"
	Eveline		17				"
787	James	BRUMFIELD	20	Laborer		25	"
	Louisa		19				"
788	E. B.	HUGGINS	36	Laborer		50	N. C.

	Name		Age	Occupation	Real	Pers.	Birthplace
789	S. D.	WADDLE	43	Carpenter		100	N. C.
	Winny		44				Tenn.
	James	MOONEYHAM	10				"
	Calvin		13				"
790	Lewis	WILLIS	36	Farmer		125	"
	Mary A.		24				Tenn.
	George W.		5				"
	Sarah E.		3				"
	Adeline		6/12				"
791	Martin	LINTZ	36	Farmer		737	Tenn.
	Nancy		35				"
	Mary J.		15				"
	Elizabeth		56				"
792	John	FRESHOUR	92	No Occupation		80	Md.
	Catharine		88				Pa.
	Alexander	MALOY	24	Laborer			Tenn.
793	James	HIXON	23	Farmer		100	Tenn.
	Mary		21				N. C.
	Ashby		2				Tenn.
	William		1				"
794	John M. A.	BURNETT	36	Farmer	1,200	1,083	N. C.

Page 109   CATO   12 July 1860

	Name		Age	Occupation	Real	Pers.	Birthplace
	Jane E.		32				Tenn.
	Margaret		5				"
	Wm. C.		3				"
	Mary C. R.		1				"
795	James P.	NELSON	25	Farmer		400	S. C.
	Caroline		17				Tenn.
796	Elizabeth	BRADFORD	44			75	N. C.
	Albert		20				N. C.
	Marian (m)		15				Tenn.
797	John	FULTZ	71	Fortune Teller		25	Not Known
	Malinda		40				Tenn.
	Henry		17	Laborer			"
	Luna (m)		15				"
	Augustus		12				"
	Devorick		9				"
	Nicholas		3				"
798	P. M.	WILLIAMS	47	Carpenter		723	"
	Sarah		46				"
	James		28	Shoemaker			"
	William		23	Laborer			"
	George W.		21				"
	Sarah		17				N. C.
	Douglas		16	Laborer			"
799	A. C.	HUFF	41	Farmer	15,000	3,180	Tenn.
	Narcissa L.		38				N. C.
	Swan B.		17	Laborer			Tenn.
	James T.		15	"			"

Name		Age	Occupation	Real	Pers.	Birthplace	ıplace
Francis E. J.		13				"	'
John J.		10				"	
Andrew F.		6				"	
Eliza C.		4				"	
David P.		1				"	
Sarah	BURNETT	25				N. C.	
A. J.	MUSICK (mul)	15	Fieldhand			"	'
Amos	PRAYTER	26	Laborer		50	N. C.	
Sarah		24				Tenn.	
Nancy J.		5				"	
Lydia		4				"	
Jos. J.		2				"	
Calvin		10/12				"	
110					13 July 1860		
Franklin	MILLER	23	Laborer		40	Tenn.	
Rhoda		23				"	
Nancy J.		1/12				"	
Wm. C.	BURNETT	58	Farmer	5,000	2,826	N. C.	
Lydia		52				"	
Jane		29				"	
Isaac	CLEMENS	61	Farmer	1,000	1,102	N. C.	
Judia		54				"	
Jane E.		18				Tenn.	
John	SEXTON	30	Laborer			"	
Mary C.		34				N. C.	
Sarah E.		8				Tenn.	
James B.		6				"	
Nancy E.		4				"	
Eliza C.		2				"	
J. M.	BURNETT	46	Farmer	20,001	13,000	N. C.	
Judith C.		34				Tenn.	
Stephen A.		14				"	
Swan L.		12				"	
John E.		10				"	
Mary F. E.		8				"	
Eliza E.		6				"	
Susannah A.		4				"	
Joseph J.		3				"	
James H.		11/12				"	0
Rachel	WADDEL	32	Teacher			N. C.	
James S.	TAYLOR	21	Laborer		40	S. C.	
Mary E.		18				N. C.	
Mary C.		1				Tenn.	
Mary A.	PRAYTER	40			60	N. C.	
Jackson		16				N. C.	
Martha		14				"	
Amanda		12				Tenn.	
Hester N.		10				"	
John	PRAYTER	70				N. C.	

	Name		Age	Occupation	Real	Pers.	Birthplace
808	J.J.	BURNETT	35	Farmer	4,000	3,882	N. C.
	Mary L.		28				Tenn.
	J. E.		6				"
	Stephen F.		4				"
	Jesse A.		2				"
Page 111							13 July 1860
	Francis D. C.		9/12				Tenn.
809	Calup	REESE	42	Farmer		311	Tenn.
	Catharine		43				Pa.
	John H.		17	Laborer			Tenn.
	Sarah M.		15				"
	Amanda E.		11				"
	Wm. L.		6				"
	Jacob A.	TOBA	8				"
	Susannah A.		5				"
	Henry F.		3				"
	Mary A.	TOBY	25				"
810	James	ROBERTS (mwy)	21	Laborer		100	N. C.
	Nancy E.		21				Tenn.
811	Zackey	BIBLE	23	Farmer	200	100	Tenn.
	Lyda J.		17				N. C.
	Mary E.		3/12				Tenn.
812	(Blurred)	WOODY	88	Farmer		100	N. C.
	Barshaba		38				S. C.
	Narcissa		11				Tenn.
	Susannah		9				"
	Martin		3				"
	Margaret		11/12				"
813	Wills	WOODEY	32	Farmer	600	535	N. C.
	Sarah A.		31				"
	Stephen H.		7				Tenn.
	Elizabeth		6				"
	Lavina		1				"
814	Wm.	KNIGHT	32	Farmer	200	172	"
	Sarah E.		32				N. C.
	John R.		11				Tenn.
	Sanders		9				Tenn.
	Margaret		7				"
	Stephen B.		5				"
	Matilda J.		5				"
815	IRY	BALL	32	Farmer	1,500	370	Tenn.
	Mary		24				"
	Spicy (f)		12				"
	Benjamin		19				"
	Alfred		7				"
	Isaac		6				"
Page 112				TAYLORSBURG			13 July 1860
	Jacob		5				Tenn.
	Martha		1				"
816	Martha	BALL	72			75	Va.

- 92 -

	Name		Age	Occupation	Real	Pers.	Birthplace
817	Binghame	KNIGHT	25	Farmer		270	Tenn.
	Matilda		18				"
	Nancy		2				"
	Richard		1				"
	Elizabeth		60				N.C.
818	Green	WOODY	40	Farmer	600	355	N. C.
	Margaret		38				"
	Wily		16				Tenn.
	Talten		11				"
	Nathan		10				"
	Christina		8				"
	Tilman		5				"
	Johishan (?)		4				"
	James		4/12				"
819	Eli	McMAHAN	28	Farmer	800	489	Tenn.
	Sarah		24				"
	N. J.		4				"
	Mahaly		3				"
820	John	BLACK	20	Laborer			Tenn.
	Martha J.		21				N. C.
	James A.		7/12				Tenn.
821	Smith	TEAGUE	28	Farmer	300	230	N. C.
	Mary		29				Tenn.
	Edward		11				"
	Rubin		4				"
	Sarah		1				"
822	Robert	GREEN	21	Farmer	400	100	N. C.
	Lydia		23				"
	Sarah E.		1				Tenn.
823	Wyat	JONES	64	Farmer	1,600	450	N. C.
	Hannah		61				"
	William		29	Laborer			N. C.
	Wiley		17	"			Tenn.
	Margaret	CLARK	17				"
824	Thomas	SMITH	22	Laborer		166	Tenn.
	Calvin		5				N. C.
	John L.		3				Tenn.
Page 113						14 July 1860	
	Adaline		2				Tenn.
	Rachael		1				"
825	Marvel	JONES	33	Farmer	300	365	N. C.
	Neisa		23				Tenn.
	Lydia		7				"
	Malinda		5				"
	Susannah		3				"
	Stephen		2				"
	Milburn		4/12				"
826	William	GREEN	32	Laborer	300	197	N. C.
	Martha		32				"
	James		9				Tenn.

	Name		Age	Occupation	Real	Pers.	Birthplace
	William		6				N. C.
	Dennis		4				Tenn.
	Silas		2				"
	Margaret		2/12				"
827	Umphrey	KILPATRIC	44	Farmer		270	N. C.
	Sarah		40				Tenn.
	Matilda		18				"
	James		17	Laborer			"
	Adaline		13				N. C.
	Cassa		12				Tenn.
828	Lewis	KILPATRIC	20	Laborer		50	N. C.
	Louisa		24				Tenn.
	Jane		3				N. C.
	Sarah		1				N. C.
829	Adamga	BALL	46	Farmer		200	Tenn.
	Mary		42				N. C.
	Mary J.		18				Tenn.
	John		16				"
	Samuel		12				"
	Maranda		14				"
	Martha		9				"
	Auslom (?)(m)		6				"
	Mary		5				"
	Dica		1				"
	Nancy	BALL	60				N. C.
	Sarah		23				Tenn.
	John	TURNEY	4				"
830	Hugh S.	CLARK	22	Farmer	300	220	"
Page 114							14 July 1860
	Rebecca J.		19				Tenn.
831	Isaac	MILLER (mwy)	21	Farmer	300	50	"
	Rachel		20				"
832	John	HALL	22	Laborer			"
	Elizabeth		18				"
833	G. W.	GREEN	26	Farmer		75	N. C.
	Lucinda		27				N. C.
834	Solomon	PRICE	30	Farmer	150	140	"
	Lydia		26				"
	John		9				"
	Lydia A.		5				"_
	Nancy		2				"
	Elizabeth		1/12				"
	Jane		68				"
835	Joel	SMITH	52	Farmer	1,000	715	N. C.
	Cyntha		45				"
	Narcissa		16				Tenn.
	Nancy		13				"
	Tolbert		10				"

	Name		Age	Occupation	Real	Pers.	BIRTHPLACE
836	Uriah	BANKS	55	Farmer		178	N. C.
	Margaret		20				Tenn.
	Moses		13				"
	Mary		12				"
	James		10				N. C.
	Lydia		8				Tenn.
837	James P.	PRICE	35	Farmer	100	285	N. C.
	Jinnetta		28				"
	Eliza C.		10				Tenn.
	Joseph		8				"
	William		6				"
	Mary J.		Blank				"
	Lucinda L.		1				"
838	Sol	WILLIAMS	56	Farmer	200	750	N. C.
	Lucinda		55				Tenn.
	James		33	Laborer			"
	Matilda		18				"
	McKiney		13				"
839	Moses A.	TEAGUE	26	Farmer	100	118	N. C.
	Wenny		21				Tenn.
	Harriet J.		4				"

Page 115 — TAYLORSBURG — 14 July 1860

	Name		Age	Occupation	Real	Pers.	BIRTHPLACE
	Nancy		2				Tenn.
840	Lewis	CATE	33	Farmer	300	50	Tenn.
	Rachael		33				N. C.
	Isaac		14				Tenn.
	Mary J.		11				"
	John R.		4				"
841	Edmon	RAMSEY	22				Tenn.
	Thosdocia		21				"
	William		1				"
842	John	HENDERSON	27	Farmer	600	170	S. C.
	Elizabeth J.		22				N. C.
	James J.		3				Tenn.
	Mary		2				"
	Cordelia		11/12				"
843	Wm. P.	MOORE	21	Farmer	200	50	Tenn.
	Elizabeth		24				"
844	William	HENDERSON	24	"			"
	Elizabeth		23				S. C.
	Nancy		1/12				Tenn.
845	James W.	MURRY	36	Farmer	800	503	N. C.
	Susannah		31				"
	Russel G.		13				"
	John W.		11				"
	Sarah		10				"
	James W.		6				Tenn.
	Nancy J.		5				"
	Elizabeth		3				"
	Wm.	REINS	27	Laborer			"
846	Alman	COGIN	46	Farmer		228	N. C.
	Rebecca		38				Tenn.
	George W.		7				"

	Name		Age	Occupation	Real	Pers.	Birthplace
	John		5				"
	Annie		3				"
	Thomas		1/12				"
847	Elizabeth	MOORE	50			50	Tenn.
	Ellender		25				"
	Mahaly		16				"
	Malinda		13				"
	Mary J.		5				"
	Margaret A.		3				"

Page 116   14 July 1860

	Name		Age	Occupation	Real	Pers.	Birthplace
848	Thomas	BURCHFIELD	60	Laborer		150	Va.
	Mary		70				S. C.
	Benjamine		18	Laborer			N. C.
	Andrew	HENDERSON	21	"	250	120	N. C.
849	James	JOHNSON	24	Laborer		100	"
	Jane		19				"
850	Wm. C.	JOHNSON	26	Laborer		75	"
	Martha A.		20				
851	Richard	JOHNSON	69	Farmer	1,200	274	"
	Elizabeth		48				S. C.
	Eda		21				N. C.
	Thomas		18				"
	Elizabeth		17				"
	Richard		11				"
	Safrona		5				Tenn.
852	Nicholas	GILES	36	Farmer	500	275	"
	Jemima		38				N. C.
	Holloway		16				"
	Sarah		14				"
	Hesther		11				"
	Elizabeth		6				"
	Uriah		1				"
853	Thomas	COLDWELL	30	Farmer	200	140	N. C.
	Annie		29				"
	Solomon		6				Tenn.
	Edmon		3				"
	Nancy		1				"
	Calvin		2/12				"
	Margaret	ROLLINS	30				"
	William		3/12				"
854	John	MOONEYHAM	35	Farmer	150	100	Tenn.
	Catharine		30				"
	Wm. H.		16	Laborer			"
	Nancy C.		6				"
	James		4				"
	Jacob		4				"
	John		3/12				"
855	James	ELLISON	52	Laborer	40	50	"
	Martha F.		45				"
	Joseph		20	Laborer			"

	Name		Age	Occupation	Real	Pers.	Birthplace
Page 117				TAYLORSBURG			16 July 1860
	Christopher J.		7				Tenn.
	Linipy	WOODY	70				S. C.
856	Wm. A.	CAMBELL	43	Farmer	2,000	1,720	Tenn.
	Rachel		37				"
	Annie		10				"
	Martha		6				"
	John	BROWN	20	Laborer			N. C.
	A. J.	WILBERN	9				N. C.
	Lewis P.		7				"
857	George	TURNER	30	Farmer	100	417	S. C.
	Jane		36				Tenn.
	Elijah		6				"
	Mary A.		5				"
	James P.		4				"
	Thomas G.		1				"
858	Jonathan	WADDLE	27	Laborer		10	N. C.
	Elizabeth E.		25				Tenn.
	John A.		5				"
	Benjamine F.		3				"
	John M.		1				"
859	Eligah	FARMER	60	Farmer	100	135	S. C.
	Annie		55				S. C.
	Eligah		21	Laborer			"
	Permilia		20				"
860	John	KEYS	76	Laborer	400	590	Md.
	Permilia		33				Tenn.
	Lucinda		11				"
	Roten C. (m)		7				"
	Tennessee	(f)	5				"
	Virginia		4				"
	Solera (f)		1				"
861	Eligah P.	SEXTON	20	Laborer		30	Tenn.
	Sarah		20				N. C.
862	Alex	CLEMONS	32	Farmer	400	407	"
	Mary		23				Tenn.
	Wm. C.		1				"
863	Nelson	DOWNS	57	Farmer	450	151	S. C.
	Matilda		59				"
864	Isaac	SEXTON	52	Farmer	600	348	Va.
	Nancy		55				Va.
Page 118				CATO			16 July 1860
	Benjamine		44	Laborer			N. C.
	Benjamine	BOLYHAM	45	"			"
	Wm. H.		12				Tenn.
865	John	TURNER	22	Laborer		83	S. C.
	Nancy		20				Tenn.
	Samuel G. B.		4				"
	Thomas L. D.		3				"
	Eligah		1				"

	Name		Age	Occupation	Real	Pers.	Birthplace
866	Eligah	SEXTON	66	Laborer		83	Va.
	Sarah		55				S. C.
	Benjamine H.		20				Tenn.
	Sarah		13				"
	Samuel N.		12				"
867	Thomas J.	SEXTON	22	Laborer		50	Tenn.
	Nancy		26				N. C.
	Harriett		8				"
	Tilman		2				Tenn.
	Mary J.		7/12				"
	Wm. H.		5				"
	George A.		25	Laborer			"
868	Wm.	FRANKS	47	Farmer	1,500	210	N. C.
	Pheba		47				"
	Martha		21				"
	Joshua		19	Laborer			N. C.
	James		17	"			"
	Wm. R.		12	"			"
	Garrett B.		9				"
869	F. M.	DOWN	27	Laborer		25	N. C.
	Martha L.		23				"
	James N.		2				Tenn.
870	Wm.	WOODEY	45	Laborer		82	"
	Caroline		35				"
	Nelly		18				"
	Caroline		12				"
	Mary		9				"
	Tabitha		7				"
	Samuel		5				"
	John		3				"
871	Joseph	SUTTLES	24	Laborer		25	N. C.
	Cyntha		19				Tenn.
Page 119				CATO		17	July 1860
872	Robert	SUTTON	47	Laborer	35	100	S. C.
	Annie		18				N. C.
	Elaline		15				"
	Robert		11				"
	Francis (m)		8				"
	Sarah Ann		7				"
	Wm.	PINGATEN	3				"
	Mary	MILTON	20				"
873	Ambro	SAWYERS	54	Farmer	250	100	S. C.
	Frances		46				N. C.
	Jeramiah		18	Laborer			Tenn.
	Jennetta		16				"
	Lavitha		14				"
	Nancy		9				"
	James		6				"
	Arbell (f)		3				"
	William		26				"
	Catharine		18				N. C.

	Name		Age	Occupation	Real	Pers.	Birthplace
874	William	WRIGHT	35	Laborer		40	"
	Rebecca E.		23				Tenn.
875	Enoch	STAMY	47	Miller	1,500	410	N. C.
	Mary		52				"
876	Lewis	GRIGSBY	46	Farmer	3,000	1,660	Tenn.
	Rebecca		35				"
	Daniel		20	Laborer			"
	William		16				"
	John		11				"
	Thomas		9				"
	Wiley		6				"
	Joseph		4				"
	Laura		5/12				"
877	Benjamin	DAVIS	59	Farmer	2,000	1,475	Tenn.
	Nancy		29				"
	John		28	Laborer			"
	Thomas	RICKER	9				
878	J. J.	PENNLAND	45	Farmer	1,600	3,155	N. C.
	Ellender		32				Tenn.
	John		19				"
	Hugh		12				"
	Harriett		10				"

Page 120   CATO   17 July 1860

	Name		Age	Occupation	Real	Pers.	Birthplace
	Thomas		8				Tenn.
	Jane		7				"
	James		6				"
	Stephen		9/12				"
879	George	ELLISON	32	Laborer		10	Tenn.
	Nancy J.		22				N. C.
	James H.		8				Tenn.
	Sarah J. E.		1				"
880	John H.	STOKLY	49	Farmer	6,600	1,559	Tenn.
	Mary E.		44				N. C.
	Wm.		19				Tenn.
	Sarah		17				N. C.
	Rhoda		10				"
	James		6				"
	Julia	FOX	23				N. C.
	George	MORROW	21	Laborer			"
881	James	MORROW (mwy)	28			50	N. C.
	Jane		21				Tenn.
882	Joseph	STOKLY	24	Farmer	201	50	"
	Margaret		19				"
	Sarah		1				"
883	Harrison	MORROW	53	Farmer		300	N. C.
	Mary A.		50				"
	Elizabeth		16				"
	Martha		14				"
	Harrison P.		13				"
	Jessee (m)		24	Laborer			N. C.

	Name		Age	Occupation	Real	Pers.	Birthplace
884	John	JUSTICE	24	Farmer	225	769	Tenn.
	Margaret J.		19				"
	Stephen R.		1/12				
	Hannah L.	NICHOLS	12				
885	Wm.	COOK	55	Laborer		50	N. C.
	Annie		47				"
	Ben min F.		12				Tenn.
	Wm. H.		6				N. C.
886	John	ELLISON	39	Farmer		700	Tenn.
	Mary		35				N. C.
	Annie		12				Tenn.
	Jacob		8				"
	Jane		5				"

Page 121   CATO   17 July 1860

	Name		Age	Occupation	Real	Pers.	Birthplace
	Abraham		4				Tenn.
	Judia E.		1				"
	Jacob		55	Laborer			Pa.
	Hetta (f)		64				S. C.
887	Michal	ELLISON	58	Farmer	50	50	Pa.
	Hannah		44				S. C.
	Isaac		20	Laborer			Tenn.
	Mary		17				"
	Peter		12				"
888	John	LORWOOD	35	Farmer	200	110	N. C.
	Margaret		25				"
	Daniel		4				Tenn.
	Mary		3				"
	John		1				"
889	Jacob	REESE	39	Farmer	100	100	Tenn.
	Catherine		38				"
	William		14				"
	Isabella		13				"
	Adaline		11				"
	John A.		9				"
	Samuel		7				"
	Phillip		5				"
890	Edward	HARLEY	53	Farmer	300	300	Brigham England
	Eliza		43				Iask Engla
	Mariah	HAZLEWOOD	12				Liverpool England
891	Mary	CLARK	43		100	30	N. C.
	Hugh		19	Laborer			Tenn.
	Mary		16				"
	Nancy		12				"
	Tipton		11				"
892	Joseph	WOOD	28	Laborer	100	50	N. C.
	Jane		22				Tenn.
	Mary E.		3				"
	John H.		1				"
	Joseph M.		6/12				"

	Name		Age	Occupation	Real	Pers.	Birthplace
893	John	ELLISON	29	Laborer	100	80	Tenn.
	Juda		22				"
	Eliza J.		1				"
894	Abraham	ELLISON	28	Farmer	200	75	Tenn.
	Susannah		20				"

Page 122   CATO   17 July 1860

	Name		Age	Occupation	Real	Pers.	Birthplace
	Joseph H.		1				Tenn.
895	Mack	FOX	35	Farmer	100	140	"
	Sarah		30				Tenn.
	Mary J.		14				"
	Robert		12				"
	Alexander		9				"
	Columbus		8				"
	Julia A.		6				"
	Rufus		5/12				"
896	Alfred	REESE	30	Farmer	200	258	Tenn.
	Margaret		21				N. C.
897	James H.	ELLISON	38	Laborer		25	Tenn.
	Mary		32				N. C.
	Annie		11				Tenn.
	Wm. J.		6				"
	Francis J.	(f)	6				"
	Samuel N.		4				"
	Mary E.		3				"
	Sarah H.		5/12				"
898	Rubin	JUSTICE	58	Farmer	2,500	1,473	N. C.
	Mary		55				Tenn.
	Rubin		21	Laborer			"
899	John	HUFF (mwy)	34	Farmer		425	Ill.
	Rhoda A.		17				Tenn.
900	John	QUILLIAMS	50	Laborer		75	N. C.
	Annie		35				"
	Andrew J.		17				"
	Francis (f)		12				"
	Cassa		6				"
	Mary M. C.		4				"
	Thomas		3				"
901	Wm.	FOX	51	Farmer		350	"
	Annie		47				"
	Silas		19				"
	Martha		17				"
	Allen		11				"
	Julia		8				"
	Elizabeth		6				"
	Lowry		5				"
	Luther		3				"

Page 123   CATO   17 July 1860

	Name		Age	Occupation	Real	Pers.	Birthplace
902	Charley	STOKLY	38	Farmer	8,500	3,705	Tenn.
	Sarah		34				N. C.

	Name		Age	Occupation	Real	Pers.	Birthplace
	Mary J.		15				Tenn.
	Sarah		10				"
	Rhoda		8				"
	Susannah		7				"
	Royal		5				"
	Nancy		3				"
	Stephen		1				"
	Saphrona	BLACK	19				"
	Jane	STOKLY	74				Va.
903	Wm.	JONES	41	Farmer	1,000	750	N. C.
	Mary		35				Tenn.
	Sarah J.		14				"
	Benjamin R.		11				"
	Arther P.		9				"
	Mary E.		3				"
	Corneleus		1				"
904	Russel	JONES	34	Farmer	250	750	Tenn.
	Dica		29				N. C.
	John		6				Tenn.
	Sarah F.		4				N. C.
	Wm. A.		1				"
905	Sarah	JONES	66		2,000	475	S. C.
	Marvel M.		27	Farmer			Tenn.
906	Charles	JONES	38	Farmer	1,200	700	N. C.
	Jane		23				Tenn.
	Royal		15				"
	Mary		13				"
	Rubin		11				"
	James N.		10				"
	John		6				"
	Martha E.		4				"
	William A.		3				"
	Susannah R.		1				"
907	Thomas J.	BELL	40	Farmer	1,500	650	N. C.
	Carlene		41				"
	Nancy		20				Tenn.
	William		18	Laborer			"
	Elizabeth		16				"

Page 124   CATO   17 July 1860

	Name		Age	Occupation	Real	Pers.	Birthplace
	Ellen		14				Tenn.
	Narcissus		10				"
	Elanora		9				"
	Newton		3				"
	Margarett		2/12				"
908	Abraham	PENLAND	63	Farmer	130	40	N. C.
	Elizabeth		20				S. C.
909	Daniel C.	BRYAN	29	"	2,500	900	Tenn.
	Ellen		25				"
	William		5				"
	Rebecca		3				"
	Monroe		10/12				"
	Mary	WADDLE	20				"
	Mary	MURPHY	10				"

	Name		Age	Occupation	Real	Pers.	Birthplace
910	James S.	JONES	27	Farmer	1,300	550	"
	Mary A.		24				"
	James L. D.		3				"
	Charly		1				"
	Mary	NICHOLAS	45				"
911	N. H.	STOKELY	44	"	12,000	8,000	"
	Nancy A. R.		42				N. C.
	Royal L.		19	Laborer			Tenn.
	David		18	"			"
	Sarah J.		14				"
	Thomas R.		12				"
	Allen		10				"
	Martha A.		8				"
	Nancy H.		6				"
	Nathan		4				"
	Mary F.		2				"
912	John	GILLELAND	52	Laborer		25	N. C.
	Disa		40				"
	Elizabeth		17				"
	Harriett		14				"
	Robert		11				"
	Martha		10				"
	Rebecca		7				"
	Nancy		6				"
	Adaline		4				"
	John		10/12				Tenn.

Page 125   CATO   17 July 1860

	Name		Age	Occupation	Real	Pers.	Birthplace
913	Aaron	BIBLE	40	Farmer	600	500	Tenn.
	Sarah		28				"
	Frances (f)		9				"
	Joseph L.		2				"
914	Jesse	FOX	27	"	100	150	N. C.
	Matilda		27				"
	Fanny J.		4				Tenn.
	William A.		2				"
	Andrew J.		25	Laborer			"
915	James	LAMARR (mwy)	31	"		300	N. C.
	Jane		30				Tenn.
916	Royal	JUSTICE	37	Farmer	2,500	1,350	"
	Mary		26				"
	Margarett J.		6				"
	Susanah		4				"
	Rubin D.		2				"
	Julia A.		7/12				"
	William	CLARK	17	Laborer			"
	Louiza	NICHOLAS	16				"
	Nathaniel	YATES	57		200	300	"
	Nathaniel		24	Teacher			"
917	Silas F.	MILLER	23	Laborer		30	N. C.
	Roda		23				S. C.
	Nancy J.		2/12				Tenn.

	Name		Age	Occupation	Real	Pers.	Birthplace
918	Jacob	SCHUTSCHALL	40	"		125	"
	Nancy		28				"
	Sarah M.		12				"
	Eliza J.		9				"
	Philip		7				"
	Joseph		5				"
	Mary C.		4				"
	Nancy E.		3				"
919	James G.	MILLER	32	Farmer	33	160	N. C.
	Anna		28				Tenn.
	Mary		9				"
	Lucinda A.		5				N. C.
	George F.		3				"
	Hiram		10/12				"
920	Frank	MILLER	70	Laborer		5	N. C.
	Nancy		75				Tenn.

Page 126   CATO   17 July 1860

	Name		Age	Occupation	Real	Pers.	Birthplace
	Harvy		5				N. C.
921	Rubin	GUILLIAMS	23	Laborer		5	S. C.
	Rachel		27				N. C.
	Green		3				Tenn.
922	Edman	DOCERY	26	Farmer	500	275	"
	Mahaly J.		24				"
	Manervy A.		4				"
	Mary S.		3				"
	John D.		1				"
	Sarah	PROFFIT	26				N. C.
923	William	BRYAN	40	Farmer	4,000	6,513	Tenn.
	Lucinda		40				"
	Rebecca A.		17				"
	Mary E.		16				"
	Florence M.		10				"
	Thomas M.		9				"
	William C.		6				"
	Manerva J.		5				"
	Daniel M.		11/12				"
924	George	WOODY	23	Laborer		160	N. C.
	Eliza		26				S. C.
	Elvira J.		6				Tenn.
	Thomas J.		1				"
	Kissiah		75				N. C.
925	Robert	FOX	33	Farmer	150	100	Tenn.
	Martha		32				"
	Jefferson		11				"
	Nancy J.		6				"
	Isaac		3				"
926	Abraham	ROWLAND	65	Farmer	100	150	S. C.
	Rhoda		40				N. C.
	Minerva		30				Tenn.
	Annie		10				"

	Name		Age	Occupation	Real	Pers.	Birthplace
	John		7				"
	Jane		5				"
	Sarah		5/12				"
927	Annie	BRYAN	65		1,400	350	Tenn.
	Minerva	MOORE	36				"
	Daniel R.		15	Laborer			"
	Sarah J.		13				"

Page 127   CATO   17 July 1860

	Name		Age	Occupation	Real	Pers.	Birthplace
	William		10				Tenn.
	James		7				"
	Thomas		5				"
928	Jonathan	ABLES	23	Farmer	160	164	"
	Sophina		22				N. C.
	Mary M.		1/12				Tenn.
	Lucinda	GREEN	45				N. C.
929	Hezekiah	ABLE	52	Farmer	500	238	Tenn.
	Mary M.		45				N. C.
	Joel		14				Tenn.
	Joseph		13				"
	Moses		21	Laborer			"
930	George	CLARK	25	"			N. C.
	Susanah		21				"
931	Disa	HOLLAND	30			25	"
	John		14				Tenn.
	Julia M.		12				"
	Stephen		8				"
932	William R.	WALL	27	Miller		50	N. C.
	Louiza		33				"
	Michal		4				"
	Rosetta		2				"
933	Henry	LEE	41	Farmer	1,000	480	S. C.
	Mary		36				Tenn.
	William F.		17	Laborer			"
	Green B.		15				"
	James M.		13				"
	Jane		11				"
	Thomas J.		8				"
	Jessee B.		3				"
	Charles A.		1				"
934	Willis	ELLENBURG	45	Farmer	250	264	S. C.
	Martha		29				"
	Elvina A.		19				"
	Elizabeth		16				"
	John		11				Tenn.
	Philip		4				"
	Sarah		1				"
	Catharine		30				"
	Parinthia		8				S. C.

	Name		Age	Occupation	Real	Pers.	Birthplace
Page 128				CATO		18 July 1860	
935	Jacob	ELENBURG	68	(Blind)		5	S. C.
	Camaline		26				N. C.
	Elender		7				"
936	Allen	JONES	32	Farmer	400	179	"
	Elizabeth		29				"
	Narcissa J.		7				Tenn.
	John L.		2				"
	John	GREEN	14				"
937	William	DAVIS	50	Farmer	700	324	"
	Jemima		46				N. C.
	Nathaniel		16				Tenn.
	John		13				"
	Susanah		14				"
	Robert		10				"
	William		2				"
938	Elizabeth	ROSE	44		500	106	N. C.
	Delilah		16				S. C.
	Jane		14				"
	Mary		11	(Idiotic)			"
	Sarah		10				"
	Martha A.		7				N. C.
	Rubin	BLACK	91	None (Anxious to Marry)			S. C.
939	John	MESSER	50	Farmer	300	77	N. C.
	Cinthia		39				"
	John	BLACK	12				Tenn.
940	James	GREEN	48	Laborer		35	"
	Margarett		47				N. C.
	Nancy E.		20				Tenn.
	Sarah A.		17				N. C.
	John		9				"
	Lucinda		8				"
	George		5				"
	Roda E.		2				"
	Samuel	CALDWELL	26	"			N. C.
941	David	NIGHT	29	"		150	Tenn.
	Nancy		23				N. C.
	Mourning	KAGLE	15				Tenn.
942	John	JONES	29	"		100	"
	Elizabeth		19				"
	Green A.		5/12				"
Page 129				TAYLORSBURG		18 July 1860	
943	William	GREEN	23	Laborer		75	Tenn.
	Catharine		19				"
	Jonathan		10/12				"
944	William	RAINS	51	Farmer	1,600	379	"
	Margarett E.		21				"
	Allen		19	Laborer			"
	Isaac		15				"
	Nancy		3				"
	Rebecca		1				"

	Name		Age	Occupation	Real	Pers.	Birthplace
945	James C.	SEXTON	37	Farmer	6,000	460	S. C.
	Elizabeth		26				N. C.
	Nancy E.		14				Tenn.
	Susanah		10				"
	Mary A.		8				N. C.
	Cynthia J.		5				Tenn.
	Benj. F.		1				"
946	William L.	WILLIAMS	40	Laborer		90	N. C.
	Lucinda		32				"
	William T.		16				"
	Robert J.		6				"
	James B.		4				"
947	Alexander	CALDER	43	Minister (Lutheran)	150	140	Inverness, Scotland
	Mary M.		39				Dandee, Scotland
	Elizabeth		15				Farfar, Scotland
	Mary		10				"
	Margarett		4				Tenn.
	Eliza		2				"
948	John	DAVISON	57	Farmer	400	180	Dumfries, Scotland
	Margarett C.		50				Inverness, Scotland
949	James P.	BLACK	45	Blk. Smith	90	1,150	Tenn.
	Mary H.		42				N. C.
	John W.		16				Tenn.
	Soloman		15				"
	Elizabeth K.		13				"
	Sarah E.		11				"
	Carline		7				"
	James L.		3				"
	Margarett		2				"
	George W.		35	Laborer			N. C.
950	James	DYKE	60	Laborer			"

Page 130   TAYLORSBURG   18 July 1860

	Name		Age	Occupation	Real	Pers.	Birthplace
	Sarah		67				N. C.
951	Stephen	JONES	37	Farmer	500	150	"
	Martha		34				Tenn.
	Robert F.		12				"
	Joseph		9				"
	Mary A.		8				"
	George N.		6				"
	Margarett		2				"
952	Jacob	BIBLE	50	Farmer	500	200	"
	Anna R.		40				"
	Samuel		21	Laborer			"
	Enoch		18	"			"
	Marion (m)		16	"			"
	Elizabeth		14				"
	Mordicai		11				"
	Eliza		9				"
	Seth		4				"

	Name		Age	Occupation	Real	Pers.	Birthplace
953	Susanah	BIBLE	43		100	150	"
	Ezekiel		21	Laborer			"
	Washington		17	"			"
	Abraham		13				"
	George		11				"
	Elizabeth		9				"
	Ezra		6				"
	Aaron		5				"
954	Ezra	BIBLE	32	Farmer	800	570	Tenn.
	Elizabeth		23				"
	Thomas S.		2				"
	Benjamin F.		1				"
	George		74				Va.
955	George	MESSER	35	Farmer	500	210	N. C.
	Harriett		18				Tenn.
	William		14				"
	Cyntha		12				"
	Elizabeth		10				"
	Nancy		8				"
	Jesse (m)		2/12				"
956	Richard	PRICE	60	Laborer		75	N. C.
	Lydia		70				"
957	James	HALL	30	Laborer		40	Tenn.

Page 131   TAYLORSBURG   18 July 1860

	Name		Age	Occupation	Real	Pers.	Birthplace
	Sarah		27				N. C.
	David		9				"
	Susannah		6				Tenn.
	Lydia		4				"
	Mary		2				"
958	Benjamin	MESSER	24	Laborer		175	N. C.
	Jane		26				"
	Laura L.		2				"
	Robert P.		7/12				"
959	Benjamine	FORD	53	Farmer	1,000	325	N. C.
	Nancy		43				Tenn.
	James		17				N. C.
	Evaline		14				N. C.
	Sarah		10				Tenn.
	Elizabeth		8				"
	Lydia		6				"
	Burt		4				"
	Rubin		2				"
	Joseph		2/12				"
960	John	FORD	33	Farmer	300	150	Tenn.
	Rhoda		21				"
	William		4				"
	James A.		2				"
	David B.		2/12				"
961	Rubin	BLACK	26	Farmer	800	375	Tenn.
	Sarah		20				"
	Caroline		13				"

	Name		Age	Occupation	Real	Pers.	Birthplace
962	David	GUINN	57	Farmer	3,000	2,408	N. C.
	Rebecca		58				Va.
	Sarah C.		17				Tenn.
	Jane	HARPER	24				Tenn.
	Plesant	WORTHY	18	Laborer			"
	Martin	HARPER	2				"
963	Edward	TEAGUE	53	Farmer	500	214	N. C.
	Dreucilla		54				"
964	James M.	TEAGUE	21	Laborer		50	N. C.
	Jane		22				Tenn.
	Louisa		2				"
965	Daniel	PRICE	40	Farmer	500	155	N. C.
	Anna		35				"

Page 132   TAYLORSBURG   19 July 1860

	Name		Age	Occupation	Real	Pers.	Birthplace
	David		10				Tenn.
	Mary		8				"
	Lydia C.		7				"
	Daniel M.		5				"
	Frankie (f)		3				"
	John		1				"
966	Rany (f)	BLACK	52	Tayleress		135	N. C.
	Adam		22	Laborer		60	Tenn.
	George		18	" (Idiotic)			"
	Jane A.		15				"
	Soloman		12				"
967	John	BLACK	20	Laborer		100	Tenn.
	Jane		15				"
	James A.		5/12				"
968	Solomon	ROLLINS	45	Farmer	450	228	Tenn.
	Martha J.		32				"
	Malinda M.		13				"
	Wm. A.		14				"
	John C.		11				"
	Martha A.		7				"
	James B.		1				"
969	Thomas	LILLARD	66	Laborer		110	Va.
	Lavina		58				Tenn.
970	John	POTTER	43	Laborer		58	"
	Matilda		38				"
	Carice (m)		14				"
	Sarah		12				"
	Hezekiel		8				"
	Rachael		6				"
	Amanda		4				"
	Lydia		2				"
	Wm. D.		7/12				"
971	Solomon	MESSER	55	Farmer	600	350	N. C.
	Macca		49				"
	Christian S.		20				Tenn.

	Name		Age	Occupation	Real	Pers.	Birthplace
	Rany (f)		18				"
	Ashby		15				"
	Almedy		14				"
	Lilly		90				"
	Delilah		8				"

Page 133   TAYLORSBURG   19 July 1860

	Name		Age	Occupation	Real	Pers.	Birthplace
	Laura G.		3				Tenn.
972	George	COOK	27	Laborer		25	"
	Mary C.		26				N. C.
	Martha S.		3				Tenn.
	Frances A.	(f)	1				"
	Martha	MESSER	28				N. C.
	Margaret G.		8				Tenn.
	Mary A.		3				"
973	Isaac	GREEN	36	Farmer	300	236	N. C.
	Sarah		40				Tenn.
	Robert A.		17				"
	Elizabeth J.		15				
	Malinda C.		13				
	William		11				
	David		10				
	James		8				
	Reubin		7				
	John		5				
	William		3				
	Charles		4/12				
974	Samuel	YATES	30	Farmer	1,000	645	"
	Jane		31				"
	Ellen F.		5				
	Mary M.		3				
	Nancy C.		1				
975	Michael	PARKER	41	"	600	465	N. C.
	Hannah		35				"
	Barbara E.		11				Tenn.
	Andrew J.		9				
	Joseph R.		7				
	Joshua N.		7				
	William J.		3				
976	Susannah	WILKINS	45			15	"
	Sarah		11				
	Brues (m)		8				
977	John	PARKER	35	"	700	324	N. C.
	Deborah		35				Tenn.
	Nicholas		15	Laborer			"
	Mary J.		13				
	Samuel		4				

Page 135   TAYLORSBURG   19 July 1860

	Name		Age	Occupation	Real	Pers.	Birthplace
	Michael E.		10				Tenn.
	Susannah		9				
	James J.		7				
	Margaret		4				

	Name		Age	Occupation	Real	Pers.	Birthplace
978	Nicholas	PARKER	83	Laborer		749	Va.
	Mary		61				N. C.
979	William	SUTTLES	25	"		50	"
	Elizabeth		26				"
	Eliza E.		2				
	John		1/12				Tenn.
980	William	ELLISON	48	Farmer	400	184	"
	Mary		36				N. C.
	John		21	Laborer			Tenn.
	Nicholas		19	"			"
	Mary		14				
	Aaron		16				"
	Royal		13				
	Adda		11	(Idiotic)			"
	Hannah		7				
	Adeline		4				
	Nathan		3				
981	Serena (f)	JONES	46			25	S. C.
	Isaac A.		23	"			Tenn.
	Martha C.		6				
982	William	SMITH	29	"		100	N. C.
	Sarah C.		23				Tenn.
	William D.		5				
	Mary C.		1				
	Isabella		10				
983	Lewis	SMITH	25	"		200	"
	Louisa		23				
984	Christian	MESSER	52	"		25	N. C.
	Jane		45				"
	Angeline		24				"
	Nelly		21				"
	Anna		18				"
	Soloman		12				"
	William		7				
	Ashby		5				Tenn.
	Rachel		3				

Page 135   TAYLORSBURG   20 July 1860

	Name		Age	Occupation	Real	Pers.	Birthplace
985	David VOLENTINE (mwy)		27	Farmer	200	10	Tenn.
	Rhoda		20				"
986	Meriman	BALL	52	Laborer		5	"
	Rebecca		42				N. C.
	Sarah C.		9				Tenn.
987	Martin	DAVIS	53	"		150	"
	Sarah		48				"
	John		22	"			"
	David		15				"
	Lydia		13				
	James P.		10				
988	Alexander	DAVIS	30	"		100	"
	Kissiah		31				N. C.
	Joseph		16				Tenn.

	Name		Age	Occupation	Real	Pers.	Birthplace
	Robert		14				
	Royal		9				
989	Eliza	TURNER	46		600	150	"
	James E.		24	"			"
	Sarah C.		22				
	Martha		20				
	Reubin		17				
	William		13				
	Thomas		12				
990	L. D.	TURNER	48	"	300	10	"
991	Edward	TURNER	26	"		100	"
	Casandre		20				N. C.
	William		2				Tenn.
	Eliza		6/12				
992	William	CAMERON	32	Farmer		320	"
	Louisa		26				
	Green		9				
	John		7				
	Thomas		3				
	William		2				
993	Jonathan	ELLISON	26	Laborer		160	N. C.
	Malinda		25				
	Ellinora J.		4				Tenn.
	Benjamin F.		2				
	Johnathan		1/12				
	Mary		40				N. C.

Page 136   TAYLORSBURG   20 July 1860

	Name		Age	Occupation	Real	Pers.	Birthplace
	Margaret		60				N. C.
994	L. S.	BROOKS	25	Laborer		100	Tenn.
	Sarah		28				"
	Clariesa		1				
	Martha		59				
995	John	CAMERON	25	Farmer		325	"
	Sarah		25				
	Mary		6				
	Martha		4				
	David		1				
996	Josiah	REN	33	"		375	"
	Mary		30				"
	Nancy		13				
	Elizabeth		8				
	Abagail		6				
	Martha		5				
	James		4				
	Minerva		4/12				
997	John	CLEVENGER	37	"	4,000	1,658	"
	Letty		28				
	James		13				
	Bartlet		11				

	Name		Age	Occupation	Real	Pers.	Birthplace
	Barney		10				
	Annanias (m)		8				
	Nancy E.		6				
	Sarah		1				
998	J. W.	JACKSON	54	Bricklayer	350	330	N. C.
	Margaret		58				Tenn.
	Thomas A.		26	Teacher			"
	Jane		24				N. C.
	Louisa N.		23				Tenn.
	James A.		19	Laborer			"
	William B.		18				
	Margaret A.		15				
999	William	MESSER	24	"		80	N. C.
	Catharine		26				S. C.
	Martha E.		4				Tenn.
	Sarah J.		2				
	Elijah		1				
1000	Martin	JUSTICE	21	Farmer		95	"

Page 137   TAYLORSBURG   22 July 1860

	Name		Age	Occupation	Real	Pers.	Birthplace
	Sarah		19				Tenn.
	Joseph M.		22				
	Elbert		2				
1001	Joseph	PAGGET	58	Farmer	3,000	8,380	"
	Elizabeth		58				
	Albert		26	Farmer			"
	Margaret J.		19				
	Matilda A.		19				
	Allen M.		17	Laborer			
	Amanda		14				
1002	Job	WILEY	40	Laborer		65	"
	Eliza		29				"
	Nancy		12				"
	Calvin		7				
	Wilson		6				
	Elenora		4				
	Mary		1				
1003	Austin	WILEY	35	Farmer	600	500	Tenn.
	Elizabeth		72				"
	Robert A.		23	Laborer			"
	Rose		18				
	Columbus		6/12				"
1004	Thomas J.	CLICK	30	Farmer	400	180	"
	Mary		26				
	Martha		2/12				
	William		26	Laborer			Tenn.
1005	Jane	CLICK	48			20	"
	Mary		21				"
	Eliza		18				
	James		14				

	Name		Age	Occupation	Real	Pers.	Birthplace
1006	William	CLICK	35	Farmer	400	200	"
	Nancy		26				"
	Julia C.		2				"
	Greene (?)		8/12				"
1007	William	GRANCY	52	Laborer	600	200	N. C.
	Hannah		45				Tenn.
	William		21	Laborer			"
	Isaac		20	"			"
	George		18	"			"
	Jane		16				"

Page 138   TAYLORSBURG   22 July 1860

	Name		Age	Occupation	Real	Pers.	Birthplace
	Catharine		14				Tenn.
	Mary		13				"
	Margaret		11				"
	Henry		9				"
	William		7				"
	Hannah		3				"
1008	Samuel	HUX	56	Laborer		150	N. C.
	Sarah		40				Tenn.
	Austin		18	Laborer			"
	Spicy	(f)	16				"
	Mary		14				"
	Martha		12				"
	Sarah		9				"
	Nancy		7				"
1009	Rederick	ANDERSON	34	Carpenter	2,000	500	"
	Harriett		33				"
	Walter		6				"
	Rolphus	(m)	5				"
	Wenson	(m)	1				"
1010	James	MANTOOTH	23	Farmer	400	75	"
	Martha		25				"
	Malinda		2				"
	George W.		2/12				"
1011	William	MANTOOTH	57	Shoemaker		20	"
	Nancy		48				"
	Harriet		30				"
	Mary C.		23				"
	William		14				"
	Chamberlain		21				"
	Robert		11				"
	Claborn		9				"
	Thomas A.		8				"
	Stephen		6				"
	Lee		4				"
	Berry		5				"
1012	Henry	RUNION	56	Farmer	200	109	N. C.
	Margaret		47				Tenn.
	George H.		20	Laborer			"
	Nancy J.		18				"
	Luthan (f)		16				"

	Name		Age	Occupation	Real	Pers.	Birthplace
Page 139				TAYLORSBURG		22 July 1860	
	Margaret J.		12				Tenn.
	Amanda C.		8				"
	Thomas W. C.		7				"
	John		6				"
1013	Daniel	POTTER	20	Laborer		200	"
	Sarah J.		18				"
	Mary R.		7/12				"
	Lucinda	ROBERTS	32				S. C.
	Thomas		15	Laborer			Tenn.
	Rhoda C.		3				"
	David		3/12				"
1014	George	GORMAN	58	Laborer		300	N. C.
	Sarah		59				N. C.
	Mary		32				"
	Elizabeth		28				"
	Sarah		23				"
	Jane		21				"
	John		18	Laborer			"
	William		12				"
	Mary		8				Tenn.
	Fanza F. (m)		10				"
1015	John	STEPHENS	31	Farmer	5,000	1,895	"
	Elizabeth		72	(Blind - Spider bite)			N. C.
	Laura B.		45				Tenn.
	Augusta		30				"
1016	D. D.	BROOKS	33	Farmer	11,000	18,824	Tenn.
	Nancy		34				"
	William		10				"
	Sarah J.		9				"
	Joel		7				"
	Rachael		7				"
	Daniel		5				"
	Isaac		2				"
	Benjamin	IRONS	16	Laborer			"
1017	William	MANOR	40	Farmer		440	"
	Malinda		27				"
	Eliza		10				"
	Charles		8				"
1018	Samuel	LOUDSPIECH	64	Minister ME	4,680	7,860	"
	Judith S.		35				N. C.
Page 140				TAYLORSBURG		24 July 1860	
	John Walter		8				Tenn.
	Tolbert E.		3				"
	Roton A.		1				"
1019	J. G.	CLICK	39	Farmer		388	"
	Sarah		36				"
	William		14				"
	Jacob		10				"
	Daniel		8				"

	Name		Age	Occupation	Real	Pers.	Birthplace
	Sarah		6				"
	George		3				"
1020	Jacob	CLICK	45	Blacksmith	4,000	1,000	"
	Mary		50				N. C.
	Isaac		18	Laborer			Tenn.
	Amanda		17				"
	David		16				"
	Thomas		13				"
	Taylor		12				"
	Elizabeth		9				"
	Dolly		4				"
1021	James	NETHERTON	49	Farmer	6,240	2,635	Tenn.
	Lurana		45				"
	Catherine		19				"
	Nancy		16				"
	Jane		13				"
	Levicy		8				"
	Rhoda		6				"
	Millard Fillmore		4				"
1022	George S.	NETHERTON	21	Farmer		100	"
	Elizabeth		23				"
	George J.		1				"
1023	James J.	FOX	23	Farmer		555	"
	Martha M.		19				"
	Julia		7/12				"
1024	Charles	HUX	21	Laborer			"
	Harriet		19				"
	Benjamin B.		1				"
1025	Pleasant	ALEXANDER	35	Laborer			"
	Eveline		23				"
	Catharine		6				"
	William		3	(Idiotic)			"
Page 141				TAYLORSBURG			24 July 1860
	Eliza		2				Tenn.
1026	Toliver	SISK	25	Farmer		391	"
	Catherine		23				"
1027	Pleasant J.	BURKE	22	Farmer		344	"
	Matilda		21				"
	Lewis		2				"
	Laura		1				
	Jane	FANNI	10				
1028	Morgan	WILLIAMS	37	Blacksmith		1,065	Va.
	Mary A.		39				N. C.
	John C.	FRESHOUR	17				Tenn.
	Mary A.	FRESHOUR	12				"
	David		10				"
	Rufus	LEWIS	31	Phiscian	4,000	1,500	"

1860 U. S. CENSUS OF COCKE COUNTY, TENNESSEE

	Name		Age	Occupation	Real	Pers.	Birthplace
1029	Asberry	FOWLER	33	Farmer		223	S. C.
	Elizabeth		26				Tenn.
	Elender		4				"
	Elizabeth		2				"
	Martha J.		3/12				"
	John	HOLDER	22	Laborer	30	80	Tenn.
	Nancy J.		2/12				"
1030	G. W.	LORD	38	Carpenter	500	750	"
	Catherine		35				"
	Mary A.		9				
	Sarah		7				
	John W.		5				
	Robert G.		4				
1031	Wm. V.	BUSH	21	Farmer		240	"
	Louisa		18				
	Alennah (f)		1				
	Silus		11				
1032	William	WOOD	47	"	12,000	8,417	
	Mary		36				
	Sarah J.		13				
	Thorntin		11				
	Mariah		7				
	Harrison		5				
	John		7/12				
1033	B. L.	BOULDIN	52	Teacher	2,000	1,990	Va.
	Elizabeth	"	49				Tenn.

Page 142   TAYLORSBURG   24 July 1860

	Name		Age	Occupation	Real	Pers.	Birthplace
	Catharin	"	19				Tenn.
	Ivanna (f)		17				
	Thomas T.	"	16	Laborer			
	Wood	"	13				
	Martha	"	12				
	Margaret J.	"	8				
1034	Isaac	HARTSELL, Jr.	41	Farmer		150	"
	Elizabeth	"	41				
	David	"	20	Laborer			
	Margaret	"	16				
	Harriet	"	14				
	Elbert	"	10				
	Sarah	"	4				
	James	"	1				
	Morris	LINEBERGER	35	Grocer	400	850	"
1035	John A.	REN	33	Blacksmith	800	1,150	"
	Delilah	"	29				S. C.
	Mary E.	"	9				Tenn.
	Martha J.	"	5				
	Alexander	"	2				
	Nancy	"	3/12				
1036	James	REN	58	Laborer		35	N. C.

	Name		Age	Occupation	Real	Pers.	Birthplace
1037	James	WOOD	34	Farmer	6,755	2,475	Tenn.
	Rhoda		32				
	William		9				
	Tilghman		6				
	John		4				
	John	WOOD, Sr.	73	None	3,200	5,000	Va.
1038	James C.	FOX	24	Laborer		75	Tenn.
	Nancy		22				
	Mary J.		4				
	Martha		1				
1039	John M.	COGDELL	26	"		140	"
	Manna		22				
	Andrew		14				
	Isaac		5				
	David		1				
1040	Thomas	CURRY	30	"		75	N. C.
	Matilda M.		30				
	James T.		12				

Page 143				TAYLORSBURG		24 July 1860	
	Martha C.		10				N. C.
	John W.		7				"
	Isaac		3				Tenn.
	William M.		1				
1041	Hiram	HOLT	36	Blacksmith		50	"
	Jane		24				"
	Joseph		16	Laborer			
	Abigail		14				
	Thomas		11				
	Mary		11				
	Harriet		1				
	Abigail	REN	58			25	
	Reubin		18	"			"
1042	Thomas C.	EVANS	50	"		200	N. C.
	Mary		46				Tenn.
	George		22	"			
	William		20	"			
	Jane		18				
	Maranda		16				
	Emily		14				
	Austin		13				
	Augusta		10				
	Wiley		8				
	Robert		6				
	Mary	LITTLE	21				N. C.
1043	William	COGDELL	21	Farmer		60	Tenn.
	Rebecca		17				N. C.
	Ezekiel		6/12				Tenn.
1044	Ezekiel	FOX	62	"	1,500	1,120	"
	Sarah		60				"
	Jacob		28	"	2,100	260	"

	Name		Age	Occupation	Real	Pers.	Birthplace
1045	Jacob	DAVIS	38	"		300	N. C.
	Mary A.		38				"
	Jonathan		19	Laborer			
	Thomas		14				
	Elvira		13				
	Elizabeth		11				
	Abraham		8				
	Barbara		6				Tenn.
	John W.		8				

Page 144   TAYLORSBURG   24 July 1860

	Name		Age	Occupation	Real	Pers.	Birthplace
	Elbert E.		3				Tenn.
	Robert A.		1				
1046	Jas.	MANTOOTH	43	Laborer		200	
	Rosennan		40				
	George		17				
	Evan		14				
	Martha J.		12				
	William		11				
	Mary A.		10				
	Elizabeth		7				
	Julia		5				
	Isaac		1				
1047	John	SMITHPETER	44	Farmer	250	525	
	Sarah		38				
	Nathaniel E.		18				
	Jas. S.		16				
	Nancy		14				
	Amaneul (m)		12				
	Mary R.		9				
	Susannah L.		7				
	Louisa B.		4				
	Elizabeth M.		2				
	Daniel	PORTER	13				
1048	Wilson	HALL	75	Farmer		500	N. C.
	Nancy		45				"
	Nathaniel		18	Laborer			Tenn.
	John		15				
	Sarah		14				
	Charity	WHITSON	3				
	Margaret		23				
1049	William	EVANS	36	Farmer		425	N. C.
	Mary		24				"
	Tilghman P.		12				"
	James H.		10				
	Martha L.		8				"
	Thomas J.		3				Tenn.
	Rhoda		1				"
1050	Noah	ELLIS	21	"	1,000	150	"
	Nelly		18				"
	John		1				

Name		Age	Occupation	Real	Pers.	Birthplace
Page 145			TAYLORSBURG			24 July 1860
1051 Charity	ELLIS	51		500	150	Tenn.
Job (m)		20	Farmer			"
1052 Elias	CLEVINGER	43	"	3,000	3,625	"
Julia		38				
Angeline		17				
Nancy		14				
Mary		12				
William		14				
Robert		10				
Sarah		7				
Emma		5				
John		4				
Francis (f)		3				
Rhoda		2/12				
Nancy		80				Va.
1053 Elias	GRAY	25	"		550	Tenn.
Sena		24				Va.
Margaret		4				Tenn.
Elizabeth		2				
1054 Barksdale	HIGHTOWER	44	"		615	N. C.
Cassandra		46				Tenn.
Sarah		21				"
William		18	Laborer			"
Leander		16	"			
Susannah		14				
John E.		13				
Margaret		11				
Eda		8				
Martha		6				
Tipton		4				
Rebecca		3				
1055 Martin	CAMERON	54	Farmer		650	"
Rebecca		53				S. C.
John		19	Laborer			Tenn.
Lawson		16				"
Elizabeth		14				"
Mary		12				"
Lafayette	ALLEN	7				
Joseph (m)		5				
Lavina		4				
Page 146			TAYLORSBURG			24 July 1860
1056 Susannah	CLEVENGER	46		12,000	9,461	S. C.
Allen		17				Tenn.
William		15				
Carson		13				
Harriet J.		10				
Jerome		9				
Columbus		7				
Judson Hightower		4				

	Name		Age	Occupation	Real	Pers.	Birthplace
1057	John	LINKENFELTER	66	Farmer	2,500	8,760	Va.
	Elizabeth		56				"
	Amanda		10				Tenn.
	Theodocia (f)		9				
1058	William	MANTOOTH	42	"	4,000	1,500	"
	Ava		38				
	Elias		15				
	Louisa		13				
	Amos		11				
	Scoicha (f)		9				
	Susannah		7				
	Lucinda		5				
	Franklin		2				
1059	George	SISK	39	Farmer	100	2,275	"
	Elizabeth		37				
	Maloney V. B.		14				
	Landon C. H.		12				
	Sarah C.		10				
	Toliver		1				
1060	Robert	MANTOOTH	35	"	300	1,393	"
	Harriet		32				
	Hamilton S.		12				
	Alexander		10				
	Aaron		7				
	Martha J.		5				
	Margaret E.		3				
	Calvin		1				
	Elvira	BUSH	14				
1061	John	BURK	46	"	2,000	975	"
	Elizabeth		42				
	Martha L.		20				
	Francis M.	(m)	17	Laborer			

Page 147   TAYLORSBURG   24 July 1860

	Name		Age	Occupation	Real	Pers.	Birthplace
	Nancy		15				Tenn.
	Sarah		13				
	Mary		11				
	John M.		9				
	Green W.		7				
	Susannah		4				
	Julia		2				
1062	L. L.	ROBERTS	37	Farmer	650	800	Tenn.
	Amarentha		37				N. C.
	Zachariah		16	Laborer			"
	John L.		13				"
	George W.		11				"
	Julia N.		9				"
	William L.		7				"
	Alfred W.		5				Tenn.
	Agnes N.		2				

1860 U. S. CENSUS OF COCKE COUNTY, TENNESSEE

	Name		Age	Occupation	Real	Pers.	Birthplace
1063	Joseph	JUSTICE	23	Farmer		176	"
	Elizabeth		31				"
	Elizabeth	FRASIER	67				"
1064	Annanias	CLEVINGER	26	"	3,600	3,224	"
	James A.		5				"
	Elizabeth		2				"
	Thomas	PARK	21	Blacksmith			"
1065	A.J.	SHELL	34	Wagon Maker	800	500	"
	Margaret		26				"
	Elizabeth J.		12				"
	Mary A.		10				"
	Malinda		8				"
	Columbus		5				"
	William	MORGAN	66	Laborer		50	N. C.
1066	Rebecca	MORGAN	66				"
	William	VANCE	18	"			Tenn.
1067	Martin	FRASIER	64	"			Va.
	Lilla		51				Tenn.
	Lucinda		28				
	Elizabeth		21				
	Thomas		24	"			
	Arominta (f)		19				
	Nancy		13				
	Eliza J.		8				

Page 148   TAYLORSBURG   24 July 1860

	Name		Age	Occupation	Real	Pers.	Birthplace
	Martha E.	MANTOOTH	21				Ga.
1068	Alfred	SHELL	37	Wagon Maker	200	300	Tenn.
	Lavisca		35				"
	William		15	Laborer			
	Daniel		13				
	Leonard		11				
	Martha		9				
	Anderson		7				
	James E.		5				
	Andrew		2				
1069	Eliza W.	TAYLOR	36		650	800	"
	Hortence E.		19				
	Eugene P.		17				
	Pauline		14				
	Herbert		12				
	Ida P.		10				
	Walter P.		8				
	Edgar		5				
	Ella		11/12				
	Hannah	PORTER	30				
1070	Isaac F.	GREEN (mwy)	30	Saddler	400	300	N. C.
	Nancy H.		26				Tenn.
1071	Robert	PEARCE (mwy)	23	Mill Right			"
	Nancy H.		22				

- 122 -

	Name		Age	Occupation	Real	Pers.	Birthplace
1072	Henry	HALL	28	Laborer		100	"
	Lucinda		26				
	Martha		6				
	Caster S.		5				
	Samuel		3				
	William		1				
	Sarah	BARTON	40				N. C.
	Anna		21				Tenn.
	William		18	"			Ky.
1073	Samuel	HALL	56	Farmer	400	300	N. C.
	James		18	Laborer			Tenn.
	Elizabeth		15				
	Sarah		13				
	Allen		10				
1074	William H.	HALL	29	Farmer	200	387	"
	Nancy		22				"

Page 149   TAYLORSBURG   24 July 1860

	Name		Age	Occupation	Real	Pers.	Birthplace
	Martha		5				Tenn.
	Enos	GREEN	21	Laborer	100		"
	Sarah		18				"
1075	William	JAMES	33	"		60	N. C.
	Lucinda		27				Tenn.
	Samuel		6				
	William		4				
	Isaac		3				
	Martha		6/12				
1076	Toliver	SISK	63	Farmer	19,550	3,130	Va.
	Nancy		60				"
	Lydia		23				Tenn.
	James		22				
	Martha		18				
1077	Elizabeth	WOOD	36		2,000	1,750	"
	Daniel F. C.C.		14				
	Andrew J.		12				
	Eliza J.		10				
1078	John F.	STANBERY	47	Merchant	2,000	9,190	"
	Richard		37				
	Samuel H.		20	Merchants Clerk			
	Mary L.		3				
	Sarah		1				
1079	Robt. P.	CURETON	49	Tailer	800	700	"
	Nancy E.		30				N. C.
	Jerushua		78				Va.
1080	William	VINSON	80	Farmer	15,000	5,525	Del.
1081	Vinet	FINE	50	"			Tenn.
	Elizabeth		42				
	William V.		21	Laborer			
	Lydia M.		13				
	Allen C.		11				
	Jane		6				

	Name		Age	Occupation	Real	Pers.	Birthplace
	Emily M.		4				"
	Russel		2				"
1082	Pleasant	LOYD	65	Farmer	6,000	1,031	Va.
	Elizabeth		37				Tenn.
	Pleasant		6				
	Isaac		4				
	Thorton		3				

Page 150   TAYLORSBURG   24 July 1860

	Name		Age	Occupation	Real	Pers.	Birthplace
	Lee F.		7/12				Tenn.
	Henry	RUNION	17	Laborer			
	Mary		12				
1083	John	MANTOOTH	71	Farmer	5,000	2,172	Va.
	Margaret		55				N. C.
	Nancy Williams		8				Tenn.
1084	Elizabeth	FOWLER	50		300	500	N. C.
	Elija		27	"			S. C.
	Narcissa		20				"
	Mary		18				"
1085	Berry	NETHERTON	51	"		650	Tenn.
	Elizabeth		19				"
	Sarah		8				
	Mary		1				
	Joseph	RUNNION	16	Laborer			
1086	Anderson	COOK	50	Farmer		240	"
	Lucinda		30				"
	John		8				"
	James		6				"
	Rebecca		5				"
	Margaret		1				"
1087	Enoch	NETHERTON	71	"	3,430	731	"
	Jane		56				S. C.
	Elizabeth		40	(Idiot)			Tenn.
	Moses		37				"
	Harrison		20				"
	Sarah J.		17				"
	Mary	BRADY	22				"
	Abigail		4				
	Caleb		1				
1088	Joseph	JOHNSON	63	Miller	2,400	1,190	S. C.
	Phebe		62				Tenn.
	Nancy		28				"
1089	Alexander	McNABB	38	Grocer	200	450	"
	Elizabeth		36				
	Rhoda M.		13				
	Nancy		10				
	Cynthia E.		8				
	Martha C.		6				
	Sarah A.		1/12				

	Name		Age	Occupation	Real	Pers.	Birthplace
Page 151				TAYLORSBURG			25 July 1860
1090	William	JOHNSON	40	Farmer		250	Tenn.
	Rachael		38				
	Benjamin		11				
	Henry		9				
	Mary		7				
	William		8/12				
1091	Ashby	WOOD	45	"	3,000	2,800	"
	Martha		33				
	Allen		19	Laborer			
	Rhoda		16				
	William		14				
	Lucy		13				
	Ashby		4				
	Mary		3				
	Albert		5/12				
1092	William	KELLY	83			50	Va.
	Phebe		74				"
1093	John	MANTOOTH	24	Farmer		273	Tenn.
	Mary J.		19				"
	George		1				
1094	Samuel	FRASIER	32	Laborer		100	"
	Cylvania		31				
	Michael		13				
	Harriet		12				
	Caroline		10				
	Lucinda		8				
	Mary J.		6				
	William E.		1				
1095	Lawson	MANTOOTH	33	"		300	"
	Mahala		32				
	John		11				
	Sarah E.		10				
	Lewis		8				
	Lawson		7				
	Permilia		6				
	Andrew H.		3				
	Amada (f(		1				
1096	Margaret	LEE	73		1,000	326	"
	Margaret	GORMON	25				"
Page 152				TAYLORSBURG			25 July 1860
	Mark	HOLDER	23			50	Tenn.
1097	Joseph	McMULLEN	52		2,500	2,576	N. C.
	Elizabeth		53				"
	Henderson		22	Laborer			
	Samuel		18				Tenn.
	James		15				"
	Elizabeth		10				
1098	James	McNABB	55	Farmer	10,000	1,711	"
	Nancy		45				
	Mary		21				

	Name		Age	Occupation	Real	Pers.	Birthplace
	Enoch L.		18				
	Nancy		15				
	James		12				
	John		10				
	Charity		7				
	Seabenran (m)		3				
1099	Green	CAMERON	60	Farmer		471	"
	Martha		55				
	Mary		24				
	Jane		20				
	Alexander		19	Laborer			
	Elizabeth		18				
	Thomas		10				
1100	John	LEWIS	22	"		100	"
	Lavina		24				N. C.
	Harrison		2				Tenn.
1101	Joab	BLACKWELL	64	Farmer	5,000	1,925	N. C.
	Cycha		45				Tenn.
	George	GRAY	26	Laborer			
	William		16	Laborer			
	Phebe		14				
	Willis		12				
1102	Margaret	GRAY	40				"
	Bartlet		22				
	Alexander		18				
	John		16				
	Elizabeth		14				
	Margaret		13				
	George W.		12				
	James		9				

Page 153   TAYLORSBURG   25 July 1860

	Name		Age	Occupation	Real	Pers.	Birthplace
1103	Grantham	DAVIS	50	Farmer		100	N. C.
	Rebecca		30				S. C.
	Lucinda		15				Tenn.
	Narcissa		11				
	Arnold		9				
	Margaret		7				
	Jacob		4				
	Polly A.		1				
	Rattleford	(m)	1				
1104	Robert	RUTHERFORD	64	Laborer		68	"
	Elizabeth		64				
1105	Jesse	CLAYTON	23	"			S. C.
	Martha		20				Tenn.
	William		1				
1106	William	WOODY	60	Farmer	200	75	N. C.
	Berlinda		40				"
	William J.		20	Laborer			"
	Jane O'Neal		10				"

	Name		Age	Occupation	Real	Pers.	Birthplace
	Zeb	DAVIS	20			5	"
	Rebecca		26				"
	Thomas		2				
1107	James	ALLEN	35	Farmer		25	Va.
	Eliza		25				N. C.
	Mary		8				Tenn.
	William		6				
	John		5				
	Margaret		3				
	Malissa		1				
	Elizabeth	McMULLEN	82				N. C.
1108	Alexander	FINE	24	"		400	Tenn.
	Malissa C.		19				"
	William		1				
1109	Nancy	ALLEN	27				Va.
	Sarah J.		7				Tenn.
	John		6				
	Julia	HARTSEL	48				Va.
1110	Alexander	SISK	32	"	5,500	1,200	Tenn.
	Mary		27				"
	Lewis C.		7				"
	James P.		5				"

Page 154   TAYLORSBURG   25 July 1860

	Name		Age	Occupation	Real	Pers.	Birthplace
1111	John	BALLEW	34	Laborer		60	S. C.
	Nancy		27				Tenn.
	William		11				
	Mary		8				
	Susan		5				
	Fanny		1				
1112	Minerva	RUTHERFORD	38	Seamstress		250	"
1113	Lucinda	RUTHERFORD	30			225	
	Daniel		12				
	Fanny		11				
	Joseph		9				
1114	John W.	RECTOR	25	Blacksmith		300	"
	Catharine		27				
1115	Daniel	GRAY	24	Farmer		675	"
	Nancy		24				
	Elizabeth		1				
1116	Anderson	FOX	46	Carpenter	1,500	773	"
	Susan		42				
	Ezekiel		22	Laborer			
	Julia		18				
	Matthew		16	"			
	Mary		13				
	Howard		11				
	Anderson		9				
	Elias		7				
	Frank		6				
	John		3				
	Harriet		13				

	Name		Age	Occupation	Real	Pers.	Birthplace
1117	Creed F.	BEWLEY	24	"		668	"
	Fanny F.		23				
	Walter M.		3				
1118	Isaac	HARTSELL, Sr.	74	Farmer	2,000	1,800	"
	Jane		32				"
	Elizabeth		30				"
	Emaline		3				
1119	John	FRASIER	30	"		100	"
	Letty		27				
	Maranda		10				
	Austin		8				
	Elizabeth		4				

Page 155 · TAYLORSBURG · 25 June 1860

	Name		Age	Occupation	Real	Pers.	Birthplace
	Ellinora		1				Tenn.
1120	Thomas	MANTOOTH	42	Farmer		320	"
	Lavina		32				"
	Eliza		23				
	Aurelius (m)		10				
	Hugh		8				
	Eliza		2				
1121	William	BURK	35	"	2,000	915	"
	Charity		33				
	Elisha		11				
	Margaret		9				
	James		7				
	Elizabeth		6				
	Lydia		4				
	Malissa		3				
	William		3/12				
1122	William	HUMBARD	32	Laborer		375	"
	Amanda		28				
	Emma		10				
	Matilda		8				
	James		5				
	Mary		1				
1123	James	MANTOOTH	53	Shoemaker	1,000	425	"
	Mary		49				
	Robert		14				
	Mary J.		9				
	Charity	BURK	13				
	William		4				
1124	William	MANTOOTH	30	Farmer		450	"
	Josephine		24				
	Margaret J.		3				
	Elizabeth		2				
1125	Anderson	FOX	30	Distiller		161	"
	Nancy		24				
	Sarah		9				
	William		7				
	Eli		6				

	Name		Age	Occupation	Real	Pers.	Birthplace
	Jackson		2				
	Mary		2/12				
1126	Noah	JAMES	32	Laborer		175	N. C.
Page 156				WILTON SPRINGS			25 July 1860
	Nancy		40				Tenn.
	Jane	WORTH	16				"
	William		13				
	Minerva		9				
1127	John	WILLIAMS	63	Farmer		25	"
	Rebecca		33				N. C.
	William		12				Tenn.
	Isham		21	Laborer			
	Joel		9				
	Thomas		3				
	Elihu		1				
1128	Sidney	PRICHARD	24	"		25	"
	Margaret		22				N. C.
	John		1				Tenn.
	Ransom	HICKS	20	"			N. C.
1129	David R.	BRITTON	33	Merchant		4,000	Tenn.
	Mahala A.		31				"
	Mary A.		10				
	Florence A.		5				
	Jessie R. (f)		1				
1130	Malcom	McNABB	47	Farmer	16,500	30,940	"
	Sarah A.		44				Ga.
	George R.		21	Mercht.			Tenn.
	Russel A.		18	Laborer			
	William O.		16	"			
	Martha J.		14				
	Catharine		8				
	Sarah R. F.		2				
1131	Joel	WILLIAMS	46	"		25	"
	Sarah		30				N. C.
	John		16	"			Tenn.
	Robert		14				
	Rebecca		12				
	Isam		9				
	Anderson		7				
	Sarah		5				
	Margaret		3				
	Nancy J.		2/12				
1132	James	VINSON	60	Farmer	2,000	703	"
	Hetty		60				"
Page 157				WILTON SPRINGS			26 July 1860
	Thomas D.		30	Laborer			Tenn.
	Loucinda		21				"
	Sarah		16				"

	Name		Age	Occupation	Real	Pers.	Birthplace
1133	Garet	McNABB	55	Farmer		1,410	"
	Loucinda		55				"
	Margaret		18				"
	George W.		16	Laborer			"
	Wm. G.		14				"
	Sarah		10				"
1134	Wm.	VINSON	50	Farmer		350	"
	Mary		36				"
	Malinda		14				"
	Julia		12				"
	Murry		10				"
	S. Juda (f)		8				"
	Creed		6				"
	Dora		4				"
	Luther		1				"
1135	James	MANTOOTH	29	Farmer		730	"
	Malissa		25				"
	Mary		1				"
	Ellen		5/12				"
	Tilmon		14				"
1136	Miton	DAVIS	35	Laborer		10	Va.
	Mary		28				Tenn.
	William A.		7				"
	Sarah		5				"
	Susan		2				"
1137	John	QUALLS	50	Laborer		25	N. C.
	Sarah		26				"
	Eli		16				"
	Sarah		14				"
	Robert		13				"
	John		11				"
	Mary		7				Tenn.
	Malinda		6				"
	Martha		4				"
	Margarett		8/12				"
1138	Margaret	McNABB	75			3,860	Va.
1139	Robert	MANTOOTH	35	Blacksmith		421	Tenn.

Page 158   WILTON SPRINGS   16 July 1860

	Name		Age	Occupation	Real	Pers.	Birthplace
	Eveline		32				Tenn.
	Jackson		13				"
	Thomas		11				"
	Sarah		6				"
	Margaret		5				"
	Peissena		2				"
1140	Wm. E.	McNABB	26	Farmer	2,500	727	"
	Mary		22				"
	James		3				"
	Jerome		2				"
	Sarah	McNABB	52				"

	Name		Age	Occupation	Real	Pers.	Birthplace
1141	James C.	McNABB	28	Farmer	2,500	625	"
	Margaret		26				"
	Charles		5				"
	James		1				"
1142	John	McNABB	52	Farmer	4,000	2,400	"
	Elizabeth		42				"
	Elvira		25				"
	Samuel		22	Laborer			"
	Campbell		19	"			"
	Harriett		17				"
	Mary I.		14				"
	Elizabeth		10				"
1143	John	BAKER	37	Farmer	5,000	3,782	Ga.
	Margarett		22				Tenn.
	Sarah		13				"
	Thomas I.		11				"
	John		8				"
	Catherine		6				"
	Jerome		4				"
	Virginia		2				"
	Florence		6/12				"
	Isaac	HOOPER	22	Laborer			"
1144	John	McNABB	38	Farmer (Deaf & Dumb)	1,600	3,641	"
	Martha		33				Ill.
	Lenard		15				Miss.
	George F.		8				Tenn.
	William		2				"
	Catherine	LEWIS	19				"
1145	William	DENTON	46	Miller		140	"

Page 159   WILTON SPRINGS   26 July 1860

	Name		Age	Occupation	Real	Pers.	Birthplace
	Mary		40				Tenn.
	Sarah		6				"
	Albert I.		4				"
	Martin		1				"
1146	David	LILLARD	33	Cabinet Maker	350	1,053	"
	Elizabeth		30				"
	Obedecene		13				"
	Helen		11				"
	Thadis (m)		8				"
	Mary		7				"
	Elizabeth		5				"
	Britton		3				"
	Julia		1				"
1147	Perrin	GILES	40	Distiller		75	"
	Rebecca		37				"
	Margaret E.		13				"
	James		11				"
	Matilda		9				"
	Catherine		6				"
	Hester		4				"
	Henry		2				"

	Name		Age	Occupation	Real	Pers.	Birthplace
1148	Wesley	MORRIS	30	Laborer		40	Ga.
	Mary		30				N. C.
1149	Matilda	STINNETT	25				Tenn.
	William		4			10	"
	Matilda		1				"
1150	Wm.	McGAHA	40	Farmer	200	125	"
	Catherine		22				"
	Charles		13				"
	Allen		11				"
	Robert		9				"
	William		8				"
	Jackson		5				"
1151	Jos. M.	SUTTON	26	Laborer		25	"
	Elizabeth		27				"
	Mary		8				"
	George		5				"
	Anderson		4				"
	Samuel		2				"
	Joseph		1				"

Page 160   WILTON SPRINGS   26 July 1860

	Name		Age	Occupation	Real	Pers.	Birthplace
1152	John	GILLILAND	52	Farmer		131	Tenn.
	Eliza		47				"
	John		21				"
	James		19				"
	Mary		13				"
	Oren		14				"
	Elizabeth		11				"
	Noah		5				"
1153	Cornelias	LARGE	28	Farmer	500	245	"
	Nancy		21				"
	Jonathan		1				"
1154	Wm. M.	JINKINS	29	Laborer			"
	Barbary		25				"
	Baxter H.		2				"
1155	Phillip	JINKINS	45	Farmer	350	198	"
	Rachel		32				N. C.
	Low Harvy		15				Tenn.
	Wm. C.		15				"
1156	Chrisly	WEBB	22	Laborer			"
	Cida C.		24				"
	James M.		7				"
	Mary		3				"
	Jane		2				"
1157	Willis	JOHNSON	30	Laborer		75	N. C.
	Eliza I.		21				"
	Jas. R.		6				"
	Susanna E.		4				"
	Mary S. E.		2				Tenn.
	Martha		2/12				"

	Name		Age	Occupation	Real	Pers.	Birthplace
1158	Rhuben	WILLIAMSON	44	Farmer		190	"
	Elizabeth		39				"
	James P.		19				"
	Joseph		17				"
	Eli		14				"
	Nancy		10				"
	Lewis		3				"
	Jesse (m)		1				"
1159	Anderson	McMELLON	30	Farmer	1,000	1,419	N. C.
	Martha		27				Tenn.
	Joseph		10				"

Page 161   WILTON SPRINGS   26 July 1860

	Name		Age	Occupation	Real	Pers.	Birthplace
	Elias A.		8				Tenn.
	Lydia		7				
	Elizabeth		5				
	Eliza		3				
	Noah		1				
1160	G. W.	VOSS	32	Farmer	200	80	N. C.
	Mary		43				"
	Robert		10				
	Margarett		7				
	Emiline		6				
	Rachel		2				
	Manning		5/12				Tenn.
	Susan	WILLIAMS	90				N. C.
1161	George	SHULTS	31	"	2,000	1,168	Tenn.
	Elizabeth		29				
	Felix		2				
	Susannah J.		6/12				
	Stephen	WHITEHEAD	10				
1162	Russel	JENKINS	40	"	800	305	"
	Laurena		47				S. C.
	Permilla		15				Tenn.
	Nancy		13				
	Asa (m)		11				
	George W.		10				
	Edward		9				
1163	John M.	GILES	27	"		125	"
	Nancy		28				"
	Milford		9				"
	Thomas		5				"
	Matilda		2				
1164	Isaac	LINDSY (mwy)	21	Laborer		25	"
	Bershaba		18				"
1165	Wilson	McMAHAN	38	Farmer	2,000	616	"
	Jane		28				"
	Theodocia	(m)	13				"
	Marcus		9				
	Sarah		7				
	McKinny		6				
	Breckenridge		2				

	Name		Age	Occupation	Real	Pers.	Birthplace
1166	William	TINKER	50	"	800	1,375	"

WILTON SPRINGS 26 July 1860

	Name		Age	Occupation	Real	Pers.	Birthplace
	Elizabeth		50				Tenn.
	Margaret M.		16				
	Margaret		4				
1167	Samuel	TINKER	27	Farmer		389	"
	Catharine		22				
	William		8/12				
1168	Joseph	McMULLEN	23	"	300	280	"
	Catharine		22				"
	William		8/12				"
	Harrison	DEBUSK	18	Laborer			
1169	William	GILLILAND	27	Farmer	150	123	"
	Rebecca		23				
	Isaac		5				
	Mark		4				
	William		2				
	Malinda		4/12				
1170	Benjamin P.	HOPKINS	50	"	2,500	1,130	"
	Ruth		51				Ky.
	Jacob		21	Laborer			Tenn.
	Gipson		21	"			
	Joseph		17	"			"
	Baxter		14				
	Ellison W.		12				
	Israel		10				
1171	Anderson	HOPKINS	30	"		450	"
	William		6				
	Soloman		4				
	Eli M.		2				
1172	Richmond	HILL	49	"	500	150	N. C.
	Rhoda		24				Tenn.
	Delilal		13				N. C.
	Joseph N.		12				Tenn.
	Lewis R.		9				
	James G.		8				
	John A.		5				
	Nancy		3				
	Benjamin	HOPKINS	24	Laborer		310	
1173	Francis M.	TINKER	27	Farmer		389	"
	Mildred		23				"
	William N.		3				"

WILTON SPRINGS 26 July 1860

	Name		Age	Occupation	Real	Pers.	Birthplace
1174	John	WILLIAMS	62	Farmer	800	2,000	N. C.
	Rachel		47				Tenn.
	William		34	(Idiotic)			"
1175	William	LINDSY	47	"	500	440	"
	Phebe E.		45				
	Rachael		19				

	Name		Age	Occupation	Real	Pers.	Birthplace
	John W.		16	Laborer			
	Nancy E.		15				
	William G.		14				
	Jackson F.		12				
	Lucinda		10				
	Baxter H.		5				
	Phebe E.		4				
1176	John	COLE	23	Farmer		100	"
	Nancy		20				
	Soloman		2				
	Anna E.		1				
	Anna	COLEMAN	45				
	Adaline	COLE	18				
1177	William N.	SMITH	46	Minister (Bapt.)	500	500	S. C.
	Nancy		46				N. C.
1178	John	RAMSEY	57	Farmer	450	100	"
	Mary		46				Tenn.
	Isaac		12				"
	Jesse (f)		10				
	Sarah		8				
	Nancy		6				
	Mary		4				
1179	John	RAMSEY, Jr.	21	Laborer		272	"
	Theodocia		20				
	Rose		1				
1180	John C.	ROLLINS	62	"		50	S. C.
	Sarah		62				N. C.
	Abagail		16				Tenn.
	Landon		13				
1181	John I.	McGAHA	34	Farmer	200	75	"
	Cretia		25				
	Mary A.		9				
	Samuel		6				
	Isaac		4				

Page 164   WILTON SPRINGS   26 July 1860

	Name		Age	Occupation	Real	Pers.	Birthplace
1182	Vardin	WHITEHEAD	21	Laborer		75	N. C.
	Margaret		24				"
	William I.		2				Tenn.
	Tipton		70				N. C.
1183	Jesse	BAXTER	34	Farmer	300	313	Tenn.
	Sarah		32				"
	Willis		13				
	James		11				
	Jane		10				
	William H.		6				
	Perry		5				
	Mary		3				
	Lydia		1				
	William	McMAHAN	32		175		"

	Name		Age	Occupation	Real	Pers.	Birthplace
1184	Wilson	WILLIAMS	32	Laborer		100	"
	Matilda		26				"
	John		7				
	Samuel		5				
	Rhoda		4				
1185	James	McMAHAN	51	Farmer	300	500	N. C.
	Mary		44				Tenn.
	McKinney		14				
	Rhoda		12				
	George		10				
	Mary		6				
	Margaret		4				
	James		2				
	Perry		8/12				
1186	John	McMAHAN	23	"	300	300	"
	Anna		20				
	Samuel		9/12				
1187	Mitchell	SMITH	51	"	200	464	S. C.
	Anna		55				"
	Sarah J.		27				Tenn.
	Mary C.		25				"
	Thomas		24	Laborer			"
	Fanny E.		17				"
	Mary	LEATHERWOOD	83				N. C.
1188	William	RAMSEY	27	"		50	Tenn.
	Emaline		21				"

Page 165   WILTON SPRINGS   26 July 1860

	Name		Age	Occupation	Real	Pers.	Birthplace
	Lavina		3				Tenn.
	Wilson		1				"
1189	Robert	McGAHA	60	Farmer	800	1,014	N. C.
	Elizabeth		56				Tenn.
	William		21	Laborer			"
	Ritty (f)		17				
	Isaac		16				
	Malcom		14				
	Sarah A.		9				
1190	John	McGAHA (mwy)	23	Farmer		100	"
	Eliza		28				N. C.
1191	Jonas	PHILLIPS	34	"	1,000	330	Tenn.
	Sarah		28				"
	Martha		14				N. C.
	James		12				"
	Jonas		9				"
	Joseph		7				"
	Margaret		6				Tenn.
	Mary		3				
	Elizabeth		1				

	Name		Age	Occupation	Real	Pers.	Birthplace
1192	John	HARRISON	40	"		715	"
	Anna		43				
	Sarah		21				
	Martha		17				
	Thomas		13				
	Nancy		11				
	Elizabeth		9				
	William B.		5				
	Mildred		7				
	Nancy		2				
1193	William	McKINNEY	35	Laborer		250	N. C.
	Darcus		25				"
	Jeremiah		6				"
	Candus (f)		4				"
	Dorcus		1				"
1194	Joseph	GILLILAND	29	Farmer	500	260	"
	Elizabeth		25				"
	James		9				"
	Mary		7				Tenn.
	Allen		5				"

Page 166　　　　　　　　　　　　WILTON SPRINGS　　　　　　　26 July 1860

	Name		Age	Occupation	Real	Pers.	Birthplace
	Harriet		3				Tenn.
1195	Jonas	PHILLIPS	79	Laborer		150	Va.
	Nancy		45				Tenn.
	Eliza	BENNER	17				
1196	Caleb	JENKINS	35	Farmer			"
	Martha		39				
	John		16	Laborer			
	William H.		12				
	Cynthia		8				
	Elizabeth		6				
	Matilda		3				
	Nancy		3/12				
1197	Nathaniel	GILES	27	Farmer		700	"
	Matilda		24				"
	Anderson		1				
1198	Jesse	GILES	71	Laborer		50	Va.
1199	Logan	JOHNSON	70				S. C.
	Elizabeth		70				N. C.
	Mary		25				"
1200	Joel	JENKINS	54	Farmer	500	550	Tenn.
	Mary		38				N. C.
	Rhoda		27				Tenn.
	Abraham		24	Laborer			"
	Toliver		16				"
	Wilson D.		14				"
	Sarah		12				"
	Jane	ROMINES	15				"
	Samuel		12				
	Butler	JENKINS	21	"			N. C.

	Name		Age	Occupation	Real	Pers.	Birthplace
1201	Robert	McGAHA, Jr.	24	"		330	Tenn.
	Harriet		26				
	William		10				
	Anna		4				
	Rhoda		1				
1202	Lemuel	WHITLOCK	59	Farmer	100	75	S. C.
	Racy(f)		52				"
	Amanda		12				Tenn.
	William		7				"
1203	Thomas	CARVER	49	"	200	200	"
	Sarah		44				Va.

Page 167   WILTON SPRINGS   26 July 1860

	Name		Age	Occupation	Real	Pers.	Birthplace
	Lucinda		21				Tenn.
	Nancy		16				"
	Mary A.		15				
	Sarah J.		15				
	Malinda		11				
	Thomas		8				
	Jesse (m)		5				
	John		3				
1204	Joel	DENNIS, Jr.	32	Farmer	600	280	"
	Matilda		30				"
	Robert		11				"
	Elizabeth		3				
1205	Henry	VOLENTINE (mwy)	27	Laborer		65	"
	Mary		27				
1206	William	VOLENTINE	69	Farmer		200	N. C.
	Rebecca		58				Tenn.
	Darcus		30				
	Elizabeth		27				
	Robert		23	Laborer			"
	Sarah		22				"
	Holloway		7				
	Wm. M.		6				
	Anderson		3				
1207	Abraham	HOPKINS	33	Farmer		420	"
	Nancy		33				
	Lafayette		12				
	Benjamin		10				
	Amanda		8				
	Moses		7				
	Fletcher		5				
	Serena		1				
1208	James	HAROLD	34	"	1,000	515	N. C.
	Theodocia		28				Tenn.
	Enoch		10				
	Rosannah		8				
	Theodocia		5				
	Sanders		1				
	John	WHITLOCK	16	"			N. C.

	Name		Age	Occupation	Real	Pers.	Birthplace
1209	Zacharich	STYLES	53	Laborer		125	"
	Minnie J.		64				Va.

Page 168   WILTON SPRINGS   26 July 1860

	Name		Age	Occupation	Real	Pers.	Birthplace
1210	Augustus	JENKINS	50	Farmer	900	500	Tenn.
	Ruth		66				Va.
1211	Reubin	HARRISON	65	"	600	200	N. C.
	Elizabeth		64				Tenn.
	Margaret		43				"
1212	Adam	HARRISON	38	"	800	313	"
	Jane		25				"
	Elizabeth		14				
	Jane		12				
	Joseph		10				
	Margaret		6				
	Sarah		4				
	John		1				
1213	Russell	HARRISON (mwy)	23	"		440	"
	Elizabeth		20				
1214	James	HARRISON	24	Laborer		100	"
	Nancy		21				"
	Martha		4				
	Elizabeth		2				
	Partillia		7/12				
1215	Sarah	STYLES	32			30	"
	Lavina		9				
	Aera (m)		7				
	Thomas		4				
1216	James	YARBER	43			130	N. C.
	Margaret		35				Tenn.
	Sarah		15				
	Rebecca J.		13				
	Jackson		11				
	Darcus		9				
	Elizabeth		7				
	William		5				
	Jacob		2				
1217	John	SUTTON	40	Farmer	300	147	"
	Elizabeth		44				"
	Mahal (m)		21	Laborer			
	Mary		17				
	Andrew		13				
	Jackson		11				
	Thomas		8				

Page 169   WILTON SPRINGS   26 July 1860

	Name		Age	Occupation	Real	Pers.	Birthplace
	Joseph		10				N. C.
	Mark		6	(Idiotic)			Tenn.
1218	Phillip	STYLES	24	Laborer	100	50	"
	Esther		23				"
	John		2				
	Martha		10/12				

	Name		Age	Occupation	Real	Pers.	Birthplace
1219	Joseph	SUTTON	83	Farmer	300	90	"
	Elizabeth		80				
	Russel		20	Laborer (Blind)			"
	Silas		3				
1220	Joseph CAMPBELL Jr. (mwy)		22	"		120	"
	Mildred		20				
1221	Margaret	RAINS	42		75	50	Mo.
	John		20	"			Tenn.
	Balam		17	"			
	Carter		15	"			
1222	Jane	LINEBARGER	47			50	"
	Mary		23				"
	Martha		18				
	Alfred		14				
	Susannah J.		12				
	Polly		2				
1223	Jeremiah	JENKINS	31	Farmer		175	N. C.
	Emiline		27				Tenn.
	Malinda		10				
	Elizabeth		8				
	Anderson		6				
	Cana (m)		5				
	John		3				
1224	Thomas R.	CATON	40	"	1,000	1,051	N. C.
	Margaret		39				Tenn.
	John		19	Laborer			
	Robert		18	"			
	Stephen		14				
	Giles		12				
	Green B.		9				
	Rebecca		6				
	George		3				
	William C.		5/12				
1225	James	VOLENTINE	37	Farmer	500	983	"

Page 170   WILTON SPRINGS   26 July 1860

	Name	Age	Occupation	Birthplace
	Green	12		Tenn.
	Isaac	9		"
	Mary	7		"
	James	5		"
	Elizabeth	2		"
	William	20	Laborer	"

	Name		Age	Occupation	Pers.	Birthplace
1226	Jacob H.	SHIELDS	32	"	150	"
	Rebecca		28			
	John J.		5			
	Robert		4			
	Elizabeth		2			
1227	Green	VOLENTINE	34	Farmer	189	"
	Elizabeth		29			
	Nancy		6			
	Martha		4			
	Robert		1			

	Name		Age	Occupation	Real	Pers.	Birthplace
1228	Robert VOLENTINE	(mwy)	23	"	150	122	"
	Elizabeth		19				
1229	Holloway	BAXTER	33	"	600	528	"
	Margaret		33				
	John		12				
	William A.		10				
	James		8				
	Rhoda		4				
	Dove (f)		2				
1230	Daniel	JAMES	24	Laborer		312	"
	Mary		30				
	William		2				
	Jane		2/12				
	Isaac	HARTSELL	13				
	George		11				
1231	Samuel	GREEN	34	"		50	"
	Mary		30				N. C.
	Sarah		14				Tenn.
	Hannah		12				"
	John		11				
	Mary		7				
	William R.		6				
1232	John	BAXTER	42	Farmer	1,200	328	"
	Allen C.		11				

Page 171   WILTON SPRINGS   26 July 1860

	Name		Age	Occupation	Real	Pers.	Birthplace
	John		9				Tenn.
1233	Jesse	WEBB	40	Farmer		100	"
	Barshaba		20				
	Minerva		14				
	George		8				
1234	James P.	WATERS	53	"		169	N. C.
	Elizabeth		56				"
	Joseph P.		19	Laborer			
	James		18				
	William H.		14				
	David		9				
1235	James	BAXTER, Sr.	66	Farmer	1,200	639	Ga.
	Rhoda		63				N. C.
	Sanders		24	Laborer			Tenn.
1236	Perry	BAXTER (mwy)	22	"		100	"
	Miland		21				
1237	James	BAXTER, Jr.	27	Farmer	100	100	"
	Mary		27				
	Fanny		4				
	Nancy		8/12				
1238	James	WEBB	37	Laborer		20	"
	Anna		35				
	Deborah		14				
	Dillard		12				

	Name		Age	Occupation	Real	Pers.	Birthplace
	Joseph		10				
	Nancy		6				
	William		2				
1239	Robert	GILLILAND	26	"		75	"
	Martha		19				
	Sarah		14				
	Esther		1				
1240	Sinia	PHILLIPS	40				"
	Elizabeth		18				
	Jemina		20				
	James		16	Laborer			
	Sarah		15				
	Nancy		11				
	Mary		9				
	Margaret		7				
	Eliza J.		2				

Page 172   WILTON SPRINGS   26 July 1860

	Name		Age	Occupation	Real	Pers.	Birthplace
1241	Samuel B.	ADAMS (mwy)	38	Farmer	300	221	Tenn.
	Ellender		25				
1242	Margaret	CANUP	58	Spinster		3	N. C.
	Eliza		17				Tenn.
	Elizabeth		15				
	James		11				
	Martha		9				
	Christley (m)		6				
1243	Jesse	RAMSEY	40	Laborer		125	"
	Sarah		39	(Blind)			
	Anna		20				
	Nancy		18				
	Jane		16				
	William		13				
	Delilah		11				
	James		9				
	Rhoda		6				
	George W.		3				
1244	Samuel	McGAHA, Jr.	24	"		150	"
	Anna		19				
	John		9/12				
1245	Joseph	WEBB	69	Farmer	2,000	784	"
	Barshaba		67				Va.
	Jane		22				Tenn.
	Mary		21	(Idiotic)			
	James	PHILLIPS	15	Laborer			"
	Sarah		12				
	Caroline		11				
1246	Mary	WEBB	35			50	
	John		13				
	James		11				
	Lavina		9				
	Alexander		8				
	Martha		6				
	Henderson		4				

	Name		Age	Occupation	Real	Pers.	Birthplace
1247	Isaac	McGAHA	54	Farmer	400	502	"
	Markey (f)		55				N. C.
	Susanah		18				Tenn.
	William		15	Laborer			"
	Isaac		12				

Page 173 — WILTON SPRINGS — 26 July 1860

	Name		Age	Occupation	Real	Pers.	Birthplace
	James R.		12				Tenn.
1248	John	WEBB	32	Farmer		90	"
	Margaret		24				
	Rhoda		10				
	Mildred		12				
	William		8				
	Caroline		6				
	Abraham		2				
	Elizabeth		5/12				
1249	E. M.	FRANKLIN	40	"	500	236	S. C.
	Margaret		39				N. C.
	James H.		18	Laborer			"
	John H.		16				"
	William		14				
	Darcus		11				
	Margaret L.		9				
	Sarah J.		5				
1250	William	McMAHAN	45	Farmer	1,600	1,500	Tenn.
	Rhoda		39				
	Henderson		20	Laborer			
	Joseph		18	"			
	Allen		17	"			
	Anderson		15	"			
	Rachael		10				
	Jane		4				
	Wilson		3				
	Jane	GILES	30				
1251	William	SMITH	25	"		200	
	Sarah		30				N. C.
	Thomas		7				Tenn.
	Levinda (f)		5				
	Mildred		2				
1252	James	WILLIAMS	29	"		75	"
	Darcus		24				"
	Clara E.		6				
	Reubin W. A.		4				
	Diliah		3				
	Partillia M.		1				
1253	Samuel	RAMSEY (mwy)	24	Farmer	240	178	Tenn.
	Nelthy		23				S. C.

Page 174 — WILTON SPRINGS — 27 July 1860

	Name		Age	Occupation	Real	Pers.	Birthplace
1254	William	HARRIS	35	Farmer		635	Tenn.
	Mary		37				N. C.
	Elizabeth		12				Tenn.

	Name		Age	Occupation	Real	Pers.	Birthplace
	Deborah		10				"
	Martha		8				
	Owen		5				
	Lydia		2				
	Phebe		1				
1255	Sarah	JONES	52			100	N. C.
	Elvira		20				Tenn.
	Anna		17				
	Mary		14				
1256	James	ROLLINS	35	Farmer	500	100	"
	Nancy		35				N. C.
	Joseph M.		16	Laborer			Tenn.
	William		15				
	Sarah J.		12				N. C.
	Robert		10				Tenn.
	Calvin		7				
	Elizabeth		1				
1257	Henderson	JOHNSON	22	"		65	N. C.
	Margaret		22				Tenn.
	James		3				
	Sarah E.		1				
1258	William	HUSKY	42	Farmer	400	160	"
	Mary		30				
	Henry		11				
1259	James	RAINS	52	"	1,000	250	"
	Sarah		56				N. C.
	James		17				Tenn.
	Thomas		10				
	Amanda		8				
	Nancy		6				
	Mary	STAFFORD	20				
1260	Joseph	CAMPBELL	41	"	1,500	700	"
	Delilah		25				
	Emma		16				
	Samuel		14				
	Elizabeth		11				
	Laura		7				

Page 175   WILTON SPRINGS   27 July 1860

	Name		Age	Occupation	Real	Pers.	Birthplace
	Isaac		5				Tenn.
	Mary		80				Va.
1261	William H.	GARNER	35	Farmer	3,500	1,600	N. C.
	Cynthia		27				"
	William F.		7				Ky.
	Mildred		10/12				Tenn.
1262	John	GARNER	68	"	400	3,300	N. C.
1263	William	YARBER	24	"		75	Tenn.
	Charlotte		27				"
	Jenette		13				
	Malissa		6				

- 144 -

	Name		Age	Occupation	Real	Pers.	Birthplace
1264	Robert	SMITH	23	"	300	200	S. C.
	Mary		23				Tenn.
	Sarah		6				
	Joseph		1				
1265	Calvin	ROLLINS	26	"	500	300	"
	Malissa		22				S. C.
	John A.		4				Tenn.
1266	John	ERBY	24	"		75	"
	Caroline		20				
	William		3				
	James A.		3/12				
1267	Nelson	WILLIAMS	20	"		80	"
	Nancy J.		19				
	James P.		5/12				..
1268	Thomas	WEBB	35	"		120	"
	Anna		38				
	Jesse (m)		18	Laborer			
	Ragan (m)		16	"			
	Mary		14				
	Phebe		12				
	Joseph		10				
	John		6				
	James		5				
	Ashby		4				
	Rachael		2				
1269	Eli	WEBB	47	Farmer		150	"
	Charity		46				S. C.
	Jessee (m)		24	Laborer			Tenn.
	Samuel		17				"

Page 176   WILTON SPRINGS   27 July 1860

	Name		Age	Occupation	Real	Pers.	Birthplace
	Allen		10				Tenn.
	William		3				
	Susanah		1				
1270	Jane	JENKINS	45			175	"
	William L. D.		17	Laborer			"
	Julia		15				
	James C. D.		13				
	Martha C.		11				
	Anna		6				
1271	James P.	BALL	34	"		50	"
	Anna		18				
	Rebecca		2				
1272	Samuel	McGAHA	62	Farmer	50	75	N. C.
	Anna		69				
1273	Anderson	GROOMS	24	"	50	100	Tenn.
	Nancy J.		22				"
	John		5				
	Mary		1/12				
	Mary A.	RAMSEY	20				

	Name		Age	Occupation	Real	Pers.	Birthplace
1274	Elizabeth	MILLER	80?		50	160	N. C.
	Elizabeth	McGAHA	40				Tenn.
1275	John	RIDENS	22	"	130		"
	Rhoda		22				
	Anna		1				
1276	William	RIDENS	68	"	300	100	
	Mary		21				
1277	James A.	SMITH	26	Laborer		150	N. C.
	Jane		22				Tenn.
	William N.		3				
	Joseph		1				
1278	Jane	SMITH	75			70	N. C.
	Susanah	WHITLOCK	30				Tenn.
1279	Christian	ADAMS	29	Farmer	400	200	"
	Emaline		30				
	William		12				
	Samuel		9				
	Martha		7				
	David		6				
	Birdwell		4				
	Mansfield		2				

Page 177   WILTON SPRINGS   27 July 1860

	Name		Age	Occupation	Real	Pers.	Birthplace
	Mary		50				Tenn.
1280	George	RAMSEY	44	Farmer	250	140	N. C.
	Mary		37				"
	Louenda		17				Tenn.
	William		14				"
	John		10				"
	Mary		9				"
	Jesse (m)		2				"
	Nancy		1				"
	Mary		87				Va.
1281	Jacob	MILLER	60	Laborer		75	Pa.
	Susannah		60				N. C.
	William		21	"			Tenn.
	William	KIMSEY	14				"
1282	Mansfield	ELLIS	35	Minister-Carpenter	1,300	840	"
	Elizabeth		40				N. C.
	William		9				Tenn.
1283	James	BROTHERTON	37	Farmer		250	"
	Elizabeth		48				"
	Fanny		20				"
	Margarett		18				"
	Mary		16				"
	John		12				"
	Abraham		10				"
	Moses		8				"
	Jane		6				"
	Martha	SHELTON	20				N. C.

	Name		Age	Occupation	Real	Pers.	Birthplace
	Julia		16				"
	Elizabeth		6				Tenn.
1284	Isaac	STUART	26	Farmer	1,200	662	"
	Martha		20				"
	John M.		1				"
	Florence		2				"
1285	David	SHOULTS	21	"	2,000	1,150	"
	Nancy		26				"
	John		3				"
	Martha		2				"
	J. D.	SHOULTS	19	Laborer			"
	Jacob		59	Farmer	1,000	250	"
1286	John	SHOULTS	28	"	1,000	250	"

Page 178   WILTON SPRINGS   30 July 1860

	Name		Age	Occupation	Real	Pers.	Birthplace
	Sarah		18				Tenn.
	Robert S. R.		2				"
1287	John	ALLEN (Long)	72	Farmer	7,000	8,365	Va.
	Margaret		72				Tenn.
	Mary Jane		45				
1288	Isaac	ALLEN	42	"	6,000	5,827	"
	Mary		43				
	Elizabeth		18				
	Margaret J.		16				
	William M.		15				
	John T.		13				
	Nancy M.		12				
	Harriet		10				
	George W.		9				
	Minerva		8				
	Catharine		4				
	Martha		2				
1289	William	HOLT	43	"	700	487	"
	Nancy		40				
	William		17	Laborer			
	Christopher		15	"			
	Edom		12	"			
	Berry		8				
	Pleasant		6				
	Lavina		3				
	Mary		5				
1290	Edward	HOLT	61	Farmer	800	442	Va.
	Mary		59				"
	James		23	Laborer			Tenn.
	Obadiah		18	"			
	Howard		15	"			
	Nancy Nott		10				
1291	Soloman	FANN	45	Farmer	50	75	N. C.
	Nancy		38				"
	Lavina		18				Tenn.
	Nancy		16	(Deaf & Dumb)			"

Name		Age	Occupation	Real	Pers.	Birthplace
Mary		12	(Deaf & Dumb)			
Sarah		10	(Deaf & Dumb)			
John		6				
Lydia		1				

Page 179   WILTON SPRINGS   30 July 1860

Name		Age	Occupation	Real	Pers.	Birthplace
1292 Adam	FANN	35	Laborer		20	N. C.
Lavina		30				"
John		26				Tenn.
Lydia		4				
Susanna		2				
1293 James	HARVEY	40	Farmer		100	"
Sarah		35				
Elizabeth		18				
Drusilla		16				
John		14				
1294 Obediah	DRISKILL	30	Carpenter		500	Va.
Malinda		25				Tenn.
Catharine		5				
Marion (m)	CLIFF	19	Laborer			
Mariah		24				Va.
1295 Tilghman	BLAZER	30	Farmer		490	Tenn.
Sarah		30				
James A.		3				
Mary J.		1				
1296 Thomas	McNABB	32	"	3,500	215	"
Narcissa		26				
John		9				
Horace		1				
1297 Nicholas	DUNAGAN	70	"	3,000	2,120	Va.
1298 John	DENNIS	43	"	4,000	1,392	Tenn.
Mary		33				
Catharine		8				
Jane		6				
George		9/12				
Thomas	BENSON	15	Laborer			
1299 James	WILSON, Sr.	44	Farmer	1,500	863	S. C.
Anna		42				Tenn.
John		13				
Elizabeth		11				
Samuel		5				
Psycha (f)		3				
1300 Mark	HICKS	23				"
Rebecca		20				N. C.
Jane		1				Tenn.
Cynthia	BLACKWOOD	26				N. C.

Page 180   WILTON SPRINGS   31 July 1860

Name		Age	Occupation	Real	Pers.	Birthplace
Mary		3				Tenn.
1301 Joseph	WILSON (mwy)	26	Farmer		241	"
Nancy		18				"

	Name		Age	Occupation	Real	Pers.	Birthplace
	Mary		69				S. C.
	Sycha (f)		28				"
1302	Jane	BENSON	35			25	Tenn.
	John		17	Laborer			
	Nelly		12				
	Wilson		10				
	Lavina		7				
	Margaret		4				
	Elizabeth		2				
1303	Asa P.	LEWIS	34	"		50	"
	Susannah		34				
	Mildred		15				
1304	Abraham	DENTON	62	Farmer	5,000	4,952	"
	Nancy		54				
	William		21	Laborer			
	Isaac		19	"			
	Amanda		17				
	Sarah		14				
1395	T.F.D.A.	HARPER	31	Farmer		471	"
	Theodocia		24				"
	Mildred		7				
	William D.		6				
	Eli		4				
	Matilda		2				
	John		24	Laborer			
1306	Nathan	PRESLEY	40	Laborer			S. C.
	Mary		26				"
	Elizabeth		10				Tenn.
	Ruth		8				
	Charles		6				
	Elbert		4				
	Sarah		1/12				
	Martha		2				
1307	McKINNEY	McMAHAN	38	Farmer	3,000	2,164	"
	Nancy		18				"
	George		18	Laborer			"
	James		17				"
Page 181				WILTON SPRINGS		31 July 1860	
	Ellender		13				Tenn.
	Mary		9				
	William		5				
	Elizabeth		2				
1308	William	WEBB	54	Farmer	3,000	419	"
	Nancy		48				"
	Sarah		16				
	Susannah		12				
	Nancy		8				
	Isaac		2				
1309	Edwin	ALLEN	48	"	10,000	6,692	"
	Lydia		42				"
	Lewis		20	Laborer			"

	Name		Age	Occupation	Real	Pers.	Birthplace
1310	Samuel	ELENTON	57	"		38	Va.
	Catharin		65				"
1311	Joseph	CAMERON	25	Farmer		105	Tenn.
	Margaret		22				
	Sarah		3				
	Hiram	ALLEN	28	Laborer			
1312	James M.	LILLARD	36	Farmer		70	"
	Nancy		34				N. C.
	Mary		16				Tenn.
	Margaret		12				
	Elizabeth		10				
	James		8				
	Sarah I.		2				
1313	Wilson	ALLEN	27	Laborer		100	"
	Lydia		25				
	Mark		7				
	William		5				
1314	C. B.	McNABB	38	Farmer		360	"
	Edy		39				N. C.
	Margaret J.		19				
	Mary E.		17				
	Harriet		15				
	Elizabeth		14				
	Eliza		12				
	James		10				
	Tipton		8				
	Sarah		5				

Page 182 · WILTON SPRINGS · 31 July 1860

	Name		Age	Occupation	Real	Pers.	Birthplace
	Charles		4				Tenn.
	Jason		5/12				
1315	Allen	RAINS	35	Farmer		130	"
	Catherine		28				"
	Minda		4				"
	Harrison		2				"
1316	Jesse	ROBINSON (mwy)	22	Laborer		20	"
	Hannah		23				N. C.
1317	Sanders	McMAHAN	57	Farmer		160	"
	Ritty		40				"
	Mark		17	Laborer			Tenn.
	Sanders		14				
	Joseph		13				
	James		11				
	Elizabeth		9				
	Martha		7				
	Henderson		5				
	Crawford		2				
1318	Henderson	ALLEN	23	"		170	"
	Theodocia		22				
	Sanders		4				
	Willis		3				
	Martha		1				

	Name		Age	Occupation	Real	Pers.	Birthplace
1319	Nancy	RAINS	75		400	200	N. C.
	Hiram		24	"			Tenn.
	Alfred		22	"			
1320	Gilbert	RAINS (mwy)	20	"		25	"
	Rebecca		18				
1321	Rachel	ROBINSON	65			100	"
	Rebecca		34				
	Richard		32				
	Cassa		27				
1321	Moses	CLARK	63	"		200	S. C.
	Hannah		62				N. C.
	Manning		16				Tenn.
	Sarah		27				N. C.
	Hannah		7				Tenn.
	Moses		5				
1323	John A.	DENTON	37	Farmer		450	"
	Margaret		35				

Page 183   WILTON SPRINGS   2 August 1860

	Name		Age	Occupation	Real	Pers.	Birthplace
	William		16				
	Nancy		15				
	Margaret		13				
	Abraham		12				
	Elizabeth		10				
	Mary		9				
	John		7				
	Minerva		6				
	Martha		4				
	Isaac		2				
	Sarah		7/12				
1324	Ezekiel	SCROGGINS	32	Farmer	700	375	N. C.
	Catharine		28				Tenn.
	Susannah		8				
	Margaret		7				
	Anderson		5				
	Caleb		2				
1325	John	RAINS	37	"		100	"
	Rhoda		32				N. C.
	Joel P.		17	Laborer			Tenn.
	Nancy		15				
	Thos. W.		13				
	John C.		11				
	William		9				
	Cassander		6				
	Abagail		3				
	Rhoda		2				
	Jane	MATHIS?	55				N. C.
1326	Henry	ODELL	26	Farmer		175	Tenn.
	Mariah		25				
	Jacob		6				
	Susannah		5				
	Lafayette		3				
	John		7/12				

- 151 -

	Name		Age	Occupation	Real	Pers.	Birthplace
1327	Mark	HARPER	31	"		200	"
	Eliza		32				
	Mary		11				
	Lavina		7				
	Allen		4				
	Nancy		2				

Page 184   WILTON   SPRINGS   2 August 1860

	Name		Age	Occupation	Real	Pers.	Birthplace
	Woodfin		2/12				Tenn.
	John	RAINS	21	Laborer			
1328	Alfred	BALL	45	Farmer	3,000	1,320	"
	Mahala		46				Va.
	Alfred		20	Laborer			Tenn.
	John		17				
	Susannah		21				
	Margaret		14				
	Mary A.		12				
	Joseph		10				
	Richard		8				
	William		7				
	Euriah (m)		5				
	Margaret C.		3				
1329	Thomas	RAINS	34	"		200	"
	Minerva		33				
	Theodocia		13				
	Margaret		12				
	McKINNEY		10				
	Joel B.		5				
	Martha		3				
	Nancy A.		1				
1330	William	WEAVER	35	"	3,000	1,050	"
	Nancy		27				
	Abraham		9				
	Russell		6				
	Mary		2				
1331	William S.	BEAGLE	46			55	"
	Sarah		39				
	Julia		13				
	John A.		11				
	Alexander		8				
	Louisa E.		6				
	Mary		4				
	Isaac		1				
1332	Josiah	WILLIAMS	49	Farmer	2,000	600	"
	Jane		30				
	Isaac		1				
	Hester		5/12				
	George	WEST	12				

Page 185   WILTON SPRINGS   2 August 1860

	Name		Age	Occupation	Real	Pers.	Birthplace
1333	George W.	CRUM	40	Laborer		200	Tenn.
	Candus		40				
	John		17				

	Name		Age	Occupation	Real	Pers.	Birthplace
	Jane		15				
	Robert		10				
	Eli		8				
	Daniel		2				
1334	William	HARPER	62	Farmer	2,000	400	N. C.
	Emaline		35				"
	Rebecca		33				Tenn.
	Garland		18	Laborer			
	Matilda		15				
	Mary S.		13				
	Eliza		11				
	Margaret		9				
	Daniel		8				
	James P.		6				
	A. Johnson		3				
	Amanda		5/12				
1335	David	SHOEMAKER (mwy)	20	"		25	N. C.
	Elizabeth		18				Tenn.
1336	Caroline	SMALLWOOD	21			20	"
	Martha		7				
1337	John	ALLEN	29	Farmer	300	560	"
	Nancy		29				
	Daniel		8				
	William		7				
	Hester		4				
	Charity		2				
1338	Amon	SWANGER	39	Blacksmith		200	Ga.
	Elvira		31				N. C.
	William		9				"
	Cordelia		8				Tenn.
	Charles		5				
	Clarissa		3				
	Martha		9/12				
1339	Henry	MILLER	39	Laborer		100	N. C.
	Jane		22				"
	James		13				"
	Isaac		11				Tenn.

Page 186   WILTON SPRINGS   3 August 1860

	Name		Age	Occupation	Real	Pers.	Birthplace
	Nancy		9				N. C.
	Hannah		7				"
	Rose A.		3				"
	Eli R.		1/12				Tenn.
1340	Preston	LAYMAN	27	Farmer	4,000	445	"
	Barbara		29				
	Mary C.		4				
	George		7/12				
1341	James P.	TAYLOR	49	"	7,000	2,862	"
	Sarah		40				
	Augustas		17	Laborer			
	Margaret		14				
	Elizabeth		12				

- 153 -

	Name		Age	Occupation	Real	Pers.	Birthplace
	Sarah		10				
	Columbus		8				
	John		6				
	Matilda		2				
1342	William	HARTSELL	22	B. Smith		530	"
	Mildred		19				
1343	Mary	HOLDER	47			175	N. C.
	Willard		18	Laborer			Tenn.
	William		15				
	Harrison		14				
	George		12				
	Sarah M.		21				
1344	David	HEMBREE	44	Farmer		600	N. C.
	Adaline		47				"
	James		23	Laborer			Tenn.
	Abraham		15				
	Charlotte		13				
	Sarah A.		9				
	Miller		8				N. C.
	Lucinda		6				"
	George		2				"
1345	Joseph	HEMBREE (mwy)	19	"		20	"
	Charity		17				Tenn.
1346	William	HENRY	25	"		75	"
	Mary		26				
	Rufus		4				
	Caroline		2				

Page 187   WILTON SPRINGS   3 August 1860

	Name		Age	Occupation	Real	Pers.	Birthplace
1347	Anderson M.	ALLEN	27	Farmer		982	Tenn.
	Emaline		24				
	Martha		2				
1348	Fanny	ALLEN	47		10,000	1,881	"
	William		22				
	Lydia		20				
	Nancy		18				
	James C.		16				
	John G.		14				
1349	Russel	LILLARD	31	"	3,000	5,585	"
	Allen		9				
1350	Daniel	LEWIS	26	"		200	
	Margaret		20				
1351	Mark	LILLARD	43	"	5,000	11,505	"
	Sarah J.		34				
	Eliza "		19				
	Mary E.		18				
	Nancy M.		16				
	Charity E.		13				
	Julia F.		11				
	John F.		9				
	William G.		8				

	Name		Age	Occupation	Real	Pers.	Birthplace
	Lydia S.		7				
	Florence		5				
	Cartenden		3				
	Russel		1/12				
1352	John	LILLARD	42	"	4,000	5,674	"
	Nancy		37				
	Calvin		15				
	John D.		7				
1353	John J.	ALLEN	31	"	80	1,314	
	Elizabeth		26				
	Mary J.		7				
	William		5				
	Frances (f)		3				
	Creed		2				
1354	Samuel	BALLEW	23	Laborer		12	Va.
	Martha J.		19				"
	William		2				Tenn.
1355	Joseph	INMAN	27	Farmer		50	N. C.

Page 188   WILTON SPRINGS   3 August 1860

	Name		Age	Occupation	Real	Pers.	Birthplace
	Susannah		27				Tenn.
	Nancy J.		6				
	John		3				
	Martha		1				
1356	Jesse	CASE	23	Laborer		35	"
	Elizabeth		21				
	Henry		3				
	John		2				
1357	William	SCROGGINS	37	Farmer	200	350	"
	Eliza J.		37				N. C.
	Jacob		13				Tenn.
	John		10				
	Isaac		3				
	Elizabeth		10/12				
1358	Nelly	SMALLWOOD	26			25	"
	Rose A.		23				
	Mary		13				
	Susan		12				
	Laura		6				
	William		3				
	Thomas		2				
1359	Austin	FRASIER	27	"		300	"
	Laura		25				
1360	Mary	HOLDER	50			75	
	William		20	Laborer			
	Sarah		13				
	John		12				
	Catharine		6				
1361	Susannah		49	"			
	Isaac		13				
	William		11				

	Name		Age	Occupation	Real	Pers.	Birthplace
	Daniel		9				
	Mary C.		6				
	John		26				
	Eliza		28				
1362	Felix	McNABB	39	Farmer	4,500	1,104	"
	Nancy		39				
	Joseph		6				
1363	Morris	HARTSELL	51	"	3,000	1,680	"
	Mary		60				

Page 189   WILTON SPRINGS   3 August 1860

	Name		Age	Occupation	Real	Pers.	Birthplace
	James S.		12				Tenn.
1364	Russell	SHOEMAKER	60	Laborer		100	N. C.
	Emiline		35				"
	Robert		17	"			"
	William		13				"
	Zacharicek		11				"
	Sarah		9				"
	Rufus		5				"
	Candus		2				Tenn.
1365	George W.	HARPER	34	Farmer		375	"
	Sarah A.		32				S. C.
	Laura M.		11				Tenn.
	Lander (m)		9				
	Landon C. H.		6				
	William M.		4				
	Mary		2				
1366	John	HICKS	56	"		255	"
	Susannah		46				
	Sanders		24	Laborer			
	James		22	"			
	John		18	"			
	Charity		10				
	Moses		14				
	Nancy		12				
	William		10				
	Anderson		8				
	George		5				
1367	Royal	LANE	49	Farmer		300	"
	Ellender		48				
	Mary		19				
	Frances (f)		15				
	Royal		9				
	Ellender		6				
1368	James	DENNIS	35	"		550	"
	Margaret		33				N. C.
	Mary		7				Tenn.
	Margaret		6				
	Elizabeth		3				
	Cary (m)		1/12				

	Name		Age	Occupation	Real	Pers.	Birthplace
1369	Eliza	LARGE	35		400	425	"

Page 190   WILTON SPRINGS   3 August 1860

	Name		Age	Occupation	Real	Pers.	Birthplace
	John		11				Tenn.
	Thomas		9				
	Robert		7				
	Isaac		5				
	Allen		4				
	Ellen		61			60	S. C.
1370	Martha	GILLILAND	26			50	"
1371	Daniel	LEATHERWOOD	50	Farmer	1,000	875	"
	Elizabeth		46				Tenn.
	Thomas		24	Laborer			
	Elizabeth		23				
	Sarah		20				
	Joseph		18	"			
	Mary		17				
	Frances E. (f)		16				
	Willis L.		8				
	Nancy M.		7				
	Martha		6				
	George		5				
	Lemons (m)		3				
1372	Allen	DENNIS	37	Farmer		1,000	"
	Nancy		27				
	Joel		10				
	Margaret		8				
	Robert		6				
	Martha		4				
	Jane		1				
1373	James	WEBB	21	Laborer		125	"
	Mary E.		22				
	William		1/12				
1374	William	ODELL	27	Farmer		75	"
	Lucinda		26				
	Eliza		5				
	Nancy		3				
	Susannah		1/12				
1375	Henderson	ALLEN	22	Laborer		50	
	Nancy		19				
	Sarah		1				
1376	Anderson	PAGGET	28	Farmer	100	620	"
	Nancy A.		25				

Page 191   WILTON SPRINGS   3 August 1860

	Name		Age	Occupation	Real	Pers.	Birthplace
	Florence		5				Tenn.
	Lewis		4				
	Lander (m)		1				
1377	Zach	LEMONS	67	Laborer		50	Va.
	Sarah C.		32				Tenn.
	Ava		59				S. C.
	Joseph		11				Tenn.
	Elizabeth		1/12				

	Name		Age	Occupation	Real	Pers.	Birthplace
1378	Sarah	HUCKS	47		1,000	400	"
	Jane		13				
	Susannah		11				
	David C.		8				
1379	Joseph	WEBB	25	"		100	"
	Margaret		26				
	David C.		4				
	Mark		2				
1380	Joel W.	HUCKS	27	Farmer	600	300	"
	Charity		28				
	Sarah		7				
	Margaret		6				
	James C.		4				
	Mary J.		2				
	Anna	JAMES	54				
1381	Joel	DENNIS	74	"	2,500	680	S. C.
	Margaret		68				Tenn.
1382	Cary	DENNIS	27	"		800	"
	Lucinda		27				
	Joel		5				
	William		5/12				
1383	Robert	McMAHAN	35	"		400	"
	Nancy		31				
	Lydia		14				
	Edmon		12				
	Rebecca		8				
1383	Willis	LEATHERWOOD	50	"	1,000	500	S. C.
	Elizabeth		54				Tenn.
	Thomas		18				
	Daniel		15				
	Willis M.		12				
	John L.		10				

Page 192   WILTON SPRINGS   3 August 1860

	Name		Age	Occupation	Real	Pers.	Birthplace
	William H.		24	Laborer			
	Phillip		22	(Idiotic)			
1385	Enoch	HAROLD	60	Farmer	1,000	330	N. C.
	Rose A.		58				Tenn.
	Rebecca		21				
	John		19				
	Jesse (m)		17				
1386	John	STINNETT	27	Laborer		100	"
	Sarah		26				N. C.
1387	Collins	WILLIAMS	51	Farmer	300	400	S. C.
	Ann		47				Tenn.
	William		15	Laborer			
	Harriet		13				
	Jane		12				
	Sarah		7				

	Name		Age	Occupation	Real	Pers.	Birthplace
1388	Sanders	WILLIAMS	22	"	161	160	
	Rachael		20				
	Joel		1				
	Elizabeth		1/12				
1389	Lewis	WILLIAMS	24	"		100	
	Barbara		24				
	Nancy		7				
	Rachael		4				
	Harvey		1				
1390	William F.	BROOKS	28	Farmer		315	"
	Amanda		23				Ga.
	William		6				Tenn.
	Martha		5				
	Mary J.		3				
	John W.		8/12				
	George C.	McNABB	5				
	David A.		3				
	Martha	STEPHENS (mu)	13				Ky.
1391	James	ANDERSON	42	"		50	Tenn.
	Selina		24				
	Rose		16				
	Thomas		5				
	Alfred		2				
	Harley (?)(m)		1				
1392	Sanders	McMAHAN	31	Laborer		150	"

Page 193   WILTON SPRINGS   3 August 1860

	Name		Age	Occupation	Real	Pers.	Birthplace
	Elizabeth		23				Tenn.
	Lewis		2				
	William		6/12				
1393	James	WHITSON	23	Laborer		30	"
	Jane		20				
1394	James M.	HARTLY	40	"		50	N. C.
	Sarah J.		24				Tenn.
	Lucinda		6				
	Mary		6				
	Amanda		5/12				
1395	William	HARPER	27	Farmer	250	350	
	Sarah		22				
	John F.		4				
	Matilda		2				
1396	Ditly (m)	WHITSON	60	"	150	30	"
	Elizabeth		18				
	William		15				
1397	Calvin	ALLEN	46	"		250	
	Sarah		42				
	William A.		23	Laborer			
	George		18	"			
	Temperance		15				
	Morris		13				
	Louisa		8				

	Name		Age	Occupation	Real	Pers.	Birthplace
	Hester		6				
	Rufus		4				
	Martha		1				
1398	Cyrus	JONES (mwy)	60	Farmer	400	40	
	Lovitia		30				
	James		5				
	Lafayette		5				
	Robert		2				
1399	Thomas	JONES	35	Laborer		40	"
	Catharine		30				
	Columbus		4				
	Joel		1				
1400	Noah	BIRD	37	Farmer	2,000	900	"
	Delilah		31				
	Nancy		13				
	John D.		11				

Page 194   WILTON SPRINGS   3 August 1860

	Name		Age	Occupation	Real	Pers.	Birthplace
	James A.		7				Tenn.
	Sarah		5				
	Matilda		2				
1401	Abraham	HARTSELL	46	B.Smith	1,000	300	
	Rebecca		40				
	Brownlow		12				
	Isaac		10				
	Abraham		4				
1402	John	LANE	23	Laborer		75	
	Sarah		17				
1403	James	HICKS	50	Farmer	1,000	475	"
	Ophlia		46				
	Susannah		20				
	William		16	Laborer			
	James		14				
	Caleb		10				
	Ophlia		4				
	James W.		1				
1404	Joshua	HARTSELL	46	Farmer	1,200	580	"
	Scyntha		42				
	Elizabeth		22				
	Maranda		18				
	Eason (m)		16				
	Hannah		12				
	Russel		10				
	Joseph		6				
	Jacob		4				
	Ferdinand		1				
1405	John	KEENER	27	"	200	150	Ga.
	Mary		21				Tenn.
	William		2				
	John		18	Laborer			
	James		14	"			
	Noah M.		12				
	Harriet S.		6				

	Name		Age	Occupation	Real	Pers.	Birthplace
1406	Sims	JONES, Jr.	30	Farmer	500	260	
	Cynthia		23				
	Caleb		7				
	Ezekiel		6				
	John		3				

Page 195   WILTON SPRINGS   3 August 1860

	Name		Age	Occupation	Real	Pers.	Birthplace
	Mary A.		5/12				Tenn.
1407	Susannah	.ODELL	40		100	100	"
	Ophelia		17				
	Sarah A.		15				
	Y. J.		10				
1408	Fredrick	DENTON	40	Farmer	1,500	500	"
	Susannah		37				
	James		8				
	Nancy M.		6				
	Jane		5				
	William		4				
	Martha		1				
1409	Anderson	RUSSEL	27	Laborer		225	
	Sarah		25				
	Nancy		5/12				
1410	Ezekiel	KEENER	56		130		
	Charity		50				
1411	Abraham	KEENER	24	Farmer	500	285	
	Malinda		22				
	Laura		2				
	James		9/12				
1412	Thomas	KEENER	22	"	200	100	
	Charity		22				
1413	Carey	DENNIS	50	"	1,000	2,300	"
	Margaret		48				
	Malinda		26				
	John		24	Laborer			
	Joel		13				"
	Alexander		9				
	Carey		5				
1414	Joseph	DENNIS	20	"			"
	Lavina		17				
1415	James	WILSON	24	"		50	"
	Rachael		33				"
	Malinda		4				
	Thomas		2				
	William	LEWIS	19	"			
1416	William	LILLARD	36	Farmer	1,800	2,867	"
	Nancy		21				
	Sarah F.		4				

Page 196   WILTON SPRINGS   4 August 1860

	Name		Age	Occupation	Real	Pers.	Birthplace
	Elizabeth M.		2				
	William A.		1				

	Name		Age	Occupation	Real	Pers.	Birthplace
1417	Martin	LEWIS	47	Laborer	1,500	815	Tenn.
	Winnie		42				
	Louisa		15				
	Frelenhisen	(m)	11				
	Allen		8				
	Mildred		5				
	Carey		1				
	John	TAYLER	16				
1418	Anderson	LEWIS	23	Cabinet Maker		50	"
	Abagail		20				
	Winfield C.		7				
	Morgan		3				
1419	Nathan	MURREL	27	Farmer		226	"
	Mary		25				
	Sarah		5				
	John		3				
	Florence		1				
1420	Asa P.	LEWIS	34	"		150	"
	Susannah		34				
	Mildred		15				
	John H.		13				
	Eliza E.		3				
1421	Sanders	JENKINS	24	Laborer		220	"
	Sarah		22				
	Caswell		9/12				
1422	Abraham	DENTON, Jr.	30	Farmer		805	"
	Maranda		21				
	Susannah		4/12				
1423	Wright	BROOKS	46	"	1,000	500	S. C.
	Florence		46				Tenn.
	Elizabeth		26				
	Allen		23	Laborer			"
	Jane		22				
	Isabella	BARNET	27				
	Sarah	BROOKS	17				
	Nancy		15				
	Austin		16	Laborer			
	Eliza		9				
Page 197				WILTON SPRINGS		4 August 1860	
	Matilda		7				Tenn.
	Anderson		4				
	Laura		3				
	Lydia		8/12				
1424	David	BROOKS (mwy)	19	Laborer		350	"
	Jenetta		22				
1425	Aaron	BRYANT	41	Farmer	4,000	2,569	"
	Elizabeth		42				
	Margaret		15				
	Elizabeth		13				
	James H.		10				
	Lucinda		8				

	Name		Age	Occupation	Real	Pers.	Birthplace
	William		6				
	Harriet		2				
1426	Mary	HENRY	43			5	"
	Matilda		2				
1427	Brummet	BRYANT	46	Minister (Old Bapt.)	3,000	5,705	"
	Elizabeth		38				
	Brummet		18	Laborer			"
	Jane		14				
	Sarah		12				
	Ann		10				
	Perlina		5				
	William		2				
1428	Austin	HALL	46	Farmer	1,500	1,591	N. C.
	Elvira		46				"
	Richard	McCARTER	19	Laborer			Tenn.
	Mary	HALL	78				N. C.
1429	John	LEWIS (Bl)	60	Farmer		211	N. C.
	Nancy		60				Va.
	Margaret		20				Tenn.
1430	George	BAXTER	22	"		393	"
	Nancy		21				
	Aaron		3				
	Elizabeth		4/12				
1431	Samuel	GREGORY	46	"		188	"
	Rebecca		35				"
	Sarah		17				
	James		15	Laborer			
	Martha		14				

Page 198   TAYLORSBURG   4 August 1860

	Name		Age	Occupation	Real	Pers.	Birthplace
	Archibald		15	Laborer			
	Margaret		3				
	Henry		1				
1432	James	SHEPHEARD	35	Farmer		221	Tenn.
	Rebecca		35				
	Elihu		6				
	Cynthia		4				
	George		2				
1493	John	MURREL	42	"	3,500	2,000	"
	Temperance		45				
	William		16	Laborer			
	Sarah		14				
	James T.		12				
	Mildred		9				
	Nancy C.		7				
	Charity		5				
	Isaac A. J.		1				
1434	Jacob	DENTON	65	"		100	Tenn.
	Deborah		65				

	Name		Age	Occupation	Real	Pers.	Birthplace
1435	John P.	DENTON	26	Blacksmith		300	
	Mary		24				
	Jonathan		3				
	Frances (f)		1				
	Sarah		60				
1436	John	HATLEY	65	Miller		100	N. C.
	Elizabeth		60				
	Thomas		23	(Idiotic)			Tenn.
1437	Margaret	CLICK	45		2,000	200	"
	Mary A.		18				
	Henry		16	Laborer			
	Emaline		14				
	Dorcus		10				
	Andrew J.		8				
1438	James	ANDERSON	29	"		117	
	Julia		34				
	Eliza		11				
	Saline		9				
	Thomas		7				
	Elizabeth		6				
	William		5				

Page 199   TAYLORSBURG   4 August 1860

	Name		Age	Occupation	Real	Pers.	Birthplace
1439	Elijah	FINCHEM	21	Farmer		50	Tenn.
	Elizabeth		17				
	Harriet		1				
	Frances (f)		21				
	Wesley		1				
1440	David E.	MILLER	55	"	1,000	240	"
	Elizabeth		30				"
	William		18	Laborer			
	George W.		9				
	Robert		7				
	Nancy		4				
	Owen		2				
	Sarah		5/12				
	Joseph		5/12				
1441	Austin	GREEN	25	"		150	"
	Mary		33				
	Elizabeth		2				
1442	Samuel	DENTON	55	Farmer		50	"
	Augusta		31				
	Nelson		15	Laborer			
	Michael		11				
	William		3				
	Jane		1				
1443	James	HICKS	47	Farmer		150	
	Orphy		45				
	William		14				
	James		11				
	Caleb		8				
	Henry		5				
	Wilie		9/12				

	Name		Age	Occupation	Real	Pers.	Birthplace
1444	George	CLARK	39	Laborer		40	N. C.
	Nancy		37				"
	Mary		17				Tenn.
	Moses		15				
	Sarah		13				
	Ezekiel		10				
	Catharine		8				
	Nancy		5				
	Charity		2				
	Thomas		1				

Page 200   TAYLORSBURG   4 August 1860

	Name		Age	Occupation	Real	Pers.	Birthplace
1445	Lawson	SUTTON	33	Farmer	500	250	Tenn.
	Mary		27				
	Louise		8				
	Mildred		2				
	Jane		5/12				
	William	WOOTNEY	12				
1446	Alfred	SUTTON	59	Laborer		50	"
	Rebecca		25				"
1447	Rubin	GREEN	44	"		40	Va.
	Julia		26				Tenn.
	Harriet		12				
	James		10				
1448	Lawson	SISK	59	Farmer	2,000	2,156	Va.
	Sarah		50				Tenn.
	Branson		19	Laborer			"
	Carson		17	"			
	Addison		15	"			
	Nancy		11				
	Sarah		9				
1449	George	ROBERTS	30	Farmer	2,000	806	"
	Eliza M.		28				
	John		10				
	Emma J.		4				
	William		1				
1450	Sarah	ROBERTS	62		500	955	"
	Anna		28				
	Charity		26				
	Harriet	CATES	24				
	Texanna		4/12				
	Louisa	ROBERTS	20				
1451	Gipson	WOODS	44	"	2,500	5,456	
	James		18	Laborer			
	Nancy		17				
	Toliver		15				
	Elizabeth		13				
	Phebe		11				
	Mary D.		9				
	Fanny		8				
	John B.		6				

	Name		Age	Occupation	Real	Pers.	Birthplace
1452	John B.	DENTON	41	Farmer	2,000	2,608	"

TAYLORSBURG 6 August 1860

	Name		Age	Occupation	Real	Pers.	Birthplace
	Mary		30				Tenn.
	Thomas J.		2.2?				
	James A.		7				
	Francis M.	(m)	4				
1453	Frances (f)	DENTON	70			100	
1454	George	ALLEN	44	Farmer		218	"
	Catharine		44				"
	James		21	Laborer			Mo.
	William		15				"
	Margaret		12				Tenn.
	Sarah		10				
	Anderson		7				
	Margaret		5				
1455	Samuel	PATTERSON (Bl)	58	Farmer		414	N. C.
	Cyntha	(Bl)	63				"
	Evaline	(Bl)	33				Tenn.
	Samuel	(Bl)	14				"
	Marusha J.	(Bl)	6				"
	Mary E.	(Bl)	9				"
	Sarah	(Bl)	60				"
	Nancy	(Bl)	25				"
1456	Hamilton	LEWIS	39	Bricklayer	2,500	200	"
	Eliza J.		34				
	Elbert		10				
	Dorthula		7				
	Alla		4				
	Leanner (f)		1				
1457	William	RUTHERFORD	35	Farmer		180	"
	Ruth A.		28				
	Lewis		14				
	Eliza J.		6				
	Nancy		5				
	Rachael		3				
	William		2				
	Elizabeth		1				
1458	William	IVY	23	Laborer		20	"
	Elizabeth		15				
1459	Lewis	CLICK	59	Farmer	5,000	2,600	"
	Rachael		60				Va.
	Lewis		23				Tenn.

TAYLORSBURG 6 August 1860

	Name		Age	Occupation	Real	Pers.	Birthplace
	Jane		19				Tenn.
	William		14				
1460	James	WEBB	44	Sawyer		482	"
	Louisa		43				
	Martha		19				
	Mary		17				

Name		Age	Occupation	Real	Pers.	Birthplace
Nancy		15				
Laurena		12				
Franklin		9				
Sarah		6				
Margaret		3				
1461 Russel	BAKER	25	Farmer	600	477	"
Matilda		24				
Catharine		·3				
Mary		2				
McCorell		1				
1462 William	HATLEY	36	"	100	800	"
Nancy		40				
Orpha		12				
Elizabeth		10				
Rachael		8				
Sarah		6				
Elijah		5				
Allen		4				
Rachael	ODELL	76		250		"
1463 Houston	SISK	33	"	2,400	564	"
Louisa		30				
Anna	McGAHA	5				
1464 Jacob	TEMPLIN	63	"	3,000	1,500	"
Catharine		61				
Isaac		25	Laborer			
David		22				
Jane		20				
1465 Richard	TEMPLIN	31	Farmer	300	814	"
Mildred		28				
William F.		7				
Mary J.		5				
Isaac		1				
1466 Russel	BUTLER	25	"	400	265	"
Nancy		21				

Page 203   TAYLORSBURG   6 August 1860

Name		Age	Occupation	Real	Pers.	Birthplace
Richard		3				
John		2				
Mary		6/12				
1467 Sarah	WILSON	40		500	520	Tenn.
William		20	Laborer			"
George		17	"			
Bird (m)		12				
Joseph		13				
Mary		11				
Sarah		5				
Elizabeth	BIRD	90				N. C.
1468 David L.	DENTON	27				Tenn.
Mary J.		23				
George W.		4				
Sarah M.		3				
Joseph		2				

	Name		Age	Occupation	Real	Pers.	Birthplace
1469	Reubin	SAMPLES	28	Laborer		35	"
	Elizabeth		27				
	James N.		5				
	Josiah		4				
	George W.		9/12				
1470	E. L.	MORRIS	25	Farmer		1,300	"
	Matilda		22				
	Ellen		1				
1471	Y. J.	MORRIS	50	Minister (Bapt)	500	290	"
	Cynthia		53				Va.
	William R.		23	Merchant		1,300	Tenn.
	Caroline		18				
	Elijah		16	Laborer			
	Pleasant		14				
	Penelope		11				
	Casander		9				
1472	John	BIRD	30	Farmer	400	430	"
	Martha M.		21				
	Andrew J.		2				
	Lavina	HICKS	17				
1473	John	HICKS	32	"	1,000	320	"
	Mary		29				
	Martha		8				
	Russel		6				

Page 204   TAYLORSBURG   6 August 1860

	Name		Age	Occupation	Real	Pers.	Birthplace
	William		4				Tenn.
	John T.		1				
	David	SIMMENS	22	Laborer			"
1474	Nancy	STUART	70		400	782	"
	Fanny		40				
	Sarah		28				
	Nancy		35				
	William		25	Farmer			
	James		20	Laborer			
1475	Andrew	STUART	30	Farmer		500	
	Emaline		26				
	Rufus		5				
	Mary		4				
	Harriet		2				
	Lydia		5/12				
1476	Blackburn	SISK	51	Farmer	4,000	800	
	Eliza		23				
	Florence		19				
	Lucinda		8				
1477	Campbell	SISK	27	"		263	
	Mary J.		18				
	Blackburn		1				
1478	Mark	SISK	25	"		338	
	Margaret		20				
	Sarah		1				

	Name		Age	Occupation	Real	Pers.	Birthplace
1479	Fowler	AMBROSE (mwy)	30	Mill Right		300	"
	Elizabeth		17				
1480	William	SISK	34	Farmer		541	
	Ellen		27				
	Minerva		7				
	Leonard		2				
	Elizabeth		4/12				
	Daniel	HENRY	12				
	Margaret		11				
1481	Willis	GRAY	65	"	3,000	8,640	Va.
	Phebe		65				"
	James		87				"
1482	Francis	McGAHA	33	"	500	600	Tenn.
	Mildred		28				
	Margaret		7				
Page 205				TAYLORSBURG			6 August 1860
	William		5				Tenn.
	Sarah J.		4				"
	Joseph M.		1				"
	Nancy	MURR	60		500		Va.
1483	Isaac	BUTLER	53	Farmer	3,000	875	Tenn.
	Martha		50				
	Elizabeth		25				
	Samuel		16				
	Mildred		18				
	Martha		14				
	William		10				
	James		7				
1484	Mary	RIDENS	56		200	80	"
1485	John	BUTLER	23	Farmer		270	"
	Rose		18				
1486	Hugh	NORRIS	50	"	1,200	650	N. C.
	Harriet		33				Tenn.
	Morris		20	Laborer			
	Isaac		15	"			
	Susannah		13				
	Hannah		11				
	Nancy		9				
	Sarah E.		7				
	George W.		5				
	Martha		2				
	William		5/12				
1487	George F.	NORRIS	30	Farmer		275	"
	Mary		30				
	Samuel		12				
	James		11				
	Mary A.		10				
	Sarah J.		8				
	Elizabeth		5				
	Martha		2				

	Name		Age	Occupation	Real	Pers.	Birthplace
1488	Saml.	COCHRAN	67	"	1,500	400	"
	Elizabeth		62				Va.
	Caroline		18				Tenn.
1489	Jackson	COCHRAN	27	"		400	"
	Mary		22				
	Samuel		2				

Page 206   TAYLORSBURG   6 August 1860

	Name		Age	Occupation	Real	Pers.	Birthplace
1490	Isaac	COCHRAN	33	Farmer		320	Tenn.
	Mary A.		26				
	James W.		10				
	William A.		8				
	Martha		5				
	Margaret		3				
	John		1				
	Saml.	HICKS	62				
1491	Elizabeth	FOX	62		90	30	Va.
	Robert		33	Laborer			Tenn.
	William		21	"			
1492	Elizabeth	BRYANT	55		300	300	Va.
	Mary		25				Tenn.
	Sarah		20				
	Charles		19	"			
	Brummet		16	"			
	William W.		5				
	Margaret		3				
	Julia		1				
1493	Sarah	HICKS	60			60	"
	Nancy		27				
	Lucinda		35				
	Jonathan		26	"			
	Narcissa		7				
	Martha		5				
	Mary J.		3				
1494	James	BIRD	31	Farmer	900	600	"
	Nancy		30				
	Anderson		10				
	Albert		9				
	Mary J.		5				
	John		3				
	Noah		7/12				
1495	John	MURREL, Jr.	34	"		430	"
	Cynthia		36				
	John		17	Laborer			
	Elizabeth		15				
	Lavina		13				
	William		9				
1496	David	HICKS	26	Farmer		200	"

Page 207   TAYLORSBURG   7 August 1860

	Name		Age	Occupation	Real	Pers.	Birthplace
	Susannah		32				Tenn.
	Mary		7				"

	Name		Age	Occupation	Real	Pers.	Birthplace
	Nancy		5				"
	Lavina		1				"
1497	John	GREGORY	20	Laborer		100	"
	Jane		17				
1498	Job	MURREL	55	Farmer	4,000	1,200	Va.
	Mary		58				"
	Benjamin		22	Laborer			Tenn.
	Nancy		16				
	Job		18	"			
	Sarah		15				
1499	John	MURR	23	"		175	"
	Mary		21				
	Caroline		2				
	Austin		5/12				
1500	John	LEWIS	30	"		100	"
	Almeda		28				
	Catharine		6				
	Mary		4				
	Martha L.		1				
1501	William	OWEN	73	"		75	N. C.
	Martha		45				"
	Nancy		26				"
	Alfred		25				"
	Amanda J.		23				"
	Franklin		21				"
	John		18				"
	Mary		15				"
	Perry		13				Tenn.
	Eliza		12				
1502	Austin	BRANCH	36	Farmer	2,000	1,446	
	Lavina		33				
	Mary A.		12				
	William		10				
	Sarah		7				
	David P.		5				
	Jonathan C.		3				
	Louisa		1/12				
1503	Wilie	HICKS	40	"	1,200	450	"

Page 208   TAYLORSBURG   7 August 1860

	Name		Age	Occupation	Real	Pers.	Birthplace
	Mary		40				Tenn.
	Jane		21				"
	James D.		19	Laborer			"
	Aaron		12				"
	William		10				"
	Elijah		7				"
	Martha		5				"
	Susannah		9/12				"
1504	William	MASHBURN	63	Farmer		150	N. C.
	Lydia		57				"
	Allen		32	Laborer			

	Name		Age	Occupation	Real	Pers.	Birthplace
	Thomas		27	"			"
	Emaline		21				"
	Anderson		15				"
	Drucilla		10				"
1505	Israel	CRAWLY	45	"		40	N. C.
	Jane		36				"
	Louisa		15				"
	James		12				Tenn.
	William		9				"
	Lydia		7				"
	Mary		3				"
	Mary		65				N. C.
1506	Aaron	MASHB.ERN	27	"		40	Tenn.
	Sarah		45				N. C.
	Sarah		15				"
	Emaline		11				"
1507	Saml.	LEWIS	64	Farmer	100	520	Va.
	Susannah		54				Tenn.
	Martha		31				
	John C.		30	Laborer			
	Griffin		22	"			
	Elizabeth		24				
	James		16	"			
	Samuel		14				
	Susannah		11				
	Anderson		9				
1508	Rutherford	ROSE	46	Farmer		265	S. C.
	Elizabeth		47				Tenn.
	Mary		13				

Page 209   TAYLORSBURG   7 August 1860

	Name		Age	Occupation	Real	Pers.	Birthplace
	Lucinda		11				Tenn.
	Martha		2				
1509	Silas	OWENSBY	28	Laborer		30	N. C.
	Sarah		25				Tenn.
	Priscilla		3				
	Rutherford		9/12				
1510	Brummet	ROSE (mwy)	17	"		100	"
	Cynthia		17				
1511	Martin	ECTON	30	Farmer		280	
	Sarah		26				
	Samuel	BIRD	10				
1512	John	ECTON	70	"	100	285	"
	Elizabeth		58				
	Elizabeth		30				
	Martin		24	Laborer			
	Dricilla		22				
	Albert		22	Laborer			
	Emaline		21				

	Name		Age	Occupation	Real	Pers.	Birthplace
1513	William	DUNCAN	52	Bricklayer	1,000	300	Va.
	Catharine		28				Tenn.
	John		28	Laborer			Va.
	James		16	"			Tenn.
	Jane		18				
	Robert		14				
	William		12				
	Elizabeth		10				
	Dud (m)		3				
	Julia		1				
	William	CARTER	14				
	Edward		11				Va.
1514	Thomas	HARTGROVE	67	Farmer	1,000	880	Va.
	Matilda		60				"
	Henry		33	Laborer (Idiotic)			Tenn.
	Priscilla		32				
	Matilda		22	(")			
	William		21	"			
1515	William	ECTON	36	"		350	"
	Harriet		23				
	Mary A.		10				
	Andrew J.		8				

Page 210   TAYLORSBURG   8 August 1860

	Name		Age	Occupation	Real	Pers.	Birthplace
	Martin		6				Tenn.
	Mariah		2				
1516	William	HICKS (mwy)	23	Laborer		300	"
	Jane		18				
1517	Dennis	BIRD	58	Farmer	5,000	650	Va.
	Nancy		49				"
	John	BREEDEN	13				Tenn.
	Margaret	McGAHA	10				
1518	Perry	MURREL	30	"	350	500	"
	Elizabeth		30				
	Jane		9				
	William		7				
	Susannah		5				
	Mary A.		3				
	James		1				
1519	Peter	HUFF	49	Farmer	250	150	"
	Elizabeth		42				N. C.
	Martha		16				Tenn.
	Mary J.		15				"
	William		13				Ga.
	Stephen		10				"
	James		9				"
	Anderson		6				
1520	Nancy	HUFF	56		600	300	Va.
1521	Jefferson	DENTON	50		1,000	500	Tenn.
	Charity		42				
	Margaret		18				
	James		10				
	John		5				

	Name		Age	Occupation	Real	Pers.	Birthplace
1522	Elizabeth	DENTON	44		600	200	
1523	John	HUFF	38	"	1,000	600	
	Rebecca		31				
	Samuel		10				
	William		8				
	John		5				
	Sarah		2				
	George W.		1/12				
	Mary	POTTER	22				
1524	George	DENTON	28	"		200	"
	Nancy		18				

Page 211   TAYLORSBURG   8 August 1860

	Name		Age	Occupation	Real	Pers.	Birthplace
1525	Elijah	BREEDEN	71	Farmer	600	1,065	Tenn.
	Sarah		68				Va.
	Matilda	BIRD	30				Tenn.
1526	Nancy	LANE	72		800	270	N. C.
	Mary		28				Tenn.
	Sarah		26				
	John	WEBB	45	Laborer			"
	Elizabeth	POTTER	82				Va.
1527	Nancy	RUTHERFORD	40			25	Tenn.
	Joseph		16				"
	Elizabeth		14				
	Caroline		12				
1528	William	MURR	50	Farmer	500	575	Ala.
	Martha		22				Tenn.
	Wesley		20	Laborer			
	Nancy		18				
	Isaac		16	"			
	Noah		14				
	Albert		10				
	James		5				
	William		3				
	Joseph		1/12				
1529	James R.	DENTON	23	Farmer		300	"
	Mary		18				
	William		2/12				
1530	Anderson A.	VINSON	31	"	3,500	2,140	"
	Matilda		28				
	Winfield S.		5				
	Julia C.		3				
	Mary L.		1				
	Daniel W.		4/12				
1531	Wm.	WILLIAMS	25	Laborer		130	
	Harriet		25				
	John		2				
1532	William	GERREL	30	Farmer		704	"
	Mary		24				
	Thomas		3				
	Sarah A.		2				

	Name		Age	Occupation	Real	Pers.	Birthplace
1533	G. W.	LAREW	42	'	15,000	8,658	"
	Sarah		37				

	Name		Age	Occupation	Real	Pers.	Birthplace
	Ann E.		15				Tenn.
	Willis		13				"
	Martha S.		12				
	William		6				
	George A.		4				
1534	John	FINNEY	28	Laborer		25	N. C.
	Elizabeth		28				"
	Susannah		12				"
	William		10				"
	Thomas		8				"
1535	Wm. R.	CODY	24	"		75	"
	Lucinda		25				"
	James A.		10				Tenn.
	Elizabeth		7				
	Sarah		5				
	Cynthia		3/12				
1536	William	HUDSON	31	Farmer		87	N. C.
	Leannah		35				"
	Caroline		12				"
	Jane		6				Tenn.
	Nancy		4				
	Emaline		3				
1537	Robt.	HENRY	55	"	1,000	870	"
	Elizabeth		44				
	Luallen (m)		24	Laborer			
	Robt. H.		20	"			
	Sarah A.		17				
	John M.		14				
	Elizabeth		13				
	Margaret		11				
	Gustavus A.		8				
	Mary		6				
	William		3				
	Franklin		1/2				
1538	Thomas H.	JAMES	44	Farmer	1,600	478	S. C.
	Sarah		30				Tenn.
	Johnson		19				"
	William		17				
	Samuel		12				
	Elizabeth		11				

	Name		Age	Occupation	Real	Pers.	Birthplace
	Margaret		9				Tenn.
	Benjamin		7				
	Mahala		5				
	Loretta J.		3				
1539	William	JAMES	79	Laborer		40	Va.

	Name		Age	Occupation	Real	Pers.	Birthplace
1540	W. E.	ALLEN	31	Farmer		1,521	Tenn.
	Mary C.		19				"
	Luella A.		1				"
1541	L. S.	GORMAN	46	"	10,000	14,220	"
	Delilah		40				N. C.
1542	F. D.	CLARK	41	"	15,000	10,224	Tenn.
	Mary J.		24				
	James		8				
	Francis (m)		6				
	Robert H.		4				
	Elizabeth		1				
1543	Wm.	LANE	60	Laborer		125	"
	Mary		60				"
	Mary		40				"
1544	Joseph	RUTHERFORD	49	Farmer	2,500	I,521	
	Mary J.		35				
	William		9				
	Anne E.		7				
	Mary R.		5				
	Joseph M.		4				
	Newton M.		6/12				
	Sarah E.	HOLT	17				
1545	Richard	BATES (Bl)	35	Laborer		150	
	Elizabeth	(Mu)	25				
	Eliza	(Bl)	17				
	John	(Bl)	15				
	Sally	(Mu)	6				
	George	(Mu)	8/12				
1546	David	GORMAN	56	Farmer	6,900	4,439	"
	Ruth		42				
	George		20	Laborer			
	John		19				
	James		16				
	Jacob		14				
	Rose A.		12				

Page 214   NEWPORT   9 August 1860

	Delilah		10				Tenn.
	Juditha		9				
	Daniel		6				
	Margaret	KINGRY	31				
	Josephine		5				
1547	Alvy	GRAY	36	Farmer		345	"
	Mary		26				Va.
	Sarah		5				Tenn.
	Julia		4				"
	Fanny		8/12				"
1548	David F.	GORMAN	24	Miller		400	"
	Jane		19				"
	Elizabeth		2				"
	George		8/12				"

	Name		Age	Occupation	Real	Pers.	Birthplace
1549	Thomas	GORMAN	27	Laborer		100	
	Caron		24				Ala.
	John		8				Ga.
	Rose		5				"
	Delilah		4				"
	Geeyr (m)		1				Tenn.
	Nancy	GOODWIN	21				Ala.
1550	William	BIRD	35	Farmer	500	378	Tenn.
	Eliza J.		33				"
	Martha		12				
	Nancy M.		8				
	Sarah		6				
	Asa P.		4				
	Daniel		3				
	William		2				
1551	George A.	PRUITT	35	"		354	"
	Elizabeth		32				
	Elizabeth		9				
	James		6				
	Willard		4				
	Frank		1				
1552	Saml.	BARNS	46	"	500	150	N. C.
	Nancy		40				
	James		16				Tenn.
	Elizabeth		13				
	Samuel		8				"

Page 215   NEWPORT   9 August 1860

	Name		Age	Occupation	Real	Pers.	Birthplace
1553	John	BARNS	24	Laborer			N. C.
	Elizabeth		21				Tenn.
	Nancy		1				
1554	Cornelius	BRINKLY	42	Farmer	1,000	1,482	N. C.
	Julia		42				"
	Mary		20				N. C.
	Clementine		18				"
	Elizabeth		16				"
	Cornilia		14				"
	John		8				Tenn.
	Delilah		3				
1555	Saml.	McGINTY	44	"	4,000	1,971	N. C.
	Mary		37				Tenn.
	George		4				"
	Mary		4				"
	Nimrod	LANE	27	Laborer			"
1556	Joseph J.	ONEAL	55	Farmer	4,000	6,829	Va.
	Nancy		55				Tenn.
	William		27	Laborer			
	Margaret		17				
	Joseph		25	"			
	Nancy		15				
	Jesse (m)		14				

	Name		Age	Occupation	Real	Pers.	Birthplace
1557	James	ONEAL	22	Farmer		592	
	Orlena		19				
	John O.		1				
1558	Josiah	SAMPLE	57	"		310	Va.
	Lydia		54				"
	John		22	Laborer			Tenn.
	Elizabeth		19				
	Mary		17				
	Joseph		13				
	Reese		15	"			
	Jasper		11				
1559	Marshal	HENRY	21	"		50	"
	Nancy		19				
	Thomas		1				
	Lina		45				

Page 216 NEWPORT   9 August 1860

1560	Sarah	SMITH	50		17,000	5,150	"
	Sarah		23				
	Jeremiah		21	Laborer			
	John		19	"			
	Simon		17	"			
	Isabell		16				
	Nancy		19				
	Abagail		12				
	Sarah		100				Ga.
1561	Alex E.	SMITH	26	Farmer		4,695	Tenn.
	Amanda		21				
1562	Joseph	MANNING	54	Minister (Bapt.)	3,000	4,375	"
	Lucinda		55				
	James		34	Farmer			
1563	Mildred	MORRIS	55		7,540	7,740	"
	William F.		34	"			
	James H.		20	Laborer			
1564	William	CAFFEE	52	Farmer	5,000	1,710	"
	Sarah		31				
	William		21	Laborer			
	John		18	"			
	Sarah J.		15				
	Joshua		9				
	Louisa		7				
	Martha		4				
	Charity		2				
	Harriet		1				
	Martha	FOWLER	52				
1565	John W.	CLARK	36	Farmer	2,000	3,977	"
	Zilpha		31				
	Nancy		10				
	Lenorah		7				
	David		5				
	Mary		3				
1566	John	THOMASON	36	"	2,500	3,030	"
	Mary J.		34				
	Nancy		10				

	Name		Age	Occupation	Real	Pers.	Birthplace
	Joseph		9				
	James		2				
	Mary		22				
1567	John	ALLEN	24	"		200	"
	Elizabeth		28				

	Name		Age	Occupation	Real	Pers.	Birthplace
	James		1				
	Volentine	THOMASON	10				
1568	Moses	MANNING	36	Farmer		25	S. C.
	Nancy		58				"
	Christopher C.		16	Laborer			Tenn.
1569	John	FREE	73		150	100	S. C.
	Mary		27	(Insane)			Tenn.
1570	Price	HOLLOWAY	26	"		20	Ala.
	Elijah		3				Tenn.
	William		8/12				
1571	Isaac	BRUMLY	51	"		158	
	Mary		39				
	Susannah		19				
	Elizabeth		17				
	Robert		15				
1572	Jesse	ATCHLY	25	Farmer		427	"
	Ellen E.		25				
	Mary		5				
	Martha		3				
	Louisa		8/12				
1573	C. A.	HENRY	26	"		215	"
	Martha		22				
	Samuel		4				
	Joseph S.		1				
1574	Ellender	TAYLOR	70			177	Md.
	Marshal		17	Laborer			Tenn.
	James	VAYN	15	"			
	Ellen		13				
1575	Joseph A.	HIX	42	Farmer	3,000	4,298	"
	Ann		28				
	David B.		10				
	Martha		7				
	Sarah		5				
	William A.		3				
	Mary A.		1				
	Lee	EVANS	20	Laborer			
1576	G. W.	McKINNEY	30	"		200	S. C.
	Martha		25				"
	Elvira		1				
1577	Thomas W.	DAVIS	34	Farmer		202	N. C.

	Name		Age	Occupation	Real	Pers.	Birthplace
	Elizabeth		28				N. C.

	Name		Age	Occupation	Real	Pers.	Birthplace
	Catharine		13				Tenn.
	Mary J.		11				
	William		9				
	Franklin		6				
	Sarah		1				
1578	Stephen D.	SMITH	50	Laborer		150	"
	Mary		50				
	Nancy E.		26				
	Nicholas		24				
	Josiah		21				
	Mary E.		16				
	James		12				
	George A.		8				
1579	Joseph	HURLEY	31	Farmer	1,500	1,524	"
	Amanda		25				
	David		6				
	Barney		5				
	Meleil (?)	(m)	2				
	Jacob	ROBERTS (Bl)	50				
1580	James O.	HARRIS	50	Laborer		25	Va.
	Mary A.		18				"
	James		16	"			Tenn.
	Martha		13				
	William		24	"			Va.
1581	Daniel C.	HURLEY	32	Farmer	2,800	2,260	Tenn.
	Louisa		31				
	George W.		12				
	Caleb		11				
	Laura		6				
	Daniel		4				
	Eliza		2				
1582	Harrison	GRAY	30	"		338	"
	Elizabeth		27				
	Mary		1				
1583	Shadrach	REN	23	Laborer		250	
	Catharine		21				
	Margaret	COEN	86				Va.
1584	William	GRAY, Sr.	60	Farmer	3,300	583	"
	Fanny		57				
Page 219				NEWPORT		9 August 1860	
	Thursey		25				Tenn.
	Sarah		17				
	Newton		21	Laborer			
1585	Henry	HOLLOWAY	40	Farmer		100	N. C.
	Elizabeth		40				Tenn.
	Jane		14				"
	Thomas		13				
	Elizabeth	GRAY	25				"
1586	Abraham	FINE	71		7,500	9,506	"
	Elizabeth		65				S. C.

	Name		Age	Occupation	Real	Pers.	Birthplace
	Mary		20				Tenn.
	Francis (m)	SMITH	17	Laborer			Tenn.
1587	Rebecca	CLARK	32			5,500	"
	Mary		12				
	William		10				
	Thomas		7				
1588	Sarah C.	WILSON	70		1,200	2,978	Ga.
	Sarah C.		32			3,000	Tenn.
	James	OTTINGER	34	Farmer	1,220	2,820	"
	Laura A.		3				"
	William H.		2/12				
1589	G. W.	CARTER	51	"	25,000	11,200	"
	Nancy		42				
	Juliet		24				
	Emaline		22				
	George		19	Laborer			
	David C.		10				
	Mary		9				
	Francis (m)		8				
	Robert		7				
	Elizabeth		5				
1590	Arch	CLEVINGER	50	"		.5	"
	Rachael		45				"
	Catharine		14				
	George		12				
	Mary		10				
	Isaac		8				
	Joseph		6				
	Florence		5				
1591	Soloman	MAGUIRE	40	"		100	N. C.

	Name		Age	Occupation	Real	Pers.	Birthplace
	Lydia		35				Tenn.
	Frank		9				
	Nancy		7				
	George		1				
1592	Neverson	COLLINS	35	Laborer		40	N. C.
	Susannah		"				S. C.
	Mary J.		17				Tenn.
	Charlie		15				
	John		9				
	Caroline		6				
	William		5				
	Addison (m)		8/12				
1593	George	FREE	45	Farmer	100	25	S. C.
	Malinda		41				Tenn.
	Sarah		21				
	Mary		20				
	Jane		15				
	Elizabeth		12				
	William		9				
	George		7	(Idiotic)			

	Name		Age	Occupation	Real	Pers.	Birthplace
1594	Julia	WILLIAMS	36		200	175	"
	William		19				
	George		11				
	Margaret		4				
	Samuel		1				
1595	R. L.	MOSELY	57	Farmer	600	400	"
	Mary		45				
	Eugene		18	Laborer			
	Susannah		16				
	Hannah		15				
	Mariah		12				
	George		10				
	Luther		8				
	Sarah		7				
	William		6				
	Matilda		5				
	Mathew		4				
	Ezekel		3				
	Moses		2				
1596	Alex	MOORE	53	"		138	N. C.

Page 221   NEWPORT   9 August 1860

	Name		Age	Occupation	Real	Pers.	Birthplace
	Rachael		50				N. C.
	Adolphus		22				"
	Rebecca C.		19				"
	John T. S.		13				"
	Laura		9				Tenn.
	Jacob		6				
1597	John	HANER (Bl)	68	Farmer	500	130	"
	Sarah	(")	70				N. C.
1598	Eliza	FRAZIER (")	38			50	"
	Jacob	(")	39	Laborer			Tenn.
	Rose	(")	15				"
	Mary A.	(")	8				
	Sarah J.	(")	6				
	Marion (m)	(")	3				
1599	Pink NICHOLS	(")	46	Laborer		150	N. C.
	Lavina	(")	44				Tenn.
	Sarah	(")	19				"
	Martha	(")	17				
	Ellen	(")	15				
	John	(")	3				
	Leander	(")	11				
	Ann	(")	9				
	Catharine	(")	7				
	Mary	(")	5				
	William	(")	2				
1600	Alex MASON	(Mu)	34	Painter		500	"
	Lucy	(")	32				
	William	(")	6				
	Cynthia	(")	4				
	Mary	(")	2				
	Charlie	(")	4/12				

	Name		Age	Occupation	Real	Pers.	Birthplace
1601	Redenick	MURR	50	Laborer	100	50	S. C.
	Elizabeth		45				Tenn.
	Alexander		20				S. C.
	Christian		17				Tenn.
	Edmond		15				
	Jas. H.		9				
	Michaux		7				
	Samuel		6				
	Mary A.		3				

Page 222   NEWPORT   9 August 1860

	Name		Age	Occupation	Real	Pers.	Birthplace
1602	Charles	CASE	26	Farmer	400	173	Tenn.
	Mary E.		22				N. C.
	William M.		2				Tenn.
1603	John	HAMPTON	62	Laborer		200	Va.
	Elender		60				N. C.
	Leander		21	(Blind)			"
	David		18	Laborer			Tenn.
	Jane		84				N. C.
1604	John M.	HAMPTON	35	Farmer		80	"
	Melvina		36				"
	Sermansha (f)		11				Tenn.
	Daniel		7				
	William E.		5				
	Sarah		3				
1605	C.C.	HAMPTON	27	Laborer		100	N. C.
	Sarah		24				Tenn.
	James A.		5				
	Lewis		3				
	Elizabeth		1				
1606	Allen	BEARD	40	Laborer		150	S. C.
	Margarett		36				Tenn.
	Nancy		23				"
	John		22	Laborer			
	Eliza		12				
	Martha		8				
	Sarah		6				
	Charlotte		4				
1607	Job	WHITE	28	"		100	N. C.
	Susannah		25				"
	James		7				"
	Mary A.		4				"
1608	Isaac	LANE	38	Laborer		200	Tenn.
	Elizabeth		18				"
	Anderson		13				
	Mary		10				
	John		8				
1609	William	STRANGE	45	Farmer		942	Tenn.
	Mary		43				N. C.
	Mary J.		20				Tenn.
	William		17	Laborer			"

	Name		Age	Occupation	Real	Pers.	Birthplace
Page 223				WILTON SPRINGS		10 August 1860	
	John W.		15	Laborer			Tenn.
	Martha		13				
	Francis M.		12				N. C.
	Waddle		10				"
	Jacob		10				"
	Elizabeth		8				Tenn.
	Margarett		5				"
1610	Henry	CASE	30	Laborer		25	"
	Julia		23				
	William M.		2				
	George		3/12				
	Biddy		43				N. C.
	Elizabeth		18				Tenn.
1611	Moses	PINNEL	58	Farmer	1,500	585	N. C.
	Hannah		50				"
	Joel		22	Laborer			"
	Alexander		18	"			"
	Zitta		13				"
	Ona	HOLLOWAY	6				Tenn.
1612	Henry	TAYLOR	30	Farmer		406	"
	Mary	"	25				N. C.
	Matilda		8				Tenn.
	John		6				"
	Moses		3				
	Mary		5				
	Malissa		4/12				
1613	James	ALLEN	21	Farmer		2,420	Tenn.
	Rebecca		16				
	Mary A.		1/12				
	C.C.	CARTER	48	Farmer	15,000	500	Tenn.
1614	Wesly	DAVIS	36	Farmer		700	N. C.
	Margaret		26				"
	Crockett		3				Tenn.
	Fulton		1				
1615	William	BECK	52	Laborer		50	N. C.
	Sarah		30				Tenn.
	Solomon		16	Laborer			
	Rachael		14				
	Jacob		11				
	Mary		8				
Page 224				NEWPORT		10 August 1860	
	John C.		5				Tenn.
	Jane		4				"
	Francis D. C.	(m)	2/12				
1616	James	SAMPLES	22	Laborer		50	"
	Malinda		22				N. C.
	William		5/12				Tenn.

1860 U. S. CENSUS OF COCKE COUNTY, TENNESSEE

	Name		Age	Occupation	Real	Pers.	Birthplace
1617	William	LANE	57	Farmer		200	Va.
	Mary		57				Tenn.
	Mary		28				
1618	James	BROWN	27	Laborer		75	"
	Elizabeth		22				
	William		5				
	Martha A.		3				
	Cordelia		8/12				
1619	Phinnias	LANE	28	"		60	
	Jane		22				
	Catharine J.		6				
	James		5				
	Mary		4				
	Matilda		3				
	Sarah E.		1				
1620	John C.	CLARK	34	Farmer	12,175	24,005	"
	Margaret		41				
	Mary		13				
	Elizabeth		11				
	Catharine		9				
	George		4				
	John		1				
1621	Ezekiel G.	HAMPTON	30	Laborer		125	N. C.
	Julia		24				Tenn.
	Laura		4				
	George		7/12				
1622	Neal	McKOIG	27	"		100	"
	Cytha		22				
	Neil		2				
1623	Baker	DAVIS (Bl)	55				"
	Vina	(")	33				
	Richard	(")	6				
	Watkins	(")	4				
	Louisa	(")	22				

Page 225   NEWPORT   10 August 1860

	Name		Age	Occupation	Real	Pers.	Birthplace
	Rhoda	(Bl)	4				Tenn.
	Betsy	(")	2				"
1624	Fine (f)	GANN	37			10	
	Barnet		18				
	Allen		16				
	Marshal		14				
	Sarah		10				
	Marion (m)		6				
	William		4				
	John		2				
1625	Abigail	HENRY	61			200	Va.
	Matilda		25				Tenn.
	George W.		23				
	Fielding		19				

	Name		Age	Occupation	Real	Pers.	Birthplace
1626	Pleas	SNEED	45	Farmer		85	"
	Nancy		44				
	George		21				
	Matilda		14				
	William		8				
	Mary		4				
	Rhoda		1				
	Permilia (f)		20				
1627	Robert	SNEED	21	Laborer	100	165	"
	Mary		23				
	William		1/12				
1628	Andrew	WILSON	39	Farmer		4,308	
	Mary A.		29				
	William B.		3				
	Ellena A.		1				
1629	Martha	OGDEN	51		2,000	4,500	"
	Sophia E.		26				
	George		24				
	Elizabeth		21				
1630	Lucy	ALLEN	29			30	"
	George		12				
	Joseph		6				
1631	Delilah	SERAT	78			100	S. C.
	Nancy	HANEY	49				"
	Elizabeth		19				Tenn.
	Mary A.		17				
1632	James	ANDERSON	59	Farmer	1,000	575	Ireland
	Judith		52				Tenn.
	Nancy		24				
	Rose A.	HENRY	18				
	Thursy		1				
	Harvey	REED	5				
	Ruth		4				
	Julia		1				
	John	WILLIAMS	9				
1633	Eliza	GORMAN	36		5,000	575	"
	Thomas		8				
	Patrick	HENRY	29				
	Lina		45				
	W. W.	BIBEE	22	Saddler		500	
1634	James W.	HENRY	24	Laborer			
	Frances (f)		22				
1635	William	JACK	44	Farmer	20,000	32,427	"
	Elizabeth B.		36				
	Harriet E.		17				
	Mary R.		15				
	Samuel		13				
	Marcus		10				
	William		8				
	Julia		5				
	Charlie		3				
	Nancy		68				
	Elizabeth		32				
	Malcom		40	Hunter			

1860 U. S. CENSUS OF COCKE COUNTY, TENNESSEE

	Name		Age	Occupation	Real	Pers.	Birthplace
1636	Saml.	HANCE	50	Laborer		100	
	Samuel		18				
	Margaret		16				
	Daniel		14				
	Mary		12				
	Mary	LESTER	50				
1637	Joseph	HICKEY	52	Farmer	4,000	1,424	Va.
	Lavina		36				Tenn.
	Austin		24	Lawyer			"
	Catharine		16				
	Angeline		14				
	Susan		12				

Page 227   NEWPORT   10 August 1860

	Name		Age	Occupation	Real	Pers.	Birthplace
	Sarah		10				Tenn.
	Adaline		7				
	Martha		5				
	Rufus		1				
1638	James H.	BRYANT	43	Farmer	6,500	7,520	"
	Lucinda		32				
	Aaron B.		13				
	Annanias		11				
	Andrew		8				
	Emaline		5				
	William		3				
	Thomas		3/12				
	Martha		17				
1639	Joseph J.	KIKER	41	"	2,000	1,930	"
	Priscilla		38				
	Martha		16				
	Anderson		14				
	James		10				
	Aaron		8				
	Daniel		6				
	Martha		4				
	Leander		1				
1640	Daniel B.	DENNIS	38	"	250	240	Va.
	Nancy		26				Tenn.
	Martin		2				
	Jane		5/12				
1641	Henry	HICKEY	57	"	1,000	930	Va.
	Eve		50				Tenn.
	Preston		25	Laborer			
	Julia A.		13				
	Priscilla		11				
	Margaret		8				
	Sarah		5				
	Caroline	GREEN	35				
	William	HICKEY	81				Va.
	Susannah		84				"

	Name		Age	Occupation	Real	Pers.	Birthplace
1642	John W.	HALL	34	Farmer		400	Tenn.
	Matilda		34				
	Harriet J.		9				
	Cordelia		7				

Page 228   TAYLORSBURG   10 August 1860

	Name		Age	Occupation	Real	Pers.	Birthplace
	Mary F.		5				
	Julia H.		3				
1643	Elias	SISK	68	Farmer	1,500	1,600	Va.
	Mary		62				Tenn.
	Nancy		40				"
	Eliza		30				
	Lucinda		28				
	Blackburn		22	Laborer			
	Permilia		20				
1644	George W.	ALLEN	31	"		75	"
	Elizabeth		31				
	Blackburn		10				
	Jane		11				
	Susannah		6				
	George		4				
	Joseph		2				
1645	Saml.	BAXTER	26	Farmer	2,000	1,300	"
	Jane		20				
	Aaron		4/12				
1646	Lucinda	BAXTER	61		200	100	"
	Elijah		19	Laborer			"
	Joseph		13				
	Rufus		8				
1647	Reubin	RUTHERFORD	33	Farmer	1,200	310	"
	Elizabeth		32				
	Preston		18	Laborer			
	William		17	"			
	Nancy J.		15				
	Elizabeth		13				
	John		9				
	Julia A.		7				
	Mary		4/12				
1648	Andrew	MILLER	32	"		2,000	"
	Sarah J.		29				
	William		10				
	Joshua		8				
	Louisa		3				
	Julia	MILLER (Mu)	13				N. C.
1649	Richard	LEWIS	45			200	Tenn.
	Mary		50				N. C.

Page 229   NEWPORT   10 August 1860

	Name	Age	Birthplace
	Priscilla	16	Tenn.
	Eliza	14	
	Hamilton	12	

	Name		Age	Occupation	Real	Pers.	Birthplace
1650	William	BRYANT	27	Farmer	700	350	"
	Elizabeth		24				
	Aaron	LEWIS	12				"
1651	Isaac	CLEVINGER (mwy)	21	Laborer		100	"
	Harriet		21				
1652	Thomas	DAVIS	21	"		25	N. C.
	Margaret		18				"
1653	John	CLEVINGER	34	Farmer	1,000	520	Tenn.
	Mary A.		30				"
	Samuel		11				
	Sarah		9				
	Priscilla		8				
	Ellenera		6				
	David		4				
	Mary		2				
	Austin		1				
1654	Elizabeth	CLEVINGER	80			100	Va.
1655	Alexander	ALLEN	27	Laborer		400	Tenn.
	Nancy		18				"
1656	Lemuel	HALL	32	Farmer		450	N. C.
	Harriet		28				Tenn.
	Austin		3				
	Irena		2				
	Sarah		8/12				
	Mary	HENRY	15				
1657	William H.	GRAY	42	"		450	Va.
	Martha		39				N. C.
	Hiram		17				Tenn.
	Eliza		13				
	Minerva		8				
	Willis		6				
	Robert		5				
1568	Isaac A.	DENTON	34	Farmer		225	"
	Sarah		36				N. C.
	William		13				Tenn.
	Drucilla		8				
	Delphia		7				

Page 130   NEWPORT   10 August 1860

	Name		Age	Occupation	Real	Pers.	Birthplace
	Cornelius		2				Tenn.
	Jas.	ROADMAN	14				
1659	George W.	FINE	24	Laborer		200	"
	Sarah		18				
	Mary E.		2/12				
	William	LANE	13				
1660	William	ALLEN	34	Farmer		200	"
	Mary A.		34				"
	Lucinda		13				
	Andrew J.		10				

	Name		Age	Occupation	Real	Pers.	Birthplace
1661	Harde	LEE	62	"		225	N. C.
	Martha		60				Tenn.
1662	Albert	DUNCAN	21	Laborer		75	
	Martha		20				
	Leander		1				
1663	Hamilton	RUTHERFORD	28	"		100	"
	Margaret		28				
	Margaret		5				
	Andrew		3				
	Louisa		8/12				
1664	Abraham	FINE	72	Farmer		300	"
	Elizabeth		70				
	Margaret		30				"
	Abraham		25	Laborer			
1665	Isaac	FINE	40	"		125	"
	Louisa		22				
	Elizabeth		10				
	Mary		8				
	Martin		7				
	Lavina		5				
	Samuel		4				
	Sarah		1				
1666	James A.	GOUCH	24	"		300	"
	Jane		24				
	William		7/12				
1667	John	GOUCH	52	Farmer		300	"
	Agnes		45				"
	John N.		18	Laborer			"
	Nancy J.		10				"
1668	Jesse	DAVIS	23	Farmer		165	N. C.

Page 231   NEWPORT   10 August 1860

	Name		Age	Occupation	Real	Pers.	Birthplace
	Nancy		21				Tenn.
1669	John	GRIFFIN	52	Farmer	400	500	"
	Mary		50				N. C.
	Lee		22	Laborer			Tenn.
	James		21	"			
	Francis (m)		20	"			
	William		15	"			
	Isaac		13				
	James	RUTHERFORD	16				
1670	Mary A.	TUCKER	52		600	210	Va.
	Karen		28				Tenn.
	Mary		26				
	Marion (m)		21	Carpenter			
	Martha E.		12				
1671	William	BAILEY	25	Farmer		150	"
	Catharine		25				
	Mary J.		2				
	William		2/12				

	Name		Age	Occupation	Real	Pers.	Birthplace
1672	William	GRAY	33	"	1,000	750	"
	Jane		26				
	James F.		8				
	Harriet		4				
	Raena (f)		2				
	Jefferson	HILL	15	Laborer			
	William		13				
1673	Harvey	GRAY	31	Farmer	600	175	"
	Mary E.		28				
1674	John	McKOIG	64	Teacher		175	Inverness, Scotland
	Mary		64				S. C.
1675	John	LEWIS	31	Farmer		125	Tenn.
	Sarah		26				
	Joseph L.		10				
	George M.		6				
	Rufus		25	Laborer			
1676	Micajah	ATCHLY	29	Farmer	1,100	875	"
	Mary J.		25				
	Martha		6				
	Julia A.		5				
	Benjamin		10/12				
1677	Rachel	LEWIS	50			30	

Page 232 NEWPORT 10 August 1860

	Name		Age	Occupation	Real	Pers.	Birthplace
	Elizabeth		35				Tenn.
	Mahala		12				
	Lydia		5				
1678	Joel	DENNIS	33	Farmer	600	360	"
	Lucinda		31				
	James	VEST	10				
1679	Isaac	RAINS	45	"	95	400	
	Abagail		41				
	Joel		14				
	William		12				
	Thomas		10				
	Calvin		8				
	Martha		5				
	Mary		3				
	Eliza	WHITE	73				
1680	John	DENTON	43	"	1,200	950	"
	Sarah		17				
	Allen		20	Laborer			
	James		17	"			
	Martha		13				
	Mary		12				
	William		10				
	Malissa		5/12				
1681	Felix	LEWIS	23	Farmer	500	150	"
	Lavina		24				
	Anderson		1				
	Nancy	HAYS	45				

	Name		Age	Occupation	Real	Pers.	Birthplace
1682	Jacob	CODY	35	"		150	"
	Susannah		18				
	Margaret		15				
	William		8				
	Francis (m)		5				
	Jane		1				
1683	William R.	CODY	30	Laborer		60	"
	Lucinda		32				N. C.
	James		10				
	Elizabeth		6				
	Sarah		6				
	Cynthia		1/12				
1684	John	GRIFFIN, Jr.	24	Carpenter	300	360	

Page 233   NEWPORT   11 August 1860

	Name		Age	Occupation	Real	Pers.	Birthplace
	Nancy		28				
	Mary J.		2				
	Noah		1				
	James P.		6/12				
1685	Jackson	CLEVINGER	45	Farmer	500	150	Tenn.
	Martha		48				Ga.
	Zachariah		19				Tenn.
	Russel		10				
	Elizabeth		8				
	Mary		4				
	Zachariah	LANE	98				Va.
1686	Arch	CLEVINGER	32	"		40	Tenn.
	Sarah		21				
	Mary A.		2				
	Jackson		4/12				
1687	Alexander	CLEVINGER	44	Farmer	500	400	"
	Elizabeth		42				
	Alexander		20	Laborer			
	William		18	"			
	James		16	"			
	David		15	"			
	Richard		10				
	Martha		7				
	Arch		4				
	Darcus	PRIVETT	47				N. C.
1688	John	CLEVINGER (mwy)	23	"		120	Tenn.
	Rhoda		20				
1689	Thomas	FINE	46	"		50	"
	Elvira		30				
	Sarah		10				
	Anna		8				
	Ellen		6				
	Lucinda		4				
	Elliott		1				
1690	Mary	LANE	44			40	Ga.
	Moses		22				Tenn.

	Name		Age	Occupation	Real	Pers.	Birthplace
	Mary J.		18				
	Andrew		8/12				
1691	Elliott	SIMS	47	Farmer	1,500	900	S. C.
	Phebe		44				Tenn.

Page 234   NEWPORT   11 August 1860

	Name		Age	Occupation	Real	Pers.	Birthplace
							Tenn.
	Maranda		24				
	Anna		22				
	Martha		20				
	Mary		12				
1692	Jackson	ALLEN	61	Farmer	300	150	"
	Rose A.		43				
1693	Isaac M.	LEE	24	Laborer		15	"
	Julia A.		15				
	Martha		1				
1694	William	CLEVINGER	56	Laborer		140	
	Mary		48				
	Rufus		24	"			
	Elizabeth		23				
	John		20	"			
	Sarah		19				
	Winfield		18	"			
	Allen		17	"			
	James		14				
	Margaret		12				
	Elias		10				
	Lucinda		7				
	Mary		4				
	Emaline		1				
1695	William	FINCHEM	50	Farmer		484	N. C.
	Elizabeth		48				Tenn.
	Robert		21	Laborer			
	John		19	"			
	Eliza		16				
	Elijah		16	"			
	William		14				
	Matilda		14				
	Rebecca		11				
	Julia		9				
	Samuel		9				
	George		5				
	Elizabeth		3				
	Nancy		1				
1696	Alexander	FINCHEM	26	"			"
	Mary		20				"
	Jane		3				

Page 235   NEWPORT   11 August 1860

	Name		Age	Occupation	Real	Pers.	Birthplace
							Tenn.
	Robert		6/12				
	Elizabeth	PARKER	25				

	Name		Age	Occupation	Real	Pers.	Birthplace
1697	Elias	DAVIS	49	Farmer	400	250	N. C.
	Julia		49				"
	John		21	Laborer			"
	Jonathan		18				"
	Mary		14				Tenn.
	Minerva		11				
	Alexander		12				
	Sarah		9				
	Matilda		7				
1698	James	FINCHEM	48	Farmer		160	N. C.
	Mary		42				"
	John		18	Laborer			Tenn.
	Thomas		16				"
	Anderson		13				
	Mary		12				
	Mary	THOMAS	11				
	Alexander	FINCHEM	9				
	Matilda		7				
1699	John	FREE	25	"		70	"
	Angeline		21				
	William		2				
1700	William H.	POE	67	Farmer	700	482	Va.
	Sarah		50				Tenn.
	Pleasant C.		20	Laborer			
	Stephen		15				
	Sarah		13				
1701	John	JONES	45	Farmer	800	535	"
	Margaret		33				
	Nancy		3				
	Margaret		2				
	Rufus	JONES	20	Laborer			
1702	Samuel	WILSON	43	Farmer	2,000	4,059	N. C.
	Mary		53				Tenn.
	James	PORTER	27	Laborer			
	Ellen		19				
	Mary		1				
1703	Isaac	FREE	36	Farmer	33	60	"
	Mary		35				

Page 236   NEWPORT   11 August 1860

	Name		Age	Occupation	Real	Pers.	Birthplace
	Margaret		14				
	Elbert		13				
	Elijah		10				
	Rufus		8				
	Sarah		6				
	Isaac		4				
	Allen		1				
1704	William	PHILLIPS	28	Farmer	1,200	655	"
	Margaret		25				
	Susan		7				
	Sarah		5				
	Mary J.		4				

	Name		Age	Occupation	Real	Pers.	Birthplace
	John W. C.		1/12				
	Alexander		16	Laborer			
	Stephen		13				
1705	James	FREE	50	Farmer	600	100	S. C.
	Jane		44				Tenn.
	Elizabeth		28				
	Preston		21	Laborer			
	Anna		18				
	Jane		16				
	Henry		15	"			
	Maranda		11				
	Eliza		10				
	Howard		9				
	Cytha		5				
1706	Logan	POE	45	"		40	
	Margaret		32				
1707	Isaac	FINE	65	Farmer	150	125	"
	Anna		65				
1708	Edward	FRANCE	55	"	600	570	N. C.
	Margaret		52				Tenn.
	Joseph		32	Laborer			
	Catharine		28				
	Cordelia		26				
	William		22	"			
	Mira		20				
	David		16	"			
	Clementine		14				
	Margaret		10				

Page 237   NEWPORT   11 August 1860

	Name		Age	Occupation	Real	Pers.	Birthplace
	Mary		9				Tenn.
	Sarah		7				
1709	Albert	WILSON	43	Farmer	1,000	1,100	"
	Susannah		43				
	Jane		18				
	Sarah		3				
1710	John	FINE	45	"	1,000	300	
	Mary		28				
	William		8				
	Jane		6				
	Nancy		5				
	Robert		4				
	Mary		2				
	Aaron		2/12				
	Sarah A.	COPELAND	21				
1711	William	FRANCIS	46	"	750	200	N. C.
	Anna		32				Tenn.
	Eda		14				
	James		12				
	William		10				
	Mary		8				
	Cassa		6				
	Eliza		4				
	Margaret		2				

	Name		Age	Occupation	Real	Pers.	Birthplace
1712	Archibald	FRANCE	50	Farmer	200	700	N. C.
	Mary		80				"
	Edy		12				"
1713	James	FRANCE	48	"	300	150	"
	Delilah		46				Tenn.
	Elizabeth		15				
	Nancy		13				
	Evaline		11				
	Jane		13				
	William		7				
	Morgan		5				
	Elvira		3				
1714	Mary	DAVIS	24		700	100	
	Sarah		18				
1715	Nancy	CODY	40			20	"
	Sarah		18				

Page 238   NEWPORT   11 August 1860

	Name		Age	Occupation	Real	Pers.	Birthplace
1716	Charles A.	HARRISON	42	Farmer	25,000	24,000	Tenn.
	Anna		39				
	Montgomery		15	Laborer			
	Martha J.		8				
	Olla (m)	ALLEN	23	"			
1717	Hugh	LANE	38	Farmer		125	"
	Zilpha		40				
	John		19	Laborer			
	Sarah		14				
	Eliza		12				
	Susannah		10				
	Emma		4				
	Samuel		3/12				
1718	Stuart	ANDREWS	42	"		175	N. C.
	Eliza		43				"
	Anderson		18				Tenn.
	Catherine		16				
	Jane		14				
	Finly		12				
	Harriet		10				
	Avery (m)		6				
	Adaline		4				
	Martha		8/12				
1719	Samuel	HANCE	24	"		100	"
	Sarah		30				
	Ervin		7				
	Zilpha		5				
	Elias		4				
	Mary		2				
	Minnie	HILL	20				
	Martha		2/12				

	Name		Age	Occupation	Real	Pers.	Birthplace
1720	James	LAREW	45	Farmer	15,000	3,900	"
	Elizabeth		39				
	Mary		15				
	Catharine		13				
	Napoleon B.		8				
	Charlie		6				
	Elizabeth		4				
	Shelton		1				
	Thomas	PRIVETT	20	Laborer			

Page 239   NEWPORT   11 August 1860

	Name		Age	Occupation	Real	Pers.	Birthplace
1721	Merrit	LOLACK	43	Farmer		75	N. C.
	Martha		30				"
	John		13				"
	Mary		11				"
	Douglass		9				
	James		7				
	Richmond		4				
	Alexander		2				
1722	Mary	COLEMAN	64		2,000	6,010	Tenn.
1723	Isaac	COOPER	21	Laborer		150	
	Susannah		18				
	James		18	"			
	Joseph		17	"			
	Thomas		15	"			
	William		13				
1724	Charles	WISE	40	"		40	"
	Caroline		35				
	Peter		16				
	Andrew		14				
	Jane		9				
	Joseph		7				
	Caroline		6				
	Sarah		2				
	James		10/12				
1725	Martha	DOBBINS	90	(Blind)		25	Va.
	Elvira		45				Tenn.
1726	Mark	SCOTT	30	"		200	"
	Martha		23				
	Robert		3				
	Mark		1				
1727	John	ALLEN (of Jack)	49	Farmer	5,000	1,829	"
	Sarah		49				
	John		18	Laborer			
	Abraham		17	"			
	Sarah		15				
	Elizabeth		16				
	Elijah		14				
	Amanda		13				
	Austin		12				
	Landon		11				

	Name		Age	Occupation	Real	Pers.	Birthplace
Page 240				NEWPORT			11 August 1860
	Wiley		10				Tenn.
	Cynthia		6				
1728	Sarah A.	COFFIN	33		1,800	6,028	"
	Joseph	SMITH	9			5,101	"
	Charles C.		5				"
	Clarence		3				"
	Florida	DAWSON	5				

TOTAL FREE POPULATION 10,558

W. F. MORRIS

Asst. Marshall

1860 COCKE COUNTY MORTALITY SCHEDULE

The 1860 Mortality Schedule was taken along with the 1860 U. S. Census. It was to include all individuals who died one year prior to June 1, 1860.

Each entry lists the name, age, sex (f=female, m=male), whether married, race, month died, occupation, cause of death and how long sick before death. Since the majority of the persons listed were white, we have listed the race only for blacks and mulattos. In some cases involving slaves, the enumerator apparently listed the name of the owner and the word boy in parentheses. An example is number 2, page 1 --A. E. SMITH (boy).

Page 1.

1. A. D. SMITH, 34, m, Tn, May, farmer, consumption, 5 yrs.
2. A. E. SMITH (boy), 14, m, mulatto, slave, TN, July, farmhand.
3. A. E. SMITH (boy), 1, m, black, slave, TN, March, not known, sudden.
4. Joel GOUCHMOM, 7, m, TN, Nov., accident, sudden.
5. L. D. PORTER, 54, m, married, VA, April, clerk of court, consumption, 3 mos.
6. Catherine THOMAS (boy), 6, m, black, slave, TN, Sept., not known, 1 mo.
7. _____TOWNSEND, 70, female, widow, NC, June, unknown, 2 mos.
8. Robert CURETON, 65, March, TN, Sept., laborer, carbuncle, 4 wks.
9. P. F. KINDRICK, 38, m, married, TN, Oct., farmer, scrofulous diarhea, 3 yrs.
10. Alfred KINDRICK, 1, male, black, slave, TN, March, unknown, sudden.
11. Rachael E. PARKS, 3 days, TN, Mary, unknown, sudden.
12. Wm. A. PARKS, 1, TN, March, unknown, sudden.
13. J. W. RUSSELL, 43, male, married, SC, Oct., laborer, unknown, 8 mos.
14. Malinda STOREY, 60, widow, TN, March, scrofulous diarhea, 12 mos.
15. Martha J. HEIFNER, 22, married, TN, July, epilepsy, 13 mos.
16. Anna MANNING, 61, married, TN, July, unknown, 5 days.
17. Joseph MOORE, 1, m, TN, June, unknown, 1 yr.
18. Roda ADKINS, 2, f, TN, May, unknown, 1 mo.
19. C.M. FOX, 4/12, m, TN, Oct., croup, 1 wk.
20. P. E. DRISKILL, 10, m, TN, June, sore throat, 8 days.
21. Sarah MOORE, 47, f, TN, married, Dec., childbed fever, 4 days.
22. Amanda MOORE, 3, TN, Dec., scarlet fever, 13 days.
23. R. M. FOX, 33, m, married, TN, Oct., farmer, consumption, 14 mos.
24. _____FOX, not named, 1, female, TN, July, flux, 2 mos.
25. Thomas CARTRIGHT, 2, m, TN, Aug., flux, 3 wks.
26. Sarah CARTRIGHT, 3 days, TN, March, unknown, sudden.
27. Larkin MATHAIS, 64, m, married, SC, March, laborer, unknown, 8 mos.
28. Sarah E. CLINE, 1/12, TN, Sept., fever, 10 days.
29. Mose CURETON, 4, m, black, slave, TN, Sept., poisoned by arsnic, 4 hrs.
30. W. M. WALKER, 1, f, TN, Jan., hydraphobia, 12 days.
31. Not named WALKER, 1, f, TN, Dec., unknown, 1 day.
32. Sarah PALMER, 11/12, f, Apr., unknown, 1 day.
33. Pleasant O'NEIL, 36, m, married, Sept., farmer, accidental drowning, sudden.
34. Harriet E. JACKSON, 18, TN, Sept., fever, 25 days.
35. Augustus JENKINS, 1 day, m, TN, Dec., unknown, 1 day.

Page 2

1. William A. SHULTS, 4/12, m, TN, April, croup, 30 hrs.
2. S. McMAHAN, 4, m, TN, Aug., scarlet fever, 1 wk.
3. Hen. McMILLAN, 1/12, m, TN, Mar, croup, 4 days.
4. Lavenah HOPKINS, 1, f, TN, Oct., scarlet fever, 9 days.
*5. Amanda SISK, 2/12, f, TN, April, croup, 3 wks.
6. Thomas LLOYD, 2/12, m, TN, July, unknown, 3 days.

7. Allen CLEVENGER, 54, m, married, TN, July, farmer, galloping consumption, 3 wks.
8. John P. TAYLOR, 44, m, married, VA, June, tayloring, consumption, 18 yrs.
9. Harriet STANBERY, 2, f, black, slave, TN, Oct., croup, 36 hrs.
10. Joseph JOHNSON, 3 m, TN, Oct., croup, 1 mo.
11. Nancy HOLDER, 21, f, married, March, childbed fever, 10 days.
12. George GARMAN, 25, m, married, NC, May, laborer, consumption, 1 yr.
13. Nancy VALENTINE, 33, f, married, TN, Nov., consumption, 5 yrs.
14. Eliz. RUTHERFORD, 69, f, widow, TN, April, consumption, 18 yrs.
15. Jessee JENKINS, 50, m, married, Dec., farmer, liver complaint, 1 yr.
16. Elizabeth SISK, 2, f, July, flux, 15 days.
17. Thomas SISK, 3, m, July, flux, 14 days.
18. Susannah ALLEN, 2/12, TN, May, croup, 4 days.
19. Nancy ALLEN, 82, f, widow, VA, caused by a fall, 4 wks.
20. Charity VINSON, 75, f, married, TN, Dec., pneumonia fever, 9 days.
21. Mark DENNIS, 14 days, TN, Nov., hives, 2 wks.
22. Martha DENNIS, 2, f, TN, Jan., fever, 11 days.
23. Lou MANNING, 18, f, black, slave, NC, house girl, inflammatory bowel, 3 wks.
24. Elizabeth HICKS, 18, TN, July, fever, 1 wk.
25. Henry TUCKER, 58, m, married, VA, May, laborer, pneumonia fever, 3 wks.
26. Russell WOOD, 5/12, m, black, slave, TN, Aug., unknown, sudden.
27. John LANIER, 9 days, m, TN, June, hives, 3 days.
28. Sarah CLARK, 6, f, TN, Sept., fever, 10 days.
29. Pompy FINE, 52, m, black, slave, Aug., field hand, dropsy, 2 yrs.
30. David FINE, 15, m, black, slave, Oct., field hand, fever, 10 days.
31. James FINE, 6, m, black, slave, TN, Oct., fever, 40 days.
32. Samuel FINE, 4, m, black, slave, Sept., fever, 8 days.
33. Manerva FINE, 7/12, f, black, slave, Sept., fever, 15 days.
34. Prinus FINE, 12, m, black, slave, TN, Sept., field hand, fever, 7 days.
35. Darcus CLARK, 32, f, black, slave, TN, Sept., housegirl, fever, 3 days.

1. Cordelia DENNIS, 3, f, TN, Sept., croup, 4 days.
2. Julia S. OTTINGER, 32, f, married, TN, April, consumption, 3 yrs.
3. John GREENE, 59, m, married, SC, Jan., farmer, consumption, 16 days.
4. Sarah COOPER, 1 f, TN, May, unknown, 1 wk.
5. Elizabeth DAVIS, 24, NC, Nov., consumption, 2 yrs.
6. M. J. HOLT, 9/12, m, TN, Jan., inflammatory brain, 7 days.
7. Wm. ETHERTON, 35, m, married, March, farmer, consumption, 2 yrs.
8. Violet FAUBIAN, 65, f, black, slave, Oct., house girl, consumption. 6 mos.
9. E. S. DUNCAN, 6/12, f, TN, Oct., scarlet fever, 3 days.
10. E. J. YOUNG, 31, m, married, TN, Oct., saddler, typhoid fever, 9 wks.
11. Selena E. YOUNG, 30, f, TN, Nov., accidentally burned, 2 days.
12. Dick TEMPLIN, 25, m, black, slave, Aug., field hand, fever, 2 wks.
13. Sarah TEMPLIN, 16, black, slave, TN, June, housegirl, fever, 4 days.
14. Susannah OTTINGER, 67, married, VA, Jan., unknown, 4 days.
15. Louisa RADER, 2 TN, June, scrofula, 6 mos.
16. John EBBS, 83, married, VA, May, farmer, unknown, 2 wks.
17. Mary EBBS, 73, married, VA, May, consumption, 30 yrs.
18. James M. NEASE, 9 days, TN, June, croup, 2 days.
19. Lear FAUBIAN, 81, f, married, VA, Nov., fever, 8 wks.
20. Parthena McNABB, 49, f, TN, Jan., fever, 9 days.
21. Amanuel DeBUSK, 2/12, m, TN, March, croup, 6 hrs.
22. John OTTINGER, 6/12, TN, APRIL, CROUP, 5 hrs.
23. Elizabeth OTTINGER, 1/12, TN, June, whooping cough, 7 days.
24. M. E. CHAPMAN, 4, f, TN, Sept., scarlet fever, 2 wks.

25. Luna J. CHAMPIN, 2, m, TN, Sept., scarlet fever, 4 days.
26. Robert W. CHAMPIN, 6/12, TN, Sept., scarlet fever, 3 days.
27. Warren BROOKS, 49, m, married, SC, Nov., farmer, skull fracture in an affray, 6 days.
28. James A. BURGIN, 5/12, m, TN, Aug., flux, 4 days.
29. Wm. MOONEYHAM, 1, m, TN, Feb., inflammation of the bowels, 3 wks.
30. Jane NELSON, 1/12, TN, May, unknown, sudden.
31. Matilda WOODY, 3, TN, Feb., croup, 6 days.
32. Osborne BALL, 82, m, married, NC, May, farmer, gravel, 19 days.
33. Mary J. HALL, 1/12, TN, Jan., unknown, 1 wk.
34. Nancy CATES, 10/12, TN, April, unknown, 6 wks.
35. W. T. GILES, 2, m, TN, Jan., croup, 3 wks.

1. Elizabeth WOODY, 6/12, f, Jan., croup, 3 wks.
2. Nelly DAVIS, 50, married, TN, May, unknown, 1 yr.
3. Mary HARRISON, 9/12, black, slave, TN, Feb., fever, 2 wks.

108 deaths.

1860 U. S. CENSUS OF COCKE COUNTY, TENNESSEE

INDEX

The numbers refer to the family number. "M", followed by a number refers to that page in the mortality schedule

- A -

ABLE(S) 928, 929

ADAMS 1241, 1279

ADKINS M1

ALEXANDER 273, 1025

ALLEN 35, 492, 493, 506, 1055, 1107, 1109, 1287, 1288, 1309, 1311, 1313, 1318, 1337, 1347, 1348, 1353, 1375, 1397, 1454, 1540, 1567, 1613, 1630, 1644, 1655, 1660, 1692, 1716, 1727, M2

ALMAN 394

AMBROSE 1479

ANDERSON 38, 1009, 1391, 1438, 1632

ANDREWS 1718

ARROWOOD 430

ASENTON 784

ATCHLEY 1572

ATCHLY 1676

ATKINS 125, 131, 138

AVENTON 385

- B -

BAILEY 1671

BAILY 230

BAKER 47, 1143, 1461

BALCH 402

BALL 815, 816, 829, 986, 1271, 1328, M3

BALLEW 748, 1111, 1354

BALLENGER 14

BANKS 327, 364, 366, 761, 836

BARNES 71, 72, 76, 80

BARNET(T) 399, 694, 756, 770, 781, 799, 802, 805, 808, 1423

BARNS 1552, 1553

BARTON 1072

BASINGERS 23

BASSET 73

BATES 1545.

BAXTER 1183, 1229, 1232, 1235, 1236, 1237, 1430, 1645, 1646

BAYSINGER 376

BEAGLE 1331

BEARD 1606

BECK 1615

BELL 907

BENNER 622, 686, 1195

BENSON 1298, 1302

BEWLEY 1117

BIBEE 240, 241, 1633

BIBLE 286, 303, 331, 811, 913, 952, 953, 954

BIRD 1400, 1467, 1472, 1494, 1511, 1517, 1525, 1550

BLACK 358, 421, 539, 677, 820, 902, 938, 939, 949, 961, 966, 967

BLACKWELL 1101

BLAIR 12

BLANCHARD 701, 702

BLASER 590

BLAZER 604, 635, 641, 648, 654, 655, 656, 663, 665, 666, 672, 673, 1295

BLACKWOOD 1300

BODGUS 14

BOLCH 62, 489

BOLEYPAN 88

BOLYHAM 864

BORDEN 581

BOSWELL 227

BOULDEN 536, 666, 667

BOULDIN 1033

BOYD 523

BOYER 713

BOYIER 404

BRADFORD 796

BRADY 147, 150, 1087

BRAGDEN 696, 707

BRAGG 166

BRANCH 772, 1502

BREEDEN 1517, 1525

BREWER 398

BRIDGES 105

BRINKLY 1554

BRITTON 1129

BRIZANDIM 184, 185

BROGDEN 780

BROMFIELD 699

BROOKS 6, 80, 81, 83, 84, 85, 237, 509, 691, 708, 994, 1016, 1390, 1423, 1424, M3

BROTHERTON 104, 1283

BROWN 57, 297, 856, 1618

BRUDEN 1517

BRUMFIELD 787

BRUMLY 1571

BRYAN 909, 923, 927

BRYANT 1425, 1427, 1492, 1638, 1650

BUCKNER 130, 135, 140, 243, 263, 264, 273

BUGG 407, 408

BUNTING 343

BURCHFIELD 848

BURGEN 775, M3

BURGRES(S) 91, 145, 361

BURK(E) 1027, 1061, 1121, 1123

BURREL 483, 484

BUSH 1031, 1060

BUSTIER 461

BUTLER 1466, 1483, 1485

BYER 63

- C -

CAFFEE 1564

CAFFY 204, 209

CALDER 947

CALDWELL 940

CAMBELL 856

CAMPBELL 153, 277, 299, 1220, 1260

CAMERON 28, 992, 995, 1055, 1099, 1311

CANUP 1242

CARMIKLE 333

CARN 756

CARTER 391, 456, 1513, 1589, 1613

CARNER 1203

CARTWRIGHT 274, M1

CASE 1356, 1610

CASH 709

CASTILIES 182

CATE 840

CATES 1450, M3

CATON 1224

CHAMPIN M3

CHANDLER 537

CHAPMAN 725, 726, 744, 745, M3

CHRISTIAN 229, 275

CLARK 97, 115, 122, 123, 126, 387, 823, 830, 891, 916, 930, 1322, 1444, 1542, 1565, 1587, 1620, M2

CLAYTON 1105

CLANTHAM 457

CLEMENS 803

CLEMONS 862

CLEVENGER 997, 1056, M2

CLEVINGER 1052, 1064, 1590, 1651, 1652, 1653, 1685, 1686, 1687, 1688, 1694

CLICK 1004, 1005, 1006, 1019, 1020, 1437, 1459

CLIFF 1294

CLINE 5, 321, 334, 384, 434, M1

COCHRAN 1488, 1489, 1490

CODY 1535, 1682, 1683, 1715

COFFIN 1728

COFFMAN 473

COGBERN 613

COGBURN 579

COBLER 634

COEN 1583

COGDELL 702, 758, 786, 1039, 1043

COGIN 846

COLDWELL 853

COLE 1176

COLEMAN 1176, 1722

COLLINS 1592

COLY 523

COMPTEN 626

COMPTON 622

CONWAY 262, 288

COOK 422, 485, 651, 675, 885, 972, 1086

COOPER 103, 417, 418, 419, 595, 615, 1723, M3

COPELAND 1710

COPLEN 251

COWAN 96

CRAWFORD 11

CRAWLY 1505

CRITSELOUS 731

CRUM 1333

CRUMLEY 202, 203

CUMMINGS 495

CURETON 10, 26, 65, 324, 325, 1079, M1

CURRY 1040

- D -

DAVIS 428, 455, 521, 528, 653, 756, 877, 937, 987, 988, 1045, 1103, 1106, 1136, 1577, 1614, 1623, 1652, 1668, 1697, 1714, M3, M4

DAVISON 948

DAWSON 9, 107, 260, 261, 284, 285, 332 335, 443, 444, 452, 1728

DEAN 155

DEBUSK 643, 1167, M3

DENNIS 1204, 1298, 1368, 1372, 1381, 1382, 1413, 1414, 1640, 1678, M2, M3

DENTON 1145, 1304, 1323, 1408, 1422, 1434, 1435, 1442, 1452, 1453, 1468, 1521, 1522, 1524, 1529, 1658, 1680

DEWITT 17, 18, 753

DICKSON 141, 158, 179, 191

DIKE 326, 357, 381

DOBBINS 1725

DOCKERY 500

DOCKINS 253

DOCERY 922

DOWN 869

DOWNS 863

DRISKILL 175, 207, 215, 267, 1294, M1

DRYMAN 487, 594, 730

DUGLES 256

DUMTON 54

DUN 317, 351

DUNAGAN 1297

DUNCAN 448, 528, 1513, 1662, M3

DYKE 359, 950

- E -

EASTERLY 454, 459, 609, 623

EBBS 616, 617, 620, M3

ECTON 1511, 1512, 1515

EDINGTON 267, 278, 295

EISENHOWER 399

EISENHOUR 405, 597, 624, 626

ELENTON 1310

ELISON 409

ELKINS 296

ELLENBURG 934, 935

ELLIS 210, 211, 230, 1050, 1051, 1282

ELLISON 395, 404, 767, 855, 879, 886, 887, 893, 894, 897, 980, 993

ELLENDER 779

ELWOOD 61

ERBY 1266

ERVIN 282

ETHERTIN 547

ETHERTON 481, M3

EVANS 43, 283, 363, 390, 708, 1042, 1049

- F -

FAIRFIELD 15

FANCHER 465, 611, 679

FANCHIER 488

FANN 1291, 1292

FANNI 1027

FARMER 859

FAUBIAN M3

FAUBION 459

FAWBION 453, 521, 527, 630

FINCHEM 1695, 1696, 1698

FARNER 69, 234

FINCHUM 1439

FINE 11, 1081, 1108, 1586, 1659, 1664, 1665, 1689, 1707, 1710, M2

FINNEY 1534

FLEENER 470

FLINN 16

FORD 959, 960

FORELY 40

FOREMAN 759

FOWLER 155, 266, 378, 440, 441, 442, 445, 446, 449, 486, 1029, 1084, 1564

FOX 152, 163, 180, 188, 190, 196, 226, 246, 250, 427, 880, 895, 901, 914, 925, 1023, 1038, 1044, 1116, 1125, 1491, M1

FRASIER 1063, 1067, 1094, 1119, 1359

FRANCE 1708, 1712

FRANCIS 1711

FRANKLIN 12, 49

FRANKS 868

FRAZIER 1598

FREE 1569, 1593, 1699, 1703, 1705

FREEMAN 143

FRESHOUR 118, 556, 681, 718, 751, 792, 1028

FULTZ 797

- G -

GALLAGER 756

GAMMON 341, 342

GANN 1624

GARIS 559

GARMAN M2

GARNER 1261, 1262

GARREL 688, 690

GARRISON 34

GERREL 1532

GILBERT 287

GILES 852, 1147, 1163, 1197, 1198, 1250, M3

GILLETT 241, 245, 252

GILLILAND 912, 1152, 1169, 1194, 1239, 1370

GILLYLAND 532

GINEHENOUS 17

GLAZE 148

GOODSON 584

GOODWIN 1549

GORMAN 1014, 1096, 1541, 1546, 1548, 1549, 1633

GORRELL 53

GOSLIN 473, 555

GOUCH 1666, 1667

GOUCHMOM M1

GOWAN 769

GRAGG 89, 410, 411, 510, 528, 596, 598, 599, 600, 603, 606, 608, 614, 736

GRAHAM 114

GRANCY 1007

GRAY 1053, 1101, 1102, 1115, 1481, 1547, 1582, 1584, 1657, 1672, 1673

GREEN 349, 353, 370, 371, 822, 826, 833, 928, 936, 940, 943, 973, 1070, 1074, 1231, 1441, 1447, 1641, M3

GREGORY 1481, 1497

GRIFFIN 1669, 1684

GRIGSBY 876

GROOMS 1273

GUILLIAMS 921

GUIN(N) 136, 340, 585, 710, 721, 962

GWINN 372

- H -

HALE 417

HALL 228, 300, 301, 302, 388, 545, 565, 832, 957, 1048, 1072, 1073, 1074, 1428, 1642, 1656, M3

HAMPTON 1, 756, 1603, 1604, 1605, 1621

HANCE 1636, 1719

HANER 1597

HANEY 1631

HARDEN 439

HARLEY 890

HAROLD 1208, 1385

HARPER 247, 320, 962, 1305, 1327, 1334, 1365, 1395

HARRIS 108, 477, 492, 1254, 1580

HARRISON 352, 1192, 1211, 1212, 1213, 1214, 1716, M4

HARTGROVE 1514

HARTLY 1394

HARTSELL 1034, 1109, 1118, 1230, 1342, 1363, 1401, 1404

HARVEY 1293

HASKIN 35

HATLEY 99, 1436, 1462

HAWK 669

HAYS 683, 1681

HAYSE 526, 692

HAZLEWOOD 890

HEADRICK 475, 754

HEATH 281

HEDERICK 670

HEIFER 447

HEIFNER M1

HEMBREE 1344, 1345

HENDERSON 627, 842, 844, 848

HENRY 40, 1346, 1426, 1480, 1537, 1559, 1573, 1625, 1632, 1633, 1634, 1656

HENSTON 492

HEWING 538

HICKEY 1637, 1641

HICKS 1128, 1300, 1366, 1403, 1443, 1472, 1473, 1490, 1493, 1496, 1503, 1516, M2

HICKY 347

HIEFNER 114

HIGHTOWER 93, 1054

HILL 44, 45, 46, 474, 1172, 1672, 1719

HIX 1575

HIXON 793

HODGE 619

HOG 307, 311

HOLAWAY 387, 511, 512

HOLD 116

- Mc -

- M -

POE 1700, 1706

PORTER 24, 1069, 1701, M1

POTTER 608, 970, 1013, 1047, 1524, 1526

PRATER 113, 769

PRAYTER 800, 807

PRESLEY 1306

PRICE 834, 837, 956, 965

PRICHARD 1128

PRIVETT 1687, 1720

PROFFITT 922

PRUTT 476, 1551

- Q -

QUALLS 1137

QUILLIAMS 900

- R -

RADER 566, 567, 568, 636, 644, M3

RAGEN 4, 22

RAINS 944, 1221, 1259, 1315, 1319, 1320, 1325, 1327, 1329, 1679

RAMSEY 144, 841, 1178, 1179, 1188, 1243, 1253, 1272, 1280

RANDOLPH 8

RANKIN 20, 128

RARD 401

RAY 511

REAMS 154

RECTOR 1114

REDMAN 625

REECE 310, 451, 611, 612

REED 165, 189, 192, 193, 194, 195, 1632

REDIX 350

REESE 809, 889, 896

REEVES 409

REINS 844

REN 996, 1035, 1036, 1041, 1583

RHEA 24

RICE 743

RICKER 877

RIDENS 1275, 1276, 1484

RISSATOR 155

ROADMAN 21, 519, 522, 1658

ROBERTS 810, 1013, 1062, 1449, 1450, 1579

ROBINSON 30, 68, 751, 1316, 1321

RODES 582

ROGERS 127, 258

ROLLINS 853, 968, 1180, 1256, 1265

ROMINES 1200

ROREX 390

ROSE 938, 1508, 1510

ROSS 711

ROWLAND 936

RUNION 1012

RUNNER 586, 593, 594, 723, 733

RUNNION 1082, 1085

RUSSEL 90, 1409, M1

RUTHERFORD 1457, 1527, 1544, 1647, 1663, 1669, M2

RUTHERTON 1104, 1112, 1113

- S -

SAMPLE 1558

SAMPLES 1469, 1616

SANE 601, 602, 739

SATERFIELD 15, 386

SAWYERS 774, 873

SCHUTSIHALL 918

SCOTT 1726

SCROGGINS 1324, 1357

SCRUGGS 584, 666

SCULLY 216

SERAT 1631

SEXTON 804, 861, 864, 866, 867, 945

SHARP 589

www.ingramcontent.com/pod-product-compliance
Lightning Source LLC
Chambersburg PA
CBHW080237270326
41926CB00020B/4279